The American Assembly, *Columbia University*

THE UNITED STATES AND THE MIDDLE EAST

Prentice-Hall, Inc. *Englewood Cliffs, N.J.*

 Library of Congress Catalog Card No. 64-14027. Printed in the United States of America—C.

93833C
93832P

THE UNITED STATES AND THE MIDDLE EAST

INSTITUTE OF COMMONWEALTH STUDIES

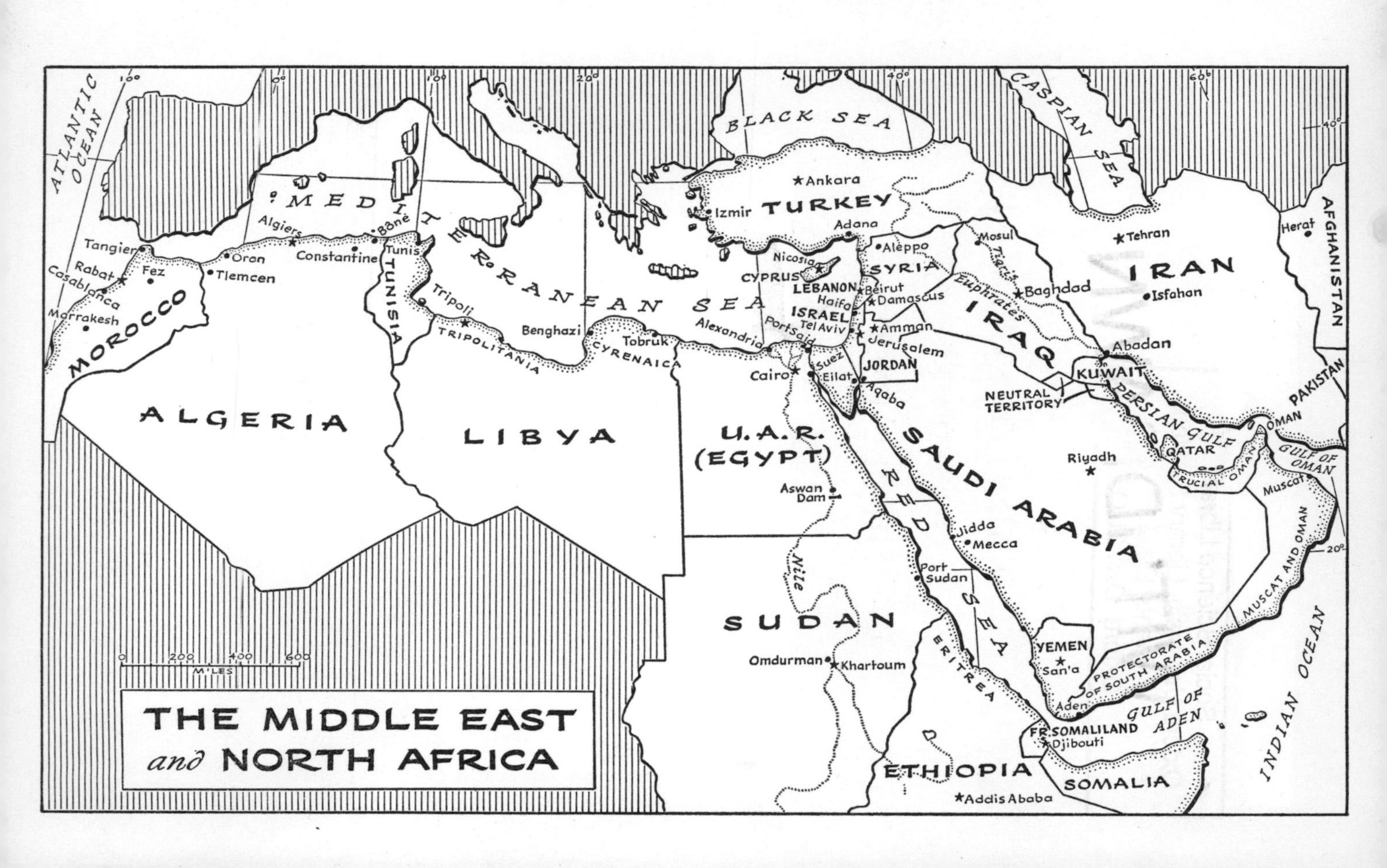
THE MIDDLE EAST
and NORTH AFRICA
0
200
400
600
MILES
ATLANTIC OCEAN
MEDITERRANEAN SEA
BLACK SEA
CASPIAN SEA
RED SEA
PERSIAN GULF
GULF OF OMAN
GULF OF ADEN
INDIAN OCEAN
MOROCCO
ALGERIA
TUNISIA
LIBYA
TRIPOLITANIA
CYRENAICA
U.A.R. (EGYPT)
SUDAN
ETHIOPIA
ERITREA
FR. SOMALILAND
SOMALIA
TURKEY
CYPRUS
SYRIA
LEBANON
ISRAEL
JORDAN
IRAQ
IRAN
AFGHANISTAN
PAKISTAN
KUWAIT
NEUTRAL TERRITORY
SAUDI ARABIA
QATAR
TRUCIAL OMAN
OMAN
MUSCAT AND OMAN
YEMEN
PROTECTORATE OF SOUTH ARABIA
Tangier
Rabat
Casablanca
Marrakesh
Fez
Oran
Tlemcen
Algiers
Constantine
Bône
Tunis
Tripoli
Benghazi
Tobruk
Alexandria
Port Said
Cairo
Suez
Aswan Dam
Nile
Omdurman
Khartoum
Addis Ababa
Djibouti
Port Sudan
Izmir
Ankara
Adana
Nicosia
Aleppo
Beirut
Damascus
Haifa
Tel Aviv
Amman
Jerusalem
Eilat
Aqaba
Mosul
Tigris
Euphrates
Baghdad
Abadan
Tehran
Isfahan
Herat
Riyadh
Jidda
Mecca
Muscat
San'a
Aden
10°
0°
10°
20°
40°
60°
40°
20°

Preface

This volume was prepared under the editorial supervision of Georgiana G. Stevens of San Francisco, as background reading for the Twenty-fourth American Assembly, Arden House, Harriman, New York, October 24-27, 1963. It was also intended for other Assembly-sponsored discussions on the subject, as well as for students and the general reading public.

At the Twenty-fourth American Assembly, as at all Assembly meetings, participants exchanged opinions and ideas on issues drawn from the chapters which follow. After three days of small group meetings they drafted in plenary session a final report of recommendations for national policy. That report is published separately as are reports of all regional Assemblies.

Neither the American Assembly nor any of the institutions cosponsoring Assembly programs takes an official position on the subjects they present for public consideration.

Henry M. Wriston
Chairman
The American Assembly

Table of Contents

Georgiana G. Stevens, Editor

Introduction: Middle East Perspectives 1

William Sands

1 Middle East Background 9

Area and Peoples, 10
Pan Arabism in Theory and Fact, 12
Attitudes of Minorities, 18
Nationalism and Neutralism, 22
The Influence of the West, 25
The Constants and the Variables, 28

William R. Polk

2 Social Modernization: The New Men 30

The Modernizers, 31
Role of Education, 40
Role of the Military, 45
Middle Class—New Style, 47
Role of Women, 49
Social Engineering Experiments, 50

A. J. Meyer

3 Economic Modernization 53

The Middle East Economy Before World War II, 53
Economic Expansion Since World War II, 54
Problems, 59
Distinguishing Features of Economic Development, 63
Prospects for the Future, 69
Summary, 76

4 *J. C. Hurewitz*
Regional and International Politics in the Middle East 78

The Return of Regional Politics, 79
Disunity in the Arab East, 82
Separatism in the Arab West, 86
The Politics of Arab Unity, 92
The Uneasy Armistice, 97
The Aligned States, 101
The Cold War, 105

5 *Harry B. Ellis*
The Arab-Israeli Conflict Today 113

Within the Middle East Itself, 114
United States Position, 117
British Role, 121
France and Israel, 122
Concentric Circle, 123
Economic Warfare: The Arab Boycott, 129
Suez Canal, 131
Jordan River Waters, 133
Arab Refugee Problem, 135
United Nations Role, 144

6 *Richard H. Nolte*
United States Policy and the Middle East 148

Groping for a Policy, 151
Wooing the Arabs 1950-1962, 156
Toward a Successful Policy, 174
Current Policy Problems, 177

Georgiana G. Stevens

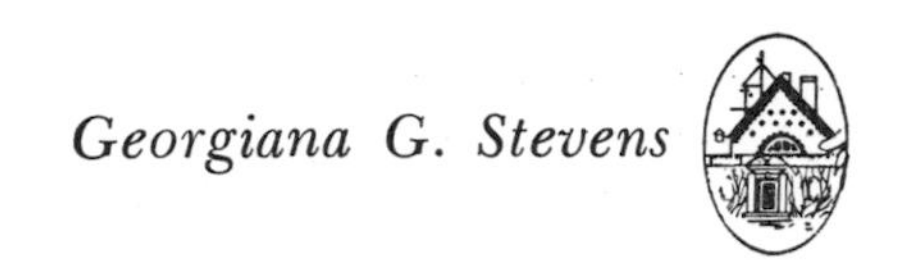

Introduction:

Middle East Perspectives

Active United States diplomatic involvement in the Middle East dates back less than twenty years. As is clear from the text of this book, American concern for strategic and commercial interests followed by many years the American educational missions first established in the area a hundred years ago. Most official business regarding the region was transacted in Constantinople until 1918; and in London or Paris from 1919 until fifteen years ago. Only Tehran and Riyadh were capitals in their own right.

In the forties, however, as an exhausted postwar Britain found it necessary to withdraw from its protective and advisory role in the Middle East, Cold War exigencies required sudden United States responsibility for its defense. This was why Washington had to improvise a policy in 1947; and why since then we have had to decide what our vital interests are in this theater of Arabic-speaking, balkanized countries which first claimed our attention during World War II.

During that war the Middle East theater comprised the countries extending eastward from Libya to the Persian Gulf. Turkey, as

GEORGIANA G. STEVENS *has lived and travelled extensively in the Middle East since World War II. During the War she was a member of the Research and Analysis Branch of the Office of Strategic Services and later of the Office of Intelligence Research, Department of State. She is the author of* The Jordan River Valley *(1956) and of* Egypt: Yesterday and Today, *(1963), and has written for* The Middle East Journal, Foreign Policy Bulletin, Christian Science Monitor, *and London* Economist.

a neutral, was just outside this theater. Iran served as the vital supply route to Russia. The Arab states, as cautious neutrals, furnished oil, transportation, air routes and services.

What is now the state of Israel was in that period a part of Palestine, still under British control. Vital intelligence functions were centered in Jerusalem, and Jewish volunteers from Palestine fought beside British Middle East armies.

America inherits responsibility

The withdrawal of the French from control of Syria and Lebanon in 1946, and Britain's successive relinquishments of its positions of strength thereafter, left a political and strategic vacuum in the entire Middle East theater. This happened at a time when the Russians were demonstrating aggressive ambitions which, had they not been challenged, would have cut free-world air routes across this vital bridge to the East; and would have put the enormous Middle East oil reserves at the disposal of Moscow. Hence, as the Cold War spread to the Islamic world, American involvement became inevitable.

The United States was ill-prepared to assume the role of protector of the region. Knowledge of its peoples was meagre among Americans twenty years ago. Vague prewar concepts of a world of noble bedouins living in black tents were strengthened by the legends of violence and chivalry recorded for the intelligentsia after World War I in the works of T. E. Lawrence. Only two groups of Americans had had experience among the Arabs in the twenties. The first group were the missionaries and teachers who had opened American schools and clinics in Turkey, Iran, Syria, Egypt and Persian Gulf outposts in the 19th century. This small company had learned Turkish, Persian or Arabic, and had learned also to bridge the more subtle communications gap between East and West. They understood the uselessness of haste and the values of indirection in negotiation with the pashas and shaikhs of the time. They also had access to some of the thoughts and aspirations of the young men who ventured into their classrooms and clinics.

The second group of Americans aware of Middle Eastern complexities were the managers and engineers of airlines and oil companies who launched these two enterprises in the Arabian Peninsula and along the routes to the Mediterranean. The practical, day-to-day contacts of these unofficial representatives gave the more perceptive of them considerable insight into Arab ways and expectations. This contact was to evolve rapidly into a cooperative sharing of skills and manpower which has enabled the Arabs to assume more and more complex functions in airlines and oil operations. (For the Americans it has led to their working themselves out of their jobs in all but the most special categories of skill.)

Political setting

None of this rapid transfer of roles could have been anticipated in the Middle East twenty years ago. At that time all the revolutionary energies of Arab leadership were directed at getting foreigners out of political control. The impact of the Western industrial example was not yet apparent. The political struggle to establish separate independent Arab states in former mandated areas was paramount.

The development of the nation-state, as it is understood in the Western world, has been a recent and unnatural process in the Near and Middle East. Historically in these Islamic countries the word *nation* has meant a religious community. Loyalties have been first to family, or tribe, next to religious profession, last to town or city. This was as true of traditional society in independent countries such as Turkey, the Arabian peninsula, and Iran, as in those under Ottoman rule which later came under European mandates.

Present day nationalism is not compatible with such a system of vertically segmented society. Today the emphasis is on building a sense of national consciousness within certain defined borders, most of which follow the frontier lines established arbitrarily by Britain and France after World War I. Thus Middle Eastern nationalism involves displacing local social and cultural patterns which have prevailed for generations.

This traditional structure has best been described as a mosaic system in which there was a division of labor between families and religious sects which gave each person an identity and a set task. Under this system there was room for all. Minorities formed their separate communities and their special occupations, and followed their separate religious and cultural practices. With the postwar drive for nationalization and the concomitant drive for industrialization and modernization, the old mosaic system has inevitably begun to disintegrate. Sons sent off to a national army or into a new industrial occupation are not likely to return permanently to the family fold. As national systems of education spread, styles of behavior and patriotism change. Thus there is a new kind of homogeneity being imposed by the modernizers as secularization and standardization take place. At the price of losing much of its colorful cultural diversity, Middle Eastern society from Morocco to Afghanistan seems destined to conform to some degree to this new pattern of nationalism.

In the 1940's, the old system still prevailed, and in that period, as the United States inherited responsibilities from European powers, our diplomats also inherited a set of unchallenged European suppositions and clichés about Middle Eastern peoples. It was genuinely believed that the natives were not restless but lazy; that their Islamic beliefs made them passive fatalists; that they did not want their European mentors to leave; that money could cure most disaffections; and that they were incapable of operating complex industries (or the Suez Canal); or of originating institutions to fit their obvious needs.

No Westerner in 1947 would have predicted that by 1964 a whole new class of young-men-in-a-hurry would be reshaping the shattered elements of the old mosaic structure of their society. In that structure for generations each craft and sect had had its unchanging separate place in city and village. Even the most optimistic observer could not have foreseen that the crews of American welders and drillers imported in the forties to construct the refineries, ports and pipelines in and out of the desert countries would be entirely replaced by agile, skilled Arabs in fifteen years. Nor was it imaginable that a whole new style of multilingual entrepreneurs, soldiers turned into managers, small landowners and socially aware teachers would appear to take over and try to make over the economies and the halting educational systems of nearly every Arab state from Morocco to Iraq.

Islamic modernization

The appearance of these activist reformers showed that fundamental changes had taken place in mentality and attitude. These involve reinterpretations of Islamic doctrine to adapt it to twentieth century circumstances. Modernists among the Islamic legal hierarchy —the *ulema*—have discovered that their faith does not conflict with a scientific approach to life, with emancipation of women, with the practice of birth control, or with a political innovation called "Arab Socialism." In short, it is possible for good Muslims to try to improve their lives with the aid of techniques and services devised by non-believers. They need not continue to fight a rear guard action against the 20th century. They may become a part of it.

In the first chapter of this book William Sands outlines this process of radical change which has taken place in Islamic thinking. From this historic development all other contemporary changes in

Middle Eastern society flow. Tracing the strands of Western influence on Arab thinking, Mr. Sands shows too, that such concepts as that of "active, willed progress" have been basic in the evolution of modern Islamic thought; but that all such borrowings have had to be reconciled with the fundamentals of Muslim faith. The resulting synthesis gives the modernists, the "new men" in Arab society today, a new sense of self-assurance, even though they remain ambivalent in their attitude toward the West.

Economic and social changes

The two chapters on modernization by William R. Polk and A. J. Meyer suggest the strength and scope of the present drive for change in Middle Eastern society. It is clear from these studies that even though trends are set, the goal of competence in the competitive modern world is barely in sight. Its achievement will be a long process, as Dr. Meyer shows in writing of the lags in development of human resources to manage natural resources. Thus even in the oil-rich states, any sort of balanced economy awaits the training of a whole generation of foremen and managers; the appearance of local investors; and the infusion of much foreign capital. The lag in management manpower can only be made up by education.

Dr. Polk describes the educational revolution now in effect throughout the Middle East. Figures for attendance at vocational schools reveal the urgent stress on technical training. He explains the role played by the military in Arab countries today. As the only technically educated middle class in such a country as Egypt, for example, the army assumes a role in the modernization process which has economic as well as political effects.

The essence of these two studies is that the "new men" are now in charge in many Arab capitals; that they have already altered the social and political pecking order so that yesterday's hierarchy, now relegated to the sidelines on pensions, already looks old fashioned. It is also evident that in all of the states involved, whatever their degree of development, the ultimate aim is some local version of the welfare state, however much individual leaders may differ on means of building it.

Regional politics

The differences over *how* to reorganize Arab society are exposed in Professor Hurewitz's review of regional politics. Much of the disunity now apparent in the region comes from its fragmented character in the period when nearly all its components were client states of different European powers. Thus British ways of doing things, including British socialist solutions to the problem of poverty, have colored the attitudes of Egypt, Iraq and the modernizers of Jordan. By contrast, French styles of doing business and of political expression have influenced Syria and Lebanon. One result, along with many others, is the present split among the Arabs over the desirability or undesirability of, for example, accepting the rigors of "Arab Socialism" as a way of life. The struggle over who shall lead, and along what lines, constitutes the present great debate over Arab unity.

Professor Hurewitz also explains how the several zones within the belt of countries from Morocco to Afghanistan have come to be drawn into closer relationships since all of them gained independence. Thus the North African states—Morocco, Algeria, Tunisia and Libya have all joined the Arab League, as has Sudan. This association, intended to strengthen the Arab position in world affairs, has led also to distinct cleavages. To the east, Turkey and Iran continue to hold aloof from Arab affairs, but they remain involved nevertheless in regional politics. Israel's successful survival, in spite of Arab efforts to isolate it, is shown to be due to its own intense dynamism, to generous foreign aid, and more recently to its expanding relations with African states.

All of the chapters dealing with internal Arab affairs show plainly that nationalism has reached a new stage and acquired new connotations. Now that independence has been attained, the kind of independence becomes important. The tendency among the economic have-nots is toward socialism, with state management of all aspects of development. The haves, particularly the oil-rich states, see other alternatives and promote their own economic independence by gradualist means. Special cases like Israel and Lebanon see their economic security as based on mixed state and private management. The notable instability of Middle Eastern governments seems unlikely to be cured while the struggle goes on over means of reaching agreed ends. But the fact that the ends are the creation of healthier, more modern and self-sustaining states is at least hopeful.

Israel's position

The most advanced state in the Middle East today is Israel. There the inheritance left by the British Mandate government has been entirely transformed to make room for the great influx of new Jewish citizens who have converged on Israel since 1948. Israel is already a socialist, democratic society, in which a mixed economy and egalitarian social structure prevail. Even though Oriental immigrants have come to outnumber the European Jews who established the state, they have not altered its fundamentally Western character. Rather they remain to be fully assimilated into the Israeli body politic. Many of Israel's internal growing pains are caused by the need to homogenize this very mixed population. Its other great internal need is to become more viable economically in a resource-poor country. Its political problems in relation to the rest of the Middle East come from its isolation as a Western-oriented state, not from the fact that its population is Jewish. They are, after all, kin to the Semitic Arabs. There is no racial barrier between the two peoples. But Israel's marked difference from its neighbors, its claims to special importance as the only real home of all world Jewry, and, in practical terms, its superior economic potential, regarded as a threat to less developed neighbors, add to its difficulties in becoming a part of Middle Eastern society. Various aspects of this situation are examined in the text of this book.

United States policy development

Looking back on United States policy development in the forties it is plain that Washington had a Palestine policy before it had a Middle East policy. The Palestine policy was shaped by profound respect for the articulate Jewish leadership and sympathy for the unspeakable horrors suffered by European Jewry under Hitler. A refuge for the remnants of European Jewry was essential. None of the belated efforts to find such refuge throughout the world met the desperate demands of Zionist leaders for the long-promised national home in Palestine.

To an American public almost totally ignorant of the contemporary setting in Palestine, and of the inevitable struggle which its division would cause, the Zionist claims seemed idealistic and fully justified. Only a minority in the United States listened to the protesting voices of those who had lived in the area. The eloquence of the Zionists and the tragic needs of the hour easily overcame the doubts of all but a few worried American officials. In the last chapter of this book Mr. Nolte reviews this phase of American policymaking and brings into focus the forces which determined it.

In the chapter on the *Arab-Israeli Conflict Today,* a serious effort has been made to take some of the heat out of this longstanding policy problem. Mr. Ellis shows that there are new dimensions to the conflict and that time has altered its character. For example, both Israelis and Arab governments agree that vocational opportunities must be opened up to a new generation of Palestine refugees now coming to maturity. This is being done at United

Nations expense. There is also, so far, a tacit acceptance of limited water withdrawals by both sides in the Jordan River water system.

The United States today continues to put the preservation of Israel high on its list of priorities in formulating Middle East policy. But it has ceased officially, as Mr. Nolte shows, to treat Israel as a client state. One reason for this is the belief in Washington that a special military treaty with Israel, for example, would further isolate it in the area and compound its difficulties. There has also been a decision not to try to force direct peace negotiations between Israel and the Arabs, as Israel urges, on the grounds that such an attempt would only further incite Arab resistance. Hence the present policy of quiet diplomacy, which forces no leader into new, irretrievable positions, along with repeated warnings by Washington against aggression from any quarter in the area.

United Nations and the rule of law

United States efforts to encourage a rule of law in the Middle East through United Nations influence and agencies have been consistent since 1945. Several of the chapters in this book bring out this aspect of American policy. They show too how the peace-keeping and relief operations conducted by the United Nations are helping to reduce tensions which would in several specific areas be otherwise unmanageable. If, in a sense, such United Nations efforts are killing the yeast in an actively fermenting region, they also quite plainly are buying time for all concerned.

This book tries to make clear why so much time is needed in this explosive area; what its people are doing with that time; and how their actions affect vital, irreducible American interests.

Neither Israel nor Iran is described specifically in these papers. Where either state is involved in the area as a whole, and with American policy problems, it is, of course, included. It is the area as such, and its prevailing atmosphere of change and conflict, which requires wider understanding if American policy there is to be relevant and constructive.

The American Assembly's purpose is to help an informed public to make up its mind about American policy. Of the many books on the Middle East appearing in this country today, none is focussed primarily on the alternatives for American policy. This set of studies attempts to supply enough highlights on major issues in the Middle East to enable the layman to find his way through its troubled but not hopeless complexities.

William Sands 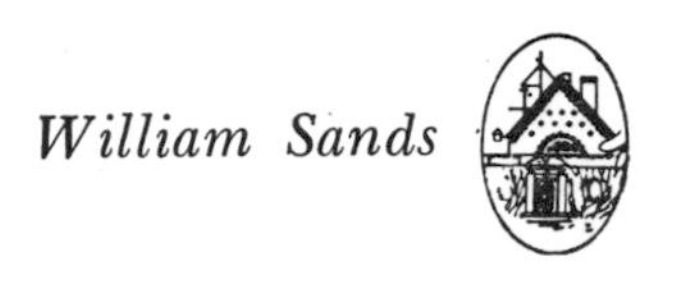

1

Middle East Background

Bedouins, noted for their bluntness, used to greet a stranger with the question *"wash int?"*—"what are you?" Only a generation ago, there were both wider and narrower answers to the question, as posed in the Middle East, than would be likely today. Depending upon circumstances, the interlocutor might then have responded that he was "Muslim," regardless of whether he was a Turk or an Arab; or he might have answered *"Anaizi,"* identifying himself by the name of his tribe, or "tinker," giving his occupation. Nowadays, in answer to the hypothetical query, the response is more likely to be—"Syrian" or "Turk" or "Iranian." The Syrian might also answer "Arab," for reasons we shall see.

So, there was an old "mosaic" in the Middle East, about which many have written. The great horizontal community was Islam—and to almost all, the overlord was the Successor to the Prophet of God—the Caliph, who was also the Ottoman Emperor. Aside from the religious minorities, who had their own head of community, and the linguistic groups, there were sharp vertical segmentations: by

WILLIAM SANDS *is Executive Director of the Middle East Institute and editor of* The Middle East Journal. *From 1941 to 1952 he was a member of the Foreign Service, serving in a number of capacities, including assignments at Jiddah, Beirut, and with two United Nations missions and as deputy Chief of Mission at Tripoli. He is a frequent lecturer and author of articles on Middle Eastern subjects. The views expressed in this paper are his own and do not necessarily represent those of the Middle East Institute or* The Middle East Journal, *neither of which takes an official stand on current issues in the Middle East.*

tribe, clan and family; by city and surrounding region; by trade, often inherited.

Today, a newer horizontal structure has arisen, and the vertical is not as sharp as it was; the formation of this process is a large part of what we examine in this book.

Area and Peoples

There are almost as many definitions of the Middle East as there are persons who write about it. Most of these definitions include Turkey and Iran, as contiguous to the rest and sharing, at least, elements of a common culture. Israel lies at the very heart of every description of the area, which was once categorized by General Eisenhower as the most strategic stretch of land in the world. There was good reason, before the Intercontinental Ballistic Missile and its implications, so to describe this great arc of the world's surface. Now, geography is no longer so important in military calculations, and it is for other reasons that we apply our study to a smaller area.

Smaller, because it is manageable under one cover. Iran, Turkey and Israel have much in common with the Arab countries, insofar as history, topography, climate and culture are concerned, but, in today's world, the "mosaic" has another dimension—nationalism and the political effects thereof, or to put it another way, people, and what they believe, are more important than mere sharing of a "land bridge" between Europe, Asia and Africa. What follows will concern the Arab states almost exclusively; this is not to mean that Turkey, Iran and Israel have less significance, but it is to pose problems singular enough in a modern context.

Unity and diversity in the Arab world

In what is perhaps the most neglected major American address, Mr. Edward Everett, at Gettysburg, posed the essential conditions for a modern political unity. To him the heart of the matter lies in "a common pride in a glorious ancestry." He named what he considered all the other factors that motivate nationalism: common origin, language, belief and law; common political interests; common history; a common interest in "this great heritage of blessings"; geographic contiguity, and even the "works of the engineer," which rearrange geographical features for better communication and economic interchange. It may be useful to examine unity and diversity in the Arab world in these terms.

The thirteen countries which now constitute the Arab League and the parts of the Arabian Peninsula, not yet completely independent, contain a population of some 90-95 millions. Their ethnographic origin it is not possible to determine in categories and percentages. Some 90 per cent of these millions speak a dialect of Arabic; approximately the same percentage is Muslim, and the vast majority of these are of the "orthodox" Sunni sect of Islam, in which belief and law are traditionally commingled.

Islam is one of the simplest of faiths as to profession—"There is no God but the one God, and Muhammad is His Messenger," is an appropriate translation. In addition to believing in the prophetic role of Muhammad and in the Koran—precepts revealed to him by God through the Archangel Gabriel—Muslims also hold that the conduct of their lives must follow certain laws laid down by the prophet in almost every aspect of their daily life. The key words are: *Sunna,* which means, roughly, customs (based on the acts, sayings and approval of the Prophet); *Sharia,* the "way," or the law; and *Islam* itself, which means submission (to God). Muslims thus follow an authoritarian doctrine, a body of teaching laid down for all circumstances of life in the seventh century. They believe in a last judgment, in predestination and in the necessity of certain ritual duties, notably prayer on one's knees five times a day; fasting during the month of Ramadan; giving of alms; and the pilgrimage to Mecca once in a lifetime if this is physically possible.

A true believer thus has a comprehensive system of laws to guide his conduct. Those who share his beliefs are part of the great religious community of Islam, who follow the same laws. This may be one of the reasons for the tenacity with which Muslims have held to their faith. Changing it means abandoning an entire way of life and a sustaining fellowship.

The modernization processes described in this volume have tended in many ways to make faith less important, diminish the practice of religion and the areas of its relevance—a development not unknown elsewhere—but membership in this community is still of the highest value. Perhaps the answer to the seeming paradox lies in the statement of one of the society's most brilliant observers: "Islam is what the Arabs have done in history." Without this, they would be but little. With it, they claim one of the world civilizations.

The second important sect of Islam, the *Shia,* the state religion of Iran, is perhaps in the majority also in Iraq and Yemen, and is an important minority in Lebanon. The theological differences are complex involving an intermediary with God, and concern this study principally because of political implications. As a minority in the Arab world, Shias have tended to be somewhat less enthusiastic about the modernizing trends to be described later. One reason for this may be that, as a minority, they tend to cling to their separateness and, therefore, to old ways that emphasize it.

The Arab states occupy a contiguous area of some 3.7 million square miles (approximately the size of China, or the United States) along the southern and eastern shores of the Mediterranean and in the Arabian Peninsula. Most of these lands are extremely arid, with occasional mountainous, coastal, and river valley stretches of watered land. The northeastern of these stretches, an arc from coastal Syria and Lebanon around, under the Turkish border and down again southeastward into Iraq, has usually been called the "Fertile Crescent," because much of it is rain fed. This geographic fact has also had political implications: Aleppo in Syria and Mosul in Iraq are closer in many ways than are Mosul and Bahgdad, or Aleppo and Damascus. Borders drawn between them are the work of hands other than their own.

Modern progress in communications has brought all these countries into contact with each other to a degree not dreamed of a generation ago.

In the midst of these lands, at the southeastern corner of the Mediterranean, is the state of Israel, which Arab nationalists have always considered a part of historic and geographic Syria, a term which includes modern Jordan and Lebanon as well. Israel today has an area of some 8,000 square miles and a population of some 2,225,000, of whom 2.0 million, approximately, are Jews and the rest largely Arabs. How this state came about and the quarrel between Jews and Arabs are the subject of a later section of this work.

All these are matters of fact; it is when we come to Everett's sentiments that the picture is less clear. Arabs have a common history which can certainly be called a "great heritage" but not since the fall of Baghdad to the Mongols in 1258 have they had even a claim to unity except as a part of an empire ruled by others. The "common pride in a glorious ancestory" is certainly a striking feature of Arab thought, but the pride has had a nostalgic flavor. It is only with this generation that the reveries on past greatness have been transformed into plans for modern expression in the form of a single nation. Even so, Arabs who share the ideal often disagree as to the means and not all share it. So the "common political interests" have to be the subject of inquiry.

Pan Arabism in Theory and Fact

The ideal of Pan Arabism is one nation, extending from the Atlantic to the Persian Gulf and incorporating all the peoples described above. Expression of the ideal is to be found in many current documents; perhaps one of the most significant, because it marked the first concrete step in this direction, is the Proclamation of the United Arab Republic (February 1, 1958). It states:

> . . . the participants feel great pride and overwhelming joy in having assisted in taking this positive step on the road to Arab unity and solidarity—a unity which had been for many an epoch and many a generation the Arabs' much cherished hope and greatly coveted objective. In deciding on the unity of both nations, the participants declare that their unity aims at the unification of all the Arab peoples and affirm that the door is open for participation to any Arab State desirous of joining them in a union or federation for the purpose of protecting the Arab people from harm and evil, strengthening Arab sovereignty, and safeguarding its existence.

After the break-up of the Syro-Egyptian union three years later, a more cautious note was struck in the United Arab Republic Constitution of 1962. But the theme remains:

> Unity cannot be nor should it be imposed. Actually, the nation's main objectives should be equally honorable in their ends and means. Therefore, coercion of any kind is contrary to unity. Not only is it an immoral act, but it also constitutes a menace to the national unity of each Arab people, and, therefore, it is a threat to the concept of the unity of the Arab Nation as a whole. Arab unity is not a uniform constitutional form that must inevitably be applied. It is rather a long path with several stages leading to the ultimate aim. . . .
>
> Any partial unity in the Arab World expressing a popular will of two or more of the Arab peoples is an advanced step towards unity, paving the way for it and extending its roots in the Arab soil. Such circumstances pave the way before the call for total Arab unity.

In the flush of the revolutions of early 1963, both the Syrian and Iraqi governments returned to the theme with vigorous language:

> if. . . the Arabs turned to and supported each other across artificial borders . . . it is because this common struggle and attitude stemmed from the belief of all Arabs that they are one nation, that their unity is the shield of their freedom. . . .

But, on a minatory note:

> The Arab people in Syria . . . will also derive important lessons from the setback of secession, thus transforming the severe trial into a lesson, and the calamity into a clear understanding of the reasons for the setback in order to uproot it.

Thus, the Syrian revolutionary government on March 14, 1963. And the Iraqi government on the next day:

> Iraqi soil is an indivisible part of the soil of one Arab homeland. The Iraqi people are a part of the one Arab nation. . . . The artificial borders planted by imperialism to divide the soil of the one homeland and the regional entities backed by the imperialist monopolies . . . are the greatest obstruction to the real interests of the masses of our people.

And, to the far west of the Arab world, Prime Minister Ahmad Ben Bella of Algeria spoke as follows on March 18, 1963:

> Algeria, which forms part of the Arab homeland and which feels its historic responsibilities towards Arab unity, cannot take a passive attitude towards the goals and ideals which set in motion the wheels of the Arab homeland. We do not need to reaffirm . . . that the goal is one and the destiny is joint.

On the occasion of the visit of President Nasser to Algiers in the summer of 1963, Premier Ben Bella, in his greeting, envisaged Algeria as "the fourth star" in the flag of the United Arab Republic.

The Tunisian Constitution of 1959, in somewhat more moderate language, refers to Tunisia's "membership in the Arab community," but declares the country to be "an integral part" of the Maghrib. King Hussein of Jordan has repeatedly stated that he would abdicate his throne if he thought his person stood in the way of true Arab unity. Such are the statements of the goals. What are the responses?

It is true that, "for many an epoch and many a generation," there had existed the ideal of a revival of Arab glory in the form of a state of their own. But, until this generation, this was a gleam in the eyes of a very few. The long Arab decline during Ottoman rule resulted in an educated élite that was small indeed, and most of the educated, until recently, were of religious background and training, who thought more in terms of a revival of the community of Islam (with Arabs as its originators and, therefore, its first citizens) than of a state based on an ethno-linguistic grouping.

Even the Arab Revolt of 1916 against the rule of the Turks

(once referred to by Arabs as "the great Arab revolution," but no longer) was a dynastic ambition of the Hashimite family in Mecca (though its ideological content was borrowed from Syrians), and extended at most to the Arabs east of Egypt and not to the whole.

In Egypt itself, the idea of gathering Arabs under one fold is new indeed. At the Versailles Peace Conference of 1919 the leader of the Egyptian "delegation," Saad Zaghlul, refused to cooperate with other Arabic-speaking delegations, claiming that his was "an Egyptian problem, not an Arab one." As Prime Minister in the twenties, Zaghlul sarcastically asked an aide—who tried to persuade him to work for Arab cooperation—how much was "zero plus zero plus zero."

A number of clubs, journals and newspapers were established during the thirties to plead the cause of one Arab nation, but the movement was largely confined to young intellectuals, many of whom took as their ideal King Feisal of Iraq. His appeal outside the eastern Arab world was almost nil.

Early in World War II, Premier Nuri al-Said of Iraq adumbrated the idea of a League of Arab States, conceived of as a loose federation of still-independent separate states. The Egyptian Prime Minister, Nahhas Pasha, borrowed and supported the idea, largely, so many observers believed at the time, as a makeweight in his power struggle with the Palace. So, the first forms were instituted. Elaborate plans for cooperation were discussed, but the poor record of cooperation among the Arabs during the Palestine War (1948-49) caused a recoil from even the trifling degree of unity obtained.

In Syria, where the idea of unity was always strongest, successive governments brought into power by *coup* after *coup d'état*, went from one pole to the other concerning plans for union. It was not until the revolutionary government of Egypt, having won kudos in the Arab world for its success in eliminating the British military presence, swung its weight toward the Arab idea that the march toward realization can be said to have begun.

It is not astonishing that an idea, later seemingly so attractive, was long in drawing a major following. As Americans, we may speculate upon the percentage of our ancestors who were exercised about independence, say, in 1775. But our founders invoked the most ancient beliefs (of Englishmen) to support their stand the next year. Among a people who, as one of its most perceptive observers has written, is still "only half-conscious politically," the lag should be less surprising.

In the full tide of the nationalist feeling in America, Everett described any argument against full union as "imaginary, factitious and transient." There were millions in America who did not think so in 1863. One of the remarkable phenomena of the Arab world today is that there is not a single major Arab figure, to the knowledge of the writer, who would deny the eventual goal of complete unity of all Arabs.

In a general way, one can distinguish three levels of current acceptance of this goal. They have subdivisions, endlessly, but they are these:

The Traditional Nationalists—Those who have declared that they loyally support Arab unity, but who, if their actions can be taken as guide, do not—or, at least, think that the dream is still far away from concrete and desirable form. Often, they are the former protagonists of a battle with the colonial, mandatory or protectorate powers, engaged then in a struggle for parochial power within the limits of the "artificial" borders (frequently compromising, frequently gaining a point here and losing another there) to whom the struggle within a larger framework is not very attractive —at their age and in an ambience to be defined as "socialism." They grew to success in a framework borrowed from Western sources, learned compromise in a parliamentary form, *ainsi dit,* and intransigence has formed a part only of their vocabulary. Many of these leaders thundered against the "imperialists" from the floor of parliament during the day and played bridge with them that night. Others are dynasts and their supporters, whom an ecumenical idea, at least in its current popular form, would probably displace. Still others are members of a religious, if not a linguistic, minority (to be discussed below) but who would still call themselves "Arab." And there are those, few perhaps in number, who once were enthusiastic about the goal but have lost the first flush. Some of them refer to the "coercion" which the Egyptian Charter of 1962 took pains to disclaim.

Federalists—By far the most splintered and seemingly the most bewildered, this second group is composed of true believers, again if past preachments and actions are a guide. They want unity, and want it now. *What* kind, and governed by *whom,* and under what principles, they have not decided. As of this writing, they are represented chiefly by the governing Baathist party representatives in Iraq and Syria, who led their countries early in 1963 to the roundtable, with Nasser and the Egyptians, came away with a ringing statement of principles (see above), and have been engaged since in making their reservations.

Pan Arabism, according to its constitution, is the chief tenet of the Baath party. Along with the ideal of unity, their program, on paper, is strikingly similar to that of the Nasser regime in Egypt: "Anti-imperialism, land reform, expropriation of foreign enterprises, increased governmental responsibility for social welfare and education, and emphasis upon enhancing the national awareness of the masses."

Upon achieving power in Syria and Iraq, an executive point of view has been visible in Baath policy. What sounded like democratic ideas in a formal "constitution" of the party have not noticeably been present in the administration. It is the opinion of many specialists that they could not win a majority in any election fairly described as "free"; and that they have depended on alliances with some younger elements in the armed forces to maintain their rule. They have repeated the principles enunciated above; their immediate concern, not unnaturally, has been to remain as governors.

The Baath governments are therefore reluctant to rush into full union now, and negotiate for something less than is desirable according to their own precepts; particularly, guarantees for a party position in the new state, the forms of representation in the federal government (by population or by state), and some protection for the parochial interests built up under differing economic systems and varying wealth and categories of resources. In short, they would settle for a small dose of the principal desideratum immediately.

Advocates of Total Unity—These are, again in general, the followers of Gamal Abdel Nasser, both in Egypt and elsewhere. Nasser, as is clear from the origins of the movement, is by no means the father of unity. But he has become, by a series of circumstances, its leader and present embodiment. The adoption by Egyptians of the idea they first had spurned; the fact that they constitute a quarter, approximately, of the Arabic-speaking peoples; what seemed, to many of the other three-quarters, Abdel Nasser's victories against the "imperialists"—all these factors, plus his personality, have combined to make him the symbol of the immediacy. This group wishes to have "complete" unity, by which they may mean a number of things, but a unity, certainly, which would have a strong central authority, minimize local differences and have a peerless leader at its head. There are some of them who are willing to wait to do this, rather than settle for a little now. If it cannot be today, then surely it will be tomorrow, and they feel they can afford the lag, since time is with them. To them, the "old men" are simply to be swept away, as compromisers with destiny, and betrayers of the cause.

What proportion of the politically conscious share the latter two points of view, it is not possible to say and, in any event, the proportions would probably change from day to day. (It should be noted, moreover, that this description of the groups applies only to Egypt and the Arabs to the east and not to North Africa, where, in spite of Ben Bella's statement cited, unity does not seem to be an immediate concern.)

Attitudes of Minorities

No country is without its minorities and the Arab countries have as rich and varied a selection as any grouping in the world—this in spite of the massive Arab Muslim majorities posited in the opening of this chapter. Historically, the Arab-Muslim record of tolerance for minorities is far better than that of European-Christian society. But the fact that religious minorities are allowed, through the *millet* (nation) system, legally to organize their own personal status (generally, matters of marriage, divorce, guardianship and inheritance) made for a feeling of separateness. This separateness was so complete that one man had only to look at another to identify him by religious community. His dress, beard or barbering of it, even his accent and vocabulary, distinguished a member of a *millet*—though the one might live directly across a very narrow street from the other. This process of identification was carried into almost every detail of daily life—occupation, diet, family custom and, of course, worship. What was to one the central fact of his religion—"the son of God"—was to the other the greatest heresy possible, *"shirk,"* or, participation in the Godhead. "God was not born and God does not father."

With the growth of modern secular nationalism, the idea of one system of law for all citizens has gained considerable ground. Reaction of the minorities to this development is mixed. In one sense, they are more fully a part of the whole under new national systems of law but, in another, they have lost old privileges which go with separation and self-constitution of community.

Two of the thirteen countries of the Arab League have substantial minorities which occupy a definite geographical area and do not consider themselves to be Arab; they are Iraq and the Sudan.

The Kurds

In Iraq, the Kurds occupy the mountainous area of the north-northeast, and may number as many as 1.5 million persons, or some 20 per cent of the population as generally estimated. Though Sunni Muslim, they speak a language closely related to Persian (and not at all to Arabic) and with their 3 to 4 million cospeakers in Iran and Turkey, who occupy a contiguous area, they consider themselves, at the least, to have a separate identity as a people. Many of them consider themselves a separate nation, and their minimum demand on Iraq is for a "voluntary fraternal union," which would include, in its implementation, provincial determination for the expenditure of oil royalties—much of which is generated in territory they consider Kurdish.

While there are Arabicized Kurds who have taken an important part in Iraqi political life, these elements in revolt feel they would be even more swallowed up in a greater Arab union than they are today in Iraq; this may be one reason for the extent of the Kurdish demands for autonomy in the spring 1963 negotiations with the Baghdad government—to gain as much as possible before it became even more difficult to assert their individuality in a larger framework. Towards the end of 1963, the rebel Kurdish leadership described the Baathist government of Iraq as "worse" than that of the assassinated Kassim.

Christians and "pagans"

In Sudan approximately one-third of the country in the south is occupied by non-Muslim and non-Arabic speaking tribes. It is not that they have any sense of nationhood of their own, but simply that they have no sense of participation in a country which calls itself Arab. As in the rest of sub-Saharan Africa, a process of Islamization is going on, accompanied by Arabicization through education, but the great majority remain pagan or Christian. Missionary spokesmen for these people complain that the government attempts to suppress their separate identity. Thus private and foreign schools have been closed, as they have also been in Syria and Egypt.

It is a tenet of Arab Nationalist theory that religion has nothing to do with the full rights of every citizen of the state. But it is also a feeling of many that, in practice, one has to be of Muslim origin (even if not religious in the practicing sense) to be a full-fledged citizen. The Coptic minority in Egypt is often adduced as proof of the thesis. The Copts are descendants of the pharaonic Egyptians, traditionally converted by St. Mark, and the very word "copt" means "Egyptian." Some 1.5 million of them, out of Egypt's 27 million, are a religious rather than a linguistic minority, but it seems to be true that they do not participate in the political life of the country to the relative extent that Muslims do. Whether this is by choice, or by exclusion, in ways subtler than law, is the argument that arises concerning minorities almost everywhere.

Jews

In Israel, the minority situation is reversed as a result of the Zionist movement for a national home in Palestine and the subsequent creation of the state in 1948. More than half of the immigration since then has come from eastern Jewry, partially as a result of an active campaign of "ingathering," and a substantial portion of their number from Arab states, particularly Iraq and Yemen. Only in North Africa are there sizeable communities left, and these are going the way of the others. In some countries, such as Lebanon and Tunisia, Jews do participate freely in public life. Most others do not or cannot. An official statement by an Arab League spokesman in 1963 on the Arab attitude towards Jews and Zionism summarizes the Arab position:

> We in the Arab world draw a distinction between Judaism and Jews on the one hand and Zionism and Israel on the other. Judaism is a religion of universal values. We regard Jews as members of a religious fellowship having no national ties with their co-religionists of other lands. Zionism, on the other hand, is a political movement of imperialist dimensions, which aspires to link all Jews, by means of ethnic and nationalistic bonds, into a worldwide nation, a 'peoplehood' having as its political center the State of Israel, in which all Jews must ultimately be 'ingathered.'

The official attitude of Israel towards its Arab minority is that they are full citizens of the state, but that the territory in which they reside, if it lies next to an Arab state, must be under security precautions and, therefore, so are its residents. Many Arabs do live in border areas. Arabs elect members to the Israeli parliament and have their own municipal governments in several places; the security restrictions to which many of them are subject, such as those on ownership of land, residence and travel, are the matter of much complaint.

Under nationalistic regimes on both sides of this conflict there seems to be poor hope that either minority can lead a life which corresponds to its aspirations.

Armenians form significant communities only in Lebanon and Syria. Though they are an ethnic, and to some extent a linguistic minority, they have participated in the political life of the two countries actively. Perhaps a primary reason for this identification is their economic stake in the well-being of the countries they now call their home. They are, relatively speaking, a prosperous group, and have benefited, particularly in Lebanon, from traditional hostility elsewhere to oppressed minorities. A large proportion of them came, two or three generations ago, from Turkey.

Scattered minorities elsewhere are not sufficiently numerous to maintain significant attitudes.

Lebanon: A special case

Lebanon is a special case in almost every category about which one would wish to examine it. Insofar as minorities go, it is more so. There is no majority in Lebanon, in a religious sense, though almost everyone speaks Arabic. It is theoretically divided, 6–5, Christian-Muslim, though there has been no census for decades now. It should be noted that the Christian-Muslim dichotomy is subdivided into numerous communities and sects, the listing of which alone would outrun our space. A recent estimate, based on identity cards, gives it a population of 2.1 million, without an ethnic or religious count.

The long European influence on the Christian community has made Lebanon a window to the West. Although Lebanese Christians were some of the earliest contributors to the ecumenical idea among Arabs, it cannot be said that most of them wish to be joined in an over-all Arab state. No percentages, by poll or otherwise, exist to quote. The Islamic Arab community, again generally speaking, feels itself more a part of Syria than of Lebanon. Some compromise was necessary, and Lebanese good sense provided one in 1943. It was agreed, between Muslim and Christian politicians, that Lebanon should continue to exist as a separate state, regardless of unity plans for others, but that it should loyally support Arab cooperation and Arab causes as agreed upon in the League of Arab States. This "national pact," so called, worked well—except for the experience of the revolt of 1958, about which one acute observer remarked that both Christians and Muslims accused the other of betrayal, and that both were perfectly right. The shock of discord over, the two parties seem to have returned to the old arrangement. It seems, in all fairness, the best for a country which has no majority.

North Africa minorities

The North African countries of Algeria and Morocco also pose a different problem—the extent to which they may be called Arab. In their long colonial presence, the French attempted to exacerbate local rivalry (divide and lose!) by emphasizing an Arab-Berber difference of origin in the population of the two. No respectable ethnography has been done to prove one point of view or another;

it is enough to say that Arabicized Berbers constitute a considerable proportion of the inhabitants. Both countries describe themselves as "Arab" in their official documents, and this should suffice for the rest of us. (A French journalist recently wrote that Ben Bella, Premier of Algeria, "likes to think of himself as an Arab." What else then?)

As to what may possibly be described as a minority, there are, or have been, several hundred thousand Europeans, most of them of French citizenship, in Tunisia, Algeria and Morocco. (There are still a number of Italians in Libya, nearly all of them in Tripolitania.) These are the remnants of European rule and play almost no part in the political life of the states, though, in places, they still have an important part in its economics. They seem destined to disappear, as these countries, either in a Maghrib union or in a greater one, shed their past.

Nationalism and Neutralism

In traditional Islamic thought, there was no *territorial* concept of loyalty and, therefore, no possibility of a nation-state. Law ran with the person, not with the border. After the borrowing of the idea of nationalism from the colonial powers in the nineteenth century, it became a weapon in the hands of Arabs to deal with the "imperialists" in the twentieth. When Arabs did take on the idea of a territorial entity totally their own, sacred as to square-mileage, they did so *à outrance*. The sowers have reaped one hundred fold, and now complain that the crop is tares instead of grain.

Any society whose principal motivation is the glorification of self—typical of nationhood and even more so when it has just come into being—is likely to feel "apart" in many ways. That this sentiment should take a neutralist form during a struggle between world powers should not surprise Americans. A certain amount of subsuming of self is necessary for any alliance—a problem our own country now faces acutely—and for new, and weaker, nations the problem is even sharper.

George Washington stated the proposition for countries such as these, faced as he was with a conflict between the major powers of his time:

> Europe has a set of primary interests which to us have none or a very remote relation. Hence she must be engaged in frequent controversies, the causes of which are essentially foreign to our concerns. Hence, therefore, it must be unwise in us to implicate ourselves by

> artificial ties in the ordinary vicissitudes of her politics or the ordinary combinations and collisions of her friendships or enmities. . . . It is our true policy to steer clear of permanent alliances with any portion of the foreign world.

As America was confronted with the rivalry between France and England, so the Arab States find themselves the objects of a struggle between the West and the Soviet Union for their favor and support. Their response has not been unanimous, and it has varied in several of the countries, according to internal politics and to the changing patterns of the politics of the larger powers.

In the years since the end of World War II and the emergence of most of these states into independence, the over-all trend has been towards neutralism. It should be remembered that most of these states have been tied to the West by previous bonds not of their making. Egypt, Sudan, Jordan, Iraq, Kuwait and Libya, in one permutation, combination or the other, had been associated with Great Britain. Algeria, Morocco, Tunisia, Syria and Lebanon had been, in different ways, tied to France. Only Saudi Arabia and Yemen, before and during World War II, had been totally free of formal obligations.

If this neutralism, then, has seemed to take an anti-Western coloring, it is at least understandable in that it was the West *from* which they were turning. A welcome to the other party was one way to say farewell to the master of the past. The undertakings which the United States, both formally and by deep sentiment, has made with Britain and France associated us with these powers beyond our power to retrieve, even if we had so wished, and which, as was inevitable, we did not.

Nasser: The symbol

Gamal Abdel Nasser has become the symbol of neutralism just as he has become a symbol of unity. Again, he has by no means been its initiator. Early in 1950, the Syrian Minister of Defense, Akram al-Hourani, stated that Arabs were friends of the Soviet Union for the same reason that they had been friends of Germany during World War II—one's enemy's enemy is one's friend.

Late in 1951, the Egyptian government of Nahhas Pasha rejected the offer of the Western powers to erect a Middle East Defense Organization, or the paradigm of NATO. Nahhas and his followers had been nominally anti-British, but had actually cooperated when important matters arose. The offer of a direct military alliance was too much even for this government to accept.

The British agreement, in 1954, to withdraw its permanent military presence in Egypt brought about a temporary feeling of good will, but two incidents early in the next year gave impetus to the movement towards neutralism with a strong anti-Western bias. The first was Iraq's adherence to a military agreement, first with Turkey, later to grow into the Baghdad Pact, which aroused the ire of Egypt and was denounced as a betrayal of the Arab cause. The second incident was Israel's large-scale attack, as reprisal, on the Gaza strip early in 1955, which led directly to the first major involvement of Egypt with the Eastern Bloc.

As the extent of the Eastern bloc arms deal with Egypt became clear, the United States and Britain, in the early summer of 1956, withdrew support for Egypt's High Dam project. Nasser's reaction in nationalizing the Suez Canal Company, a private French concern, 44 per cent of whose stock was held by the British government, marked a further cleavage with the West. Condemnation by the United States of the subsequent Anglo-French-Israeli invasion of Egypt in that autumn temporarily revived good will for the United States, but by no means for the West as an entity. And immediate economic measures by this country, considered as punitive to Egypt, sharply increased the swing to the Soviet side of neutralism.

Further efforts by the United States in 1957 and 1958 to check Arab neutralist movements in Syria, Lebanon, Jordan and Iraq (as described later in this book) resulted chiefly in a hardening of the neutralist attitude, and by the end of 1958 it could be said that most Arab nationalists considered America their enemy. Among them was the new government of Iraq which, although cool toward Nasser, had overthrown a pro-Western regime and was about to denounce the Baghdad Pact.

By their support of the High Dam Project, by their willingness to furnish arms to the Arabs, and by their frequent criticisms of Israel, the Soviet bloc gained much kudos in the Arab world during the same period.

The 1958 watershed

Since 1958, there has gradually come about more of a balance in Arab neutralism. This has occurred for a variety of reasons: the United States has resumed economic aid, principally to Egypt, and mostly in the form of food grains, to an even greater extent than before; Nasser's abrupt replies to Russian criticism of his internal anti-Communism seemed to show he was neutral only in international relations; the (principally) Baathist revolts in Iraq and

Syria have been anti-Communist in character (particularly in the former); the disenchantment with the Soviet side of the neutralist balance has vindicated the prediction of a specialist writing in 1955:

> At the present time many leaders of Middle Eastern and Asian states are still blinded by the new light from Moscow. But we may reasonably hope that in the long run, when they have had the opportunity and leisure to compare Russian and Western treatment—in what is given, how much is given, and what is required in return—the comparison will not be to our disadvantage. The principle task of Western statesmanship at this time is to make sure that there is a long run.

To generalize, again very broadly, it has been the conservatives and the reactionaries who have tended, at first, in the Arab world, to support the former colonial power (and its allies), and the liberals and radicals, at first, to support the power opposed to the former, particularly so when that power (the U.S.S.R.) had created a revolution. It was only upon the liberals' and radicals' obtaining responsibility that they realized a basic fact—the motivations of the supposedly anti-colonial power had little, or nothing, to do with their own. Thus, it has not been so much by statesmanship on the part of the Western powers, as by prudence on the part of Arab leaders, that there has been a "long run."

The Influence of the West

All this reaction to, and preoccupation with, the West leads to the question: How did the influence begin? In a way, it began with political and military facts at the end of the 18th century. The invasion of Egypt by Napoleon in 1798 is usually taken as a starting point. The dates of ideas are not so easy to pin down. An interchange between East and West has been going on at least since the time of the Phoenicians. The Crusades had equally important effects, though at that time it was more a question of influence of the East on the West than the reverse. French missionaries had been active in Lebanon since the time of Louis XIV.

But it was with Napoleon's arrival and occupation that a massive importation of ideas and institutions took place. This process has not been confined to Egypt or to the Middle East. It is a part of what William McNeill calls *The Rise of the West*. He delineates a secular trend of the impression of Western culture on non-Western ones. The latter have become convinced of the former's superiority, and have been busy adopting—and adapting—it. In a way, its ideas have gone in the holds of the same ships that carried the soldiers and the artifacts of the West. The student missions sent from Egypt largely to France, were instrumental in beginning to change ways of thought, and Muhammad Ali and his successors imported Western techniques wholesale, so that his grandson, Ismail Pasha, could say that he had made Egypt a part of Europe. The Egyptian occupation of Syria in the 1830's had transported many Western innovations there.

The idea of the nation state

It seems clear that the largest intellectual influence on Arab thought in the 19th century came from France. This influence has been brilliantly analyzed by Professor Albert Hourani in his *Arab Thought in the Liberal Age.* As he points out, the Egyptian writer, Tahtawi, one of the first of the new thinkers, dreamed of Egypt as a national state on the Western model and borrowed the territorial idea of sovereignty from Montesquieu. It was the Tunisian and Ottoman statesman, Khayr Al-Din Pasha, who rationalized the adoption of Western institutions by declaring that their purpose was really to fulfill the spirit of the sacred law. As first minister in both Tunisia and Istanbul, he did import many of the Western forms of rule.

American influence on the Arab world in the 19th century was largely exercised by missionaries and teachers at the American University of Beirut. Their influence is clearly to be found in the writings of the Lebanese Bustani who preached a new Syrian patriotism and urged the adoption of the "world of science and invention."

The idea of progress

But the more famous of the Muslim religious leaders of the 19th century also devoted themselves to the study of Western learning—again largely French—and attempted a reconciliation of Islamic and Western civilization. Jamal al-Din al-Afghani who was probably a Persian and who lived and taught all over the Middle East, learned from the French historian Guizot the idea of "active, willed progress" and preached the concept as necessary to the regeneration of a Pan-Islamic state and to the defeat of the designs of the imperial powers. Carrying on in the tradition, his follower Muhammad Abduh, who held the highest legal post in Egypt and greatly influenced Egyptian politics, adopted the positivism of Auguste Comte, the French philosopher, and its implications as to the improvability of man. These political leaders and intellectuals were impressed with the new power, particularly the armed might, of the West, as well as with their own relative stagnation or decline.

While the Arab intellectuals were absorbing Western ideas and philosophy, the political leaders of the time were gradually importing some of the trappings of the constitutional state, a process which began in the '60's and '70's. The fact that none of the Arab countries was completely independent at this time prevented the adoption of the full paraphernalia.

Woodrow Wilson's ideas on democratic rule and the liberation of nationalities ruled by the Ottoman Empire swept the Arab world immediately after World War I, but the mandate system imposed by the Western allies prevented the full play of these ideas in precisely those areas which seemed to be most ready for and receptive to them. The importation, or the imposition, of Western style constitutions and parliaments in the mandated and occupied countries did little or nothing to further the spirit under which such institutions are supposed to thrive. They resulted, in most instances, in a travesty of parliamentary government. With the disappearance of the mandates after World War II, the net effect was to leave power in the hands of small oligarchies whose members, generally speaking, had imperfect grounding in their own culture, and only a superficial understanding of the ideas of the West. Thus there were parliaments in the Fertile Crescent countries, Iraq, Syria, Lebanon, and in Egypt in the forties. Their members were drawn largely from the rich landowning class and the leaders of independence movements. Elections were rigged to keep power in the hands of this upper class—the "old men" of emerging nationalism, as viewed by their successors in the reformist, military governments of the sixties. So long as the "old men" prevailed it was impossible to alter the feudal landholding structure or to initiate land and tax reforms on modern, Western lines. Yet the façade was there, looking superficially like its Western models.

Russian influence

In all this time, Russian influence on Arab political thought seems to have been minimal. There were a few Arabs attracted by Tolstoy's brand of humanism. A small number of intellectuals have been trained in Moscow or elsewhere in Communist techniques in the last forty years or so. Only when these latter were remarkable persons in their own right (Khalid Bakdash, of Syria, for example) have they played any role in Arab thinking.

One who defected—Michel Aflaq, principal dialectician of the Baath party, originally a Communist—has used the techniques he learned in his Communist period to intellectual advantage in constructing another ideology his former tutors would consider heresy. There is a precedent. Many of the most violent anti-Western elements of the Arab world are those who were trained by Westerners and have rejected much of the thought which lay behind the training—but not the technique.

Since the process is an ever-continuing one, we cannot speak in terms of the end result of the impact of the West. At the moment, it seems fair to state that the so-called "old men," the early Arab nationalists, imported the formal apparatus of liberal Western government but not the substance. The "young men" are importing the substance of the welfare state as developed largely by European theorists, but are still engaged in a search for their own forms of government which may have little to do with government as developed in European civilization.

Meanwhile they rely heavily on army support as they experiment in methods of government. As will become apparent in this book, the reform movements in the Arab states have only been able to achieve power because they have the support of the young officers within their countries. This enables them to hold power and to coerce the populations into accepting reformist decrees, such as land distribution to peasants, compulsory education and tax payment. At the present stage such authoritarian methods seem likely to continue until a wider constituency can be developed to support modernization by more democratic means.

The Constants and the Variables

It is true in Middle Eastern diplomacy, just as it is in the rest of the world, that what may seem pressing problems at a given moment are, later, as often subsumed by other new problems as they are solved. When matters which appear to be those of utter national survival arise, others which have been important are quietly put into their place. So, with the Arab States, the *constant,* since their nominal independences beginning shortly after World War I, has been what seemed to them a struggle for "complete" sovereignty. No nation among them is an exception to this rule, though they have applied it with varying degrees of—what looks to others—severity. The struggle to fight free of mandates, then of "military presence," then of special treaty relationships, and, latterly, what they call "economic imperialism," all follow the same pattern—called in Arabic *"istiqlāl al-tamm"*—"Complete independence." Looked at in this way, the Arab-Israeli conflict becomes only another dimension of the above.

The variables are endless and unpredictable as this book will show. Who could have said, fifteen years ago, that the Hashimite and Saudi dynasties would have come together in a military alliance, after generations of bitter rivalry, or foreseen which of the other Middle Eastern governments would make temporary alliances with Western or Eastern powers, later to switch sides, or be more or less "neutral"? These are the matters that depend on "X" factors which no observer, however steeped in the facts of the area, can hope to prophesy, and it is almost useless to attempt prophecy. At the point of writing, for instance, President Nasser of the United Arab Republic believes, along with General de Gaulle and Mr. Walter Lippman, that the modern revolution in weaponry and the resultant nuclear stalemate have rendered military alliances obsolete. But it is not difficult to imagine a set of military circumstances that might change their minds and ours.

Out of all these variables, perhaps, there arises another constant—change. Political, social and economic upheaval has become the expected, and not a thing at which to be astonished, as will become clear in the following chapters.

William R. Polk 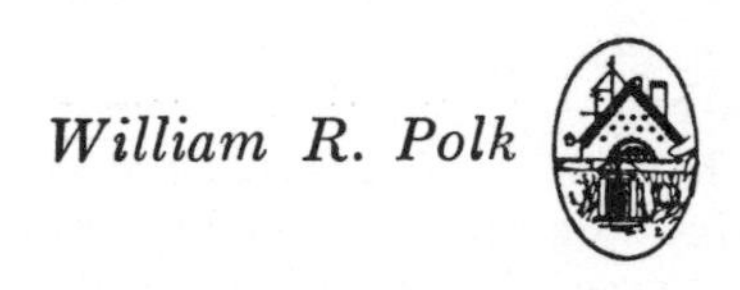

2

Social Modernization: The New Men

Western experience and tradition are the sources from which we have extrapolated such cosmopolitan modes of analysis as sociology and economics. It is natural, therefore, that we should look for the growth of a middle class as both an index of progress and as a motive force in the developing new nations. That a middle class is growing in the Middle East today is undeniable. We can perceive it in all of the indicators we use on our own society; and we can observe that its role is becoming increasingly important as men whom we classify as "middle class" have aspired to control the destinies of the several Middle Eastern states. However, our analytical experience in recent history has shown that explanations based on the middle class as we understand it in the West are inadequate to explain developments in other areas. As a result, we have sought to refine our definitions of middle class or to single out such groups as entrepreneurs and army officers to provide more useful guides. In this chapter I should like to suggest that a different system of categorization may offer a simpler and more useful insight into the

WILLIAM R. POLK *is a member of the Policy Planning Council of the United States Department of State. Until 1961, Mr. Polk was Assistant Professor of Semitic Languages and History at Harvard University, and a member of the Middle Eastern Studies Center. Among his writings on the Middle East are the following:* What the Arabs Think (*1952*); Perspective of the Arab World (*1956*); Backdrop to Tragedy: The Struggle for Palestine (*1957*).

motivations and working of the developmental process in the Middle East.

From experience with our own and similar societies, we usually divide men into strata by largely economic criteria. Other divisions have, in the past at least, been more meaningful in other societies. To analyze the actions and attitudes of other societies, social *groups* are often more useful than classes. In traditional Arab society, for example, we can relate one man to another through the family, the clan and the tribe—which are only in part kinship systems—in ways which explain conduct with more exactitude and certainty than by other means. In mixed societies, in addition, one must take account of subgroups which are separated from the rest of society by linguistic, ethnic, and/or religious frontiers—for example, the Kurds, Copts, Maronites, Shiites *et al.*

The Modernizers

In the contemporary scene, yet a further division may be helpful in our attempt to understand a society in the process of rapid transformation. This, I suggest, is a differentiation of the "new" from the "traditional" elements in society regardless of class, religion, or kinship. Both the "new men" and the traditional men can be seen to exist in all social groups and at all levels of society. Many, of course, but certainly not all, are to be found in the middle class. It appears to me that these new men form a sort of "vertical" society—composed of all classes—distinct from the traditional society. They have an inner similarity and share certain values despite the obvious differences in economic, educational and political levels of their members.

The growth of this core within Middle Eastern society is one of the most significant changes in recent years. But, viewed historically, what we observe today can be seen to be but a recent phase in a much older process.

Traditionally society is not, of course, completely static. Contemporary hallmarks of conservatism in the traditional society were, in their day, often marks of social or aesthetic advance. This is as true of social values as of such superficial signs of social usage as the fez or tarbush. Regarded by Atatürk and Nasser as the very symbol of reaction, the fez was a revolutionary innovation when introduced in the third decade of the nineteenth century to replace the more cumbersome and time-consuming turban. When the Lebanese Amir Bashir put aside his turban and affected the fez, he was symbolizing his entry into a new age; when Atatürk later banned the fez in Turkey, he was saying in effect that Turkey was to turn to the modern West and forget its Islamic past.

Likewise, indeed, on a more profound level, Islam was certainly revolutionary with new ideas on the status of women, the brotherhood of believers and the role of government in early periods. Yet, modern Middle Eastern rulers have found in Islamic values a barrier to rapid modernization and have sought in secular nationalism a replacement for some aspects of Islam. Similarly, we should expect to find, and as will be seen below do find, that the "new men" of each generation tend to fade, relatively speaking, into traditional society as they are overtaken and surpassed by each new generation. This is not necessarily to say that their role as modernizers has ended; some have come to be appreciated only long after their times. Moreover, some of the most significant innovations in the Middle East have been brought about by men who were, personally, deeply committed to the old order.

To gain some perspective on the current situation, let us turn back to the early years of the nineteenth century to examine the nature of social change.

Traditional society

Writing in the first half of the nineteenth century, that remarkable observer and student of Egyptian life, E. W. Lane, echoed the thoughts of many previous writers when he pointed to lethargy as a hallmark of the people of the Nile. Since the Egyptians could so easily support themselves on their fertile land, lacked a major incentive to devote themselves to industry and found their simple and often crude products satisfactory, they could afford the luxury of technological backwardness. The picture painted by Lane and others is of a people whose lives were minutely regulated by established custom and whose appetites were as yet unwhetted for the new and the exotic produce of the Industrial Revolution or the stimulating if disquieting ideas of the Renaissance, the Reformation or the Enlightenment.

In the Syrian hinterland (historic Syria included what is now Jordan, Israel and Lebanon) and the Iraqi basin, likewise, the people had accepted traditional approaches to life. Every man had his place in society. If that place were not entirely satisfying, it *was* God ordained. To attempt to change it was unnatural. Indeed, even the word "change" (Arabic—*ghaiyara*) carried the implication of "to corrupt" or "change for the worse." What was, was right, and the limits of acceptable human endeavor were narrow. As Professor Joseph Schacht has written:

> One ancient Arab idea, arising from the very core of the mental endowment of the Arabs . . . became the central concept of Islamic religious law and theology. . . . The Arabs were, and are, bound by tradition and precedent; they were, and are, dominated by the past. . . . Whatever was customary, was right and proper; whatever their forefathers had done, deserved to be imitated.

The facts of life lent weight to this natural bent toward conservatism. The bedouin, who lived beyond the reach of the government, along the fringes of the Great Syrian Desert, had a highly sophisticated approach to a most difficult environment. To change his pattern of life, the bedouin would be required to change his environment. Only in the way the bedouin lives and works can the extensive resources of the desert be utilized. Conditions in the desert and the surrounding steppe lands set precise limits on the ability of man and animals to stay in a single location. Rainfall, wells and pasturage are meagre, finite, and not quickly renewed, so groups of more than a score can seldom congregate for long. Nomadism is thus necessary.

Historically, as they were lured by the wealth of the sown lands or driven by the harsh unpredictability of the desert or the fury of their fellows, some bedouin have always been involved, slowly but steadily, in changing their environment and their pattern of life. Despite their many cultural and social motivations to remain free, proud and "pure," groups of bedouin drift away from the desert in a steady stream. "Sedentarization" is perhaps as old a process as nomadism. Significantly, one of the Arabic words meaning "to settle" (*quantara*) also means "to possess a hundred-weight," for when a man becomes acquisitive, he must settle.

The villager, tilling a small plot of land, consuming most of what he produced, in need of only the most rudimentary weapons, tools and consumables and fearful of outside influences, was content within his small world. The villager shared much of his culture with the bedouin, but whereas the nomad ranged widely over at least vast, if not markedly different, expanses of the world's surface, the villager stuck close to a narrow, confining world. Surrounded by kinsmen with whom he shared his means of livelihood, the villager was intent on protecting his water rights, market places, and common pasturage. Deeply wedded to his land, the villager married within his village and called it his "nation" (*watan*). Oppressed or ravaged from the one side by the rapacious nomad and, from the other, by the equally rapacious tax collector, the villager sought to retain and enjoy rather than to expand his means of livelihood. Seldom it was that he attempted to market his produce or to communicate with the world outside of the small autarkic clusters of villages that were the limits of his world.

The city dweller, likewise, was enmeshed in a world of narrow scope but known satisfactions. The mosque was his school, his club and his parliament. In craft and religious guilds and brotherhoods, his relations with his fellows were drawn tightly together. His neighbors, like those of his village cousin, were often his kinsmen. They and he were segregated from other neighborhoods by walls and were ruled internally by men at least in part of their choosing. In the city as in the village or the tribe, man was never isolated but was able to find a stable, understood and reasonably satisfying pattern of life.

The government was distant and its local agents were often foreigners, partaking of little of the local life and adding less to it. The government agent was himself a sort of nomad, camped in his headquarters, but little concerned with the life around him except in the collection of taxes.

More exposed, less secure and less integrated were the minority groups. Not the Muslim, therefore, but usually the members of the minorities were most open to change.

The British agent, Dr. John Bowring, in his report on the "Commercial Statistics of Syria" in 1839, said that he found the Muslims to be the most backward as a group since they "accumulate little capital and fail to practice the arts progressively" whereas "most of the commercial establishments . . . [were] in the hands of the Christian or Jewish population." The merchant, he wrote, "is rarely an honored being—the power of the sword and the authority of the book—the warrior and the Ulema (religious leadership) are the two really distinguished races of society. All productive labour—all usefully employed capital is regarded as belonging to something mean and secondary."

Traditionally, the Christians, particularly of the Levant, had been in contact with European missionaries and many had studied European languages. The Jews were less aided by European powers or organizations but were freed from many of the inhibitions of Islamic politics and were somewhat affected by European contacts. Moreover, the Christians and Jews were able to enter into professions which the Muslims despised. In the Levant, for example, Jews and Christians were money lenders; the men who served as the equivalent of ministers of finance to the pashas of Saida were Jews and Christians, and the prevalence of such names as Katib, Haddad, Najjar (scribe, blacksmith and carpenter) among the Christians testifies to their economic activity. The rulers of Egypt traditionally used the Copts as their tax collectors and as the cadres of their civil service. Almost a century later, in 1910, about 45 per cent of the civil service staff of Egypt was Coptic.

Yet, as a minority element, with an always insecure position in society, except in certain parts of Mount Lebanon, with a lesser stake in established society and a small commitment to the Islamic value system, the Christian was more open to change and specifically to Western influence than the Muslim or the Jew. However, the Christian, by his sect within Christianity, was selective: Maronite Catholics were not favorably disposed to Westernization at the hands of the American Protestants and were even more hostile to Westernization through the agency of Muslims. Interestingly, the British developed, but could not implement, a program of technical assistance education for their friends, the Lebanese mountain people, as early as 1841.

Egypt on the eve of change

At the end of the eighteenth century, the population of Egypt was approximately two million people. Egyptian society can be generally said to have been divided into three quite distinct groups—or two distinct social classes. The upper class was composed of the linguistically and ethnically alien military "power elite," the Mamluks, and the primarily Egyptian, religious hierarchy of Islam. The lower class, almost entirely Arabic-speaking Egyptians, was made up of the petty traders and artisans in the cities and towns and the peasant mass of the rural population. Such middle groups as existed were primarily non-Muslim—either native Copts (of whom there were about 150,000) or Jews (of whom there were apparently very few) or foreign minorities, mainly Europeans, of whom there were about 8,000. These groups were set apart from the rest of society by distinctive dress, social customs and religious practices.

All military and governmental affairs were under the control of the 12,000 Turkish Mamluks while the Egyptian, Arabic-speaking, Muslim population was confined to non-military and non-governmental affairs. The Mamluks were both more and less than "military" in our sense—they were a martial caste but they were not professional in the sense of being trained in military affairs. There is no indication that the Turkish soldiery in the eighteenth century were given any specialized education, although it is assumed that they were given the customary religious instruction.

When, in the course of the eighteenth century, a few Turks began to realize that they would need to copy some of the techniques of the West in order to defend themselves—and to overcome rivals for power—they encountered the prejudices of the religious authorities and the entrenched privileges of the traditional military elite. Neither group wanted reform since its place in society was paramount and comfortable. Such reform as the modernizers were able to bring about was primarily effected by foreign technicians. For example, even the Sultan had to hire an English engineer to help to reorganize the Ottoman fleet and a Hungarian to reform the artillery, and the Egyptian Mamluk beys followed their example slowly and grudgingly. In fact, so slowly that only a crushing defeat by the small but modern forces of Napoleon could stir a few of the leaders to try to learn from the West. Not only Muhammad Ali Pasha, the most influential and famous of these leaders, but also his domestic rivals of the time, al-Alfi Bey, Hussain Kashief al-Yahudi al-Afranji and Khusrau (later Ottoman Grand Vezir) enlisted foreigners into their semi-private armies, affected European uniforms and copied Western drill.

Muhammad Ali as modernizer

The power struggle between these men, which Muhammad Ali was to win, and between Muhammad Ali and his suzerain, the Ottoman sultan, subsequently can be seen to be, in essence, a race to acquire a usable force of "new men." The first to modernize would be the winner.

Subsequently, as he became involved in affairs beyond the frontiers of Egypt, Muhammad Ali came to realize that he needed a military force which would serve him reliably and less expensively than the foreign mercenaries in his employ. Therefore, after a troubled decade in power, he undertook seriously the Europeanization of his forces.

But where Muhammad Ali differed from his rivals was in the profundity of his understanding of power. Power, he realized, meant more than having soldiers and guns—which could simply be dangerous and expensive—but also meant having the means to clothe and feed the soldiers, to make and supply the guns and the organization to control the state. This meant building factories, training people to run them, and acquiring the financial power to pay for them. Modernization was the answer. Arsenals, dockyards, factories, hospitals, schools, a bureaucracy, all were essential if Muhammad Ali was to build the military machine which alone could insure his survival as his jealous and angry suzerain, Sultan Mahmud, tried to acquire the power to destroy him. His greatest obstacle, as Heyworth Dunne has written:

> . . . in his efforts to introduce reforms was the lack of qualified men especially in technical matters. There were no teachers or other kinds of professional men available in Egypt who could help. . . . He realized this handicap from the very beginning and in order to remedy it, he began sending missions of students to Italy as early as 1809 . . . in order to study military science, ship building, printing and engineering.

Particularly in the later years, in which the content of the studies of his missions became more academic and less concerned with the development of skilled workers, Muhammad Ali kept an extremely close check on the affairs of the students. In his letters he frequently urged the young men to report upon their studies, to hurry to return to Egypt, and upon their return, he required them to translate their textbooks into Arabic or Turkish so that others might profit from the investment made by the state.

In the course of his attempt to modernize Egyptian society, Muhammad Ali had to destroy the guild system which perpetuated the peculiar production system of the Egyptian working class as the Mamluk military order had frozen the method of fighting. Like the guild system in Europe, the guilds of Egypt were based upon long apprenticeship and were perhaps best viewed as a means of exercising social control, limiting rather than encouraging productive activity. Muhammad Ali's "new men" who learned in European industry or from technicians imported from Europe were to become the vanguard of a new system, not the apprentices of an old order.

In Egypt in the 1820's, as in America at a later date, the textile industry formed the major part of the thrust of the industrial transformation. Between 1818 and 1828, thirty cotton textile factories were opened. Additional woolen factories were opened to provide uniforms for the army. This is a development which continued in Egypt, and as late as 1952 textiles accounted for 36 per cent of the workers in establishments of ten or more workers.

Other industries lagged far behind textiles as Egypt lacked iron and coal, and here again there is continuity as in 1952, mining and manufacturing, of which textiles and food processing accounted for the bulk, still amounted to only 8 per cent of the gross national product (GNP). But in the time of Muhammad Ali as later, other factors intervened. In the 1820's and 1830's, the Egyptian military machine, with about 130,000 men under arms, required the manufacture of artillery, small arms, powder and other munitions. The growing navy, likewise, demanded and got a rapid acceleration in the manufacture of naval vessels and stores in Alexandria. Troops and those who supported them had to be fed and supplied so sugar refineries, dye works, glass blowing factories, tanneries, paper mills, and chemical works were set up throughout the country.

All of these factories were supervised, financed and controlled by the government. Many were under the immediate jurisdiction of foreign technicians but in them all Egyptians or others were trained to fill, ultimately, all the jobs. All of the personnel, including the directors, were government employees. The products were marketed by the government and all raw materials were procured by the government. Perhaps this government monopoly was necessary, as the growing and already far larger industries of Europe could swamp the area with their cheaper products, but the system, as the perceptive Egyptian writer, Moustafa Fahmy, has pointed out, did not permit the entry of a single capitalist, or entrepreneur of a Western sort, into industrial or, at times and in certain fields, commercial activity.

In order to train the new personnel required by the government for its bureaucracy and its various other technical and military activities, Muhammad Ali also began a new venture or, more correctly, series of new adventures in education. Ultimately, over 10,000 students were enrolled in various government institutions, given lodging, food and stipends at a total yearly expenditure of approximately £150 thousand or 5 per cent of the then GNP of Egypt.

In the enrollments, one can see the obviously utilitarian aims. A school of languages to train translators was opened for 225 students; a school of secretarial service for clerks was opened for 300; a polytechnic institute had 300 pupils; artillery and medical schools had 300 each; a school for infantry officers enrolled 800 and a veterinary medical school, to minister to the cavalry, absorbed 120 young men. Upon graduation, each young man was immediately taken into government service. Uniformly, and this was to remain a feature of the system as until recently, education led directly to service in the government.

The number of salaried, permanent workers in factories reached approximately 30,000 in the 1830's and over a quarter of a million others worked in smaller establishments, or at their homes, on the government account. It has been estimated that between 1816 and 1850, the total number of industrial workers was at least 400,000.

The Levant opened to the West

At this same time in the Levant, that is, the Syrian hinterland and coast, with a population of 1.3 million of whom half a million were urban, which came under Egyptian rule in 1832, rapid transformations were in process. As in Egypt, in the Levant commerce had always been an element in the economic life but a relatively secondary element.

Following the French Revolution and during the violent and greedy rule of the Ottoman pashas based in Acre and Sidon, trade had declined in the Levant. The French trading establishments were closed, the British had not at that time interested themselves in the Levant, and the American effort was minor. On the eve of the Egyptian invasion, even the British consul could not establish himself in Damascus so restrictive and xenophobic were its people. The people, as mentioned above, were content with a small world they knew and feared outsiders would destroy; they grew, built or inherited most of what they needed; and what little they got from outside was mainly from the farther East rather than from the West.

The effect of the Egyptian invasion of 1832 was to "open" the Levant to Western influence. It is useful to point out that a change in tastes and technology distinguished the Egyptian period as old ways, old tools, and old weapons were quickly judged to be outmoded. Cheap Western goods, the products of the new and booming industry of Europe, flowed into the Syrian market. Syrian handicraft industry was doomed. In the one year of 1833 an estimated 10,000 workers, mainly in textiles, were thrown out of work in Damascus and Aleppo. The smaller towns, which had often specialized, to a minor degree, in particular local products found their markets gone. Even the old caravan trade was hurt as clothing styles changed. The people of Damascus who would not allow the entry of one British official in 1830 were patronizing 107 shops retailing British goods in 1838. Even the great tribal groups in the deserts were affected as they found they could buy their headdresses and gowns more cheaply from factories at Birmingham than they could weave them. Some years later, even the chief moneylenders of Damascus and other towns were British. The flood gates, once opened by the Egyptians, were never again closed.

In Syria, as in Egypt, the army was the major agent to foster change. The soldiers were major purchasers. Officers were important investors. For the first time in Syrian history, since Byzantine times, the government, i.e. the army, undertook public works projects and gave security to the roads to foster trade and travel. As a direct result, the Levant began to be tied to the world market on a massive scale and to acquire a taste for the goods and disquieting new ideas of the West.

Failure of Muhammad Ali

It is difficult to say what might have happened in Syria—or in Egypt itself—had Egyptian rule in Syria continued. This was not to be. The major Western powers were increasingly alarmed that the threat posed by Muhammad Ali to the Sultan would force the Sultan into the arms of Russia. To get the Sultan, and his prized Straits, away from the Russian grasp, the English realized that they must weaken Muhammad Ali. Specifically, they must get the Egyptians out of Syria. Moreover, industrial England was actively in quest of markets and the restrictive practices of Muhammad Ali were frustrating British commerce. Muhammad Ali refused to allow the Commercial Code of 1838, which, having been negotiated with a weakened Sultan, was extremely favorable to foreigners, to be applied in Egyptian-controlled areas, rightly seeing in it the ruin of Egyptian industry and the de-nationalization of commerce. *Monopoly* was, in Free Trade England, almost as bad a word as *communism* is today. So, when the Egyptians had made themselves thoroughly unpopular and were in the midst of a civil war, the British assisted the Sultan in driving them out of Syria, and forced Muhammad Ali to reduce his standing armed forces from over 130,000 to 18,000. With the military *raison d'être* of the reform program removed, Muhammad Ali lost interest in the sweeping changes he had set in motion.

However, the residual effects of Muhammad Ali's rule, both in historic Syria and in Egypt, were to be felt strongly by future generations. Muhammad Ali had created, albeit for his own limited purposes, the first of the successive groups of "new men" who were to come forward in Middle East or Arab society over the next century.

Role of Education

Traditionally, in Islamic countries, primary education was not under the control of the government but was administered, taught and paid for by the religious "Establishment" or *ulema*. It was not until 1869, indeed, that the Egyptian Ministry of Education began even to inspect the primary schools and not until 1925 that, in order to meet the new Constitutional requirements for free primary education on a mass basis, it began to open half-day primary schools. Between 1925 and 1940, some 3,000 such schools were opened and ultimately enrolled almost one million children. In 1952 only 45 per cent of the children of proper ages attended schools but, following the 1952 revolution, the figure rose to 65 per cent and the present plans call for facilities for all children by 1969.

Egypt has been a pacesetter for the Arab countries in recent generations so it is instructive to observe, in some detail, trends there. Particularly in the field of education, these have been transmitted and have been formative throughout the area.

Between 1913 and 1945, school attendance in Egypt rose from 206,000 to 477,000 boys and 26,500 to 418,000 girls. In 1913, six public schools catered to 2,500 secondary students of whom none were girls whereas in 1945, 53 schools enrolled 33,000 boys and 3,000 girls; the number of private schools increased, during the same period, from five to 74. Higher schools increased their enrollment during that period from 1,500 to 15,000. The numbers, at all levels, have risen sharply since the 1952 Revolution so that, in 1960, the four Egyptian universities contained almost 87,000 students and the secondary schools graduated more students than the total enrollment in 1945.

In Kuwait, the income from oil can be graphically seen in the rise of the education budget from $90,000 in 1942 to $33 million in 1960. Other states are making major strides. Yet serious educational problems remain. The population of the Arab states is still largely illiterate, and even that part of the population which is "educated" is still largely untrained in disciplines which are readily employable.

Vocational education

But, the efforts of the modernizers in Middle Eastern countries to educate the next generation for industrial and technical occupations are already showing results. While statistics vary for the different countries they all show the same trend. Thus the *International Labour Review* for January 1963 furnishes the following figures for vocational education:

NUMBERS ATTENDING EDUCATIONAL ESTABLISHMENTS

Senior Vocational Training

Country	*Years*	*Students*	*Percentage of Girls*
Egypt	1957-58	66,007	19.9
	1958-59	83,368	21.2
Iran	1959-60	8,997	11.9
Iraq	1956-57	3,324	31.9
	1959-60	7,382	—
Israel	1956-57	12,343	29.6
	1959-60	13,388	27.4
Lebanon	1956-57	756	49.5
	1960-61	17,150	28.7
Syria	1957-58	2,656	—
	1959-60	1,134	—
Turkey	1957-58	84,842	22.7
	1959-60	5,636	19.5

More recent figures compiled by the National Science Foundation in Washington show that in 1960/1961 enrollment in preparatory and secondary *vocational* schools in four countries was:

Country	*Schools*	*Students*	*Graduates*
Egypt	181	114,693	15,277
Iraq	34	6,732	882
Jordan	14	1,281	360
Syria	32	6,830	1,147
Saudi Arabia	1,081 abroad in schools.		

These figures do not include trainees in industry or apprentices, such as those in oil installations or other plants throughout the area.

The drive for technical and vocational education throughout the Middle East has been aided during the past ten years by the Arab States Fundamental Education Center (ASFEC) operated under combined United Nations (UNESCO) and Arab League auspices at Sirsal-Layyan near Cairo. Ministers of Education, Social

Welfare, Agriculture and Rural Affairs in ten countries nominate staff members to attend this nine month cram course in literacy teaching, rural and village organization, health education, and use of modern teaching devices. About one hundred trainees a year attend ASFEC either as government bursaries or on scholarships provided by the United Nations Technical Assistance Board or the World Health Organization.

Much "training" is of course outside the educational system—for example, the British forces in Egypt employed some 80,000 skilled or semi-skilled workers in World War II. But today, the emphasis placed on science and technology, in the schools and out, has greatly increased as several countries have set out to industrialize. It was estimated in 1961, by the Higher Council for the Sciences, that 38,000 Egyptians had graduated in the natural sciences and technology from Egyptian faculties. Of these 10,000 were engineers, 9,700 agronomists, 9,000 physicians, and 5,000 scientists.

Iraqi progress

In Iraq, one of the key factors when the British established their control in the last stages of World War I was the need to create a sufficiently large cadre of skilled men to administer the country and to work its industry on acceptable terms. Particularly after the expensive revolt of 1920 had raised serious protests in London, it was decided that economy must be the rule. Therefore, the British were anxious to phase out their relatively expensive foreign personnel as rapidly as possible. The Indian clerical help they had imported during the war was, for political reasons, not regarded as a feasible alternative. However, India could be taken as a model since a small core of senior British officials set policy and supervised its execution by a local staff.

In Iraq as in India, however, the British faced what ultimately was an insolvable dilemma: they needed a skilled bureaucracy but deeply distrusted the urban "literati" who were its only native source. They felt that if this superficially Westernized group were allowed to gain control, it would corrupt the simple nobility of the "good Arabs," the bedouin, and would further impoverish the miserable peasantry. Therefore, a fine line had to be drawn between training for bureaucracy and education for government.

When they arrived on the scene in World War I, the British found that the school system of Iraq had virtually to be begun afresh; the young Turks had insisted that instructions be in Turkish in the few schools they had established in the country. The 300 Koranic schools, with an estimated 15,000 pupils were of little use in creating the "new man" needed by the bureaucracy and the developing economy; the religious minorities' community schools were judged unacceptable by the Muslim majority of the society. In their development the British put major emphasis on primary schools. Their plan was to restrict secondary education to the "select few" needed by the administration. To meet this need, they estimated that four secondary schools with approximately 400 pupils were too many. Progress was slow. In 1921, 3.03 per cent of the Iraqi budget was spent on education with only 0.6 per cent of the population registered in schools. In 1920-21 there were 88 primary schools with 8,000 students, three secondary schools with 110 students, one teachers' college with 91 students, and one higher institution with 65 students. By 1927, the government of Iraq claimed that of some 857 teachers in the public primary schools, only 300 were untrained.

Significantly, when Iraq became independent in 1932, Education was the first ministry to be taken over by the Iraqis. Almost immediately, the Iraq government embarked on a much larger program than any in the Mandate period. To assist them, an American consultant made a study of the existing system and reported that "without a public school system it is obvious to everyone that an independent nationality could not be maintained even if established." With this warning in mind, the government provided textbooks which were filled with materials aimed at fostering a nationalist feeling; the aim of history teaching, in the words of one student of the Iraqi system, was to "strengthen the national and patriotic feeling in the hearts of the pupils."

In addition to the more formal education in schools there was, of course, a major if less formal educational development in the increasing awareness of the outer world which was fostered by the presence in Iraq, Lebanon, Syria, Jordan, the Palestine Mandate and Egypt of large numbers of foreigners who brought with them distinctive habits and who, in their daily contact with numbers of natives, spread notions of the outer world. The goods and services which they imported into the countries in which they were resident and the administrative structures which they built; the industry and commerce in which they engaged, all of these tended to impart education in the broader sense of the word to the native populations.

It is instructive to compare the former mandate countries of the Middle East and other areas with those which had neither the disruptive nor the beneficial aspects of foreign rule. On a psychological level one cannot help noting that a wound has been inflicted in the "national psyche" of the former Mandate states. On the other hand, as one views such countries as Yemen, in which there has been no outside rule, one cannot help also noting the beneficial aspects of foreign tutelage. Foreign powers did leave a sense of "structure" or organization and set styles for the "new men" who alone could run them.

In addition, in Iraq, there was an early recognition that the army was a school of nationalism. In its report to the League of Nations in 1926, the Mandate Government noted that "the army is proving a valuable means of fostering a true national spirit." Even the paramilitary groups, including the Boy Scouts, played an important part in the growth of national identity on the new model. By 1930 some 12,361 Iraqi young men were enrolled in the Boy Scout movement and subsequently, in the middle 1930's, the director general of education of Iraq, inspired by the contemporary Fascist Youth Movements of Europe, encouraged the growth of the *Futuwah* Movement, in which young Iraqis were urged to break out of the lethargy of their contemporary society, to acquire from their own ancient heritage the will to be strong, and to foster in the country a new spirit. This was the very quintessence of the attempt to create a new generation which would be startlingly different from their forefathers.

It was this same spirit which subsequently caused an Egyptian army officer, Sharaf ad-Din Zabalawi, to write in an article entitled "Military Education and Character Training":

> Military life is the school of the people, it is an advanced school in public, social and national aspects of life, for the first lesson that a young soldier learns is self-denial and to exert all his efforts toward a noble cause. It is the repudiation of personal interests in favor of the public interest. Then the individual becomes a sound, ideal citizen.

It was logical that modernizers should assign this role to the army. We have seen that in the time of Muhammad Ali the army was in fact a vehicle as well as a reason for reform.

Role of the Military

Today, in many of the Middle Eastern countries, the army is viewed as the guardian of national virtue, the sole force capable of and interested in pushing forward those reforms which alone will give dignity, strength and justice. In part, the army and modernization program fulfill the role traditionally carried out by a religious movement in Islamic history as described by the great North African Arab philosopher, Ibn Khaldun. As has been suggested more recently by Professor Morroe Berger, the "image" which the military modernizers would like to project is "an industrialized, militarily powerful state, respected in the world community, composed of educated, healthful citizens, loyal to the nation state."

Traditionally, of course, this was not the case. The military establishment, as we have seen, was restricted to a very narrow stratum of the society. In Egypt, it was an alien force which did not even share the language of the population and certainly thought little of the well-being of the population. Egyptians only gradually won admission to its service and then, in the time of Muhammad Ali Pasha, usually as common soldiers. Indeed, it was not until 1936 that the Egyptian government opened the military academy to all social ranks. The nature of the change of the social composition of the army, as it grew larger and more "national," is too much a matter of public knowledge and of too recent impingement on all our thoughts to be belabored here. The change has been well put by Professor Manfred Halpern of Princeton, as one "From Praetorian Guard to Advance Guard," as the army has become conscious of the need for action. The armies, alone among the institutions of the societies, were organized along nationalist, modern lines without commitments to the past. The military alone has a defined code, a clear line of command, lines of communications, mobility, force and, ultimately, will. The better it became as an instrument of the state, the less committed it is to the state. As Halpern has perceived:

> The more the army was modernized, the more its composition, organization, spirit, capabilities, and purpose constituted a radical criticism of the existing political system. . . . In civilian politics, corruption, nepotism, and bribery loomed much larger. Within the army, a sense of national mission transcending parochial, regional, or economic interests, or kinship ties, seemed to be much more clearly defined than anywhere else in society. . . . As the army became modernized and professionalized, the traditionalist elements within the civilian sector found army service less to their taste. . . .

Whereas, in Western society, the army has tended to be equated, at least in part, with the middle class, in the Middle East until recently this has not been the case. In the first place, what we would call, on economic grounds, the middle class was often, as we have observed, in large part composed of non-Muslims or even alien minority communities. This was particularly the case in Egypt where the Copts and the large foreign communities of Greeks, Italians and others predominated in the middle reaches of the economy and society. The Egyptian middle class, in 1947, was estimated to comprise only about 6 per cent of the population or half a million people. Of these about 51 per cent were thought to be merchants, 26 per cent clerks, 19 per cent professionals and only 4 per cent businessmen.

It seems that, in part at least, the role taken upon itself by the Egyptian army has been the *creation* of a middle class. The middle class, composed of managers, administrators, teachers, engineers, journalists, scientists, lawyers and army officers are, for the most part today, employees of the state. Where new state organs have been established, they are often staffed by men who were recently army officers. For example, in Egypt the Suez Canal Authority and the Petroleum Authority are staffed by many former officers. Similarly in Sudan, Turkey and Iraq officers have assumed civilian functions.

Middle Class—New Style

Additionally, it is important to emphasize again that the middle class in the modern Middle East is rather different in several ways from the Western Middle classes we associate with the Industrial Revolution and democratic government. It is not distinguished by a dedication to private ownership (in Egypt today, for example, less than 20 per cent of investment is private), rights of self-expression, or a particular political credo. It uses and agrees to be used by the state for whose well-being it strives. And it is highly pragmatic in its approach—espousing "socialism" or whatever seems to offer solutions to baffling social problems. The key division—as suggested, is the "new" as opposed to the traditional. The "new men" of various social and economic levels share goals and values, whereas within the "middle class" there is a sharp cleavage.

Those "middle class" elements we can identify often tend to be separated from groups which share their "middleness" in economic terms, e.g. the landlords, but who are less Westernized. Thus, there is a sharp difference in politics, mode of life, and education between the "new men" and the traditionalists. When the landed or other vested interests are removed from the traditional elements in the "middle class," they can be seen to be quite different from what we would consider a middle class. The lack of a Western education effectively blocks the forward progress today of a man, even within the middle class. Additionally, men who are well trained but trained in the traditional subjects, do not have the assets to move upward socially and economically. Significantly, the acquisition of a foreign education, preferably acquired at the source, in a Western university, not a man's social rank or wealth, is the surest passport to advancement. This is the field of education in which one can note the most spectacular progress in the years since World War I in several Middle Eastern countries.

To take Iraq as an example, in 1921, nine Iraqis were sent abroad to acquire a Western education; by 1928, the number had risen to 93; by 1939, it had reached 238. By 1931, over 200 young men had spent periods of study abroad and had returned, and by 1950 the number had reached almost 2,000. In the one year of 1962, nearly 7,000 were abroad at Western schools, colleges and universities. As increased numbers were sent, and as governments committed higher proportions of money to education both on the lower and the higher levels, the social groups from which the young men and women were drawn, widened also. Thus, in education as in the army, social class became less important in the general expansion. And, perhaps more significantly, whereas education *inside* Iraq involved a limited exposure to the West in an Eastern context, the student on a mission abroad might spend upwards of eight years living in the West, acquiring new habits of life and far higher expectations; upon return, a sense of bitterness, extreme criticism and frustration was common.

Curiously, this sort of contact with an alien society seems to have affected the humble more strongly than those at the top of the social ladder. Perhaps it was partly that the young man from a humble family could more fully commit himself to a new life and more readily, because less bound, accept its ways and values and also because, upon his return from a relatively comfortable, well-paid and challenging experience, he felt more bitterly and with less protection or means of action his own, former, position.

But, those who went abroad and learned, at the prestigious source, a profession or new technical field were able to move ahead economically, politically and socially more rapidly than those who stayed behind. Thus, even men of wealth and family who stayed behind gradually became socially inferior to those of more humble origin who went abroad and returned with a marketable skill. The graduate of a Baghdad college was destined for inferior jobs, perhaps as a primary or secondary school teacher, whereas the man graduated from Oxford or Harvard could teach in the colleges, practice his profession or take a responsible government position.

Social mobility

Here it is possible to see the very sharp differentiation between the "new men" and the more traditional even when the more traditional has the advantages of social status of family and financial power. Likewise, one can observe this among the groups which we would categorize as lower class. In their study *Human Resources for Development in Egypt,* Harbison and Ibrahim distinguished several groups of workers. The largest is unskilled, landless and capital-less. The second, much smaller, are skilled or semi-skilled traditional artisans who are technologically increasingly unemployed. The third group, perhaps now less than 10 per cent are men with some degree of modern skills. Although all would be "lower class" by the sharp contrast their lives present to men of any part of the rest of the social order, they are sharply distinguished from one another by salary, regularity of employment, expectations of life, discipline, morale and world view. In Egypt, where, as in most countries of the underdeveloped world, unemployment and underemployment are common, a mechanic, for example, earns three times as much per day as a day laborer and is assured of continual employment so his real wages may be many times that of the day laborer. A similar situation exists in North Africa, as Jane P. C. Carey and Andrew G. Carey have recently explained in their *Two Developing Worlds of Morocco: A Case Study in Economic Development and Planning.* Everywhere, the differential has been very high and, apparently, the aim of a number of the Middle Eastern and North African governments is to increase it.

Role of Women

The changed status of women in the Arab states today marks one of the most radical departures from Muslim traditionalism. The dropping of the veil in Egypt and Lebanon, and its gradual disappearance in Syria and Iraq, is, like the removal of the fez, an outward sign of a fundamental break with the past. More significant is the extension of primary and secondary education for girls, co-education in some primary schools and universities, and vocational training specifically designed for girls in Egypt, Iraq and Syria. Put simply but accurately, women have come out of seclusion and the kitchen and are beginning to enter the parliaments, the universities, and the professions.

The emancipation of women in the Near East has been gradual.

American schools for girls existed in the early 19th century. The American University of Beirut opened a school of nursing in 1905 and admitted women to its Arts and Sciences school in 1924. The University of Cairo first admitted women in 1928. Today several thousand women attend the University of Damascus and University of Baghdad. Egypt's universities, includin al-Azhar, are open to women; Jordan founded a Teachers' Training College for Women at Ramallah in 1957.

UNESCO experts estimate that some 40,000 women now attend colleges or universities in the Middle East. An additional thousand are studying in the United States.

The role of women in helping to shape the modernization process in Middle Eastern society is evident on all sides. Women not only perform tasks which are traditionally feminine, such as nursing; they are prominent in many professions. Lebanon has a distinguished woman physicist, women doctors, and most recently a woman member of parliament. Jordan and Syria and Iraq have an increasing number of women teachers. Egypt has had a woman Minister of Social Affairs in the cabinet and hundreds of women in the professions of law, medicine, social work and teaching.

Other Arab countries and Iran are moving in the direction of greater freedom and responsibility for women. In Iraq, Syria, and Lebanon women vote. Their struggle for franchise in Iran has succeeded with the Shah's blessing. Here, as in many fields, the pace of modernization in Middle Eastern society is not uniform but it is clearly forward.

Social Engineering Experiments

Aware that a technologically backward and poor population is unable to form a solid base for the growth of national dignity and power (the two cherished goals of the modernizers of the Middle East) both the Iraqi and the Egyptian governments in the 1950's embarked upon attempts to create "new men" not only in the cities but also in the countryside. This was the essence of the "Liberation Province" scheme in Egypt and the resettlement and housing experiments in Iraq.

Roundly, and perhaps rightly, criticized as an economic fiasco or as an example of ambitious political planning without the requisite technological and economic foundation, "Liberation Province" does give a clue to how the government felt about the need to build a new Egyptian. In the words of the director of the Social Affairs Department, M. Gamal Zaki:

> Settlers are selected scientifically on social, medical, psychological tests. As social qualifications, applicants must possess one wife, no dependents except children, and no property; they must have been married only once, and must have finished their military service. Of 1.100 applicants so far, all have the right social qualifications, but only 382 families were accepted medically, because while most of the men were healthy enough, the women and children fell far short of the standard. Only 180 families survived the psychological test . . . of these 132 are now undergoing a six-month training, which included a three-month probation period. We must consider both people and land to be under reclamation.

The "new man" of "Liberation Province" was marked off from the traditional Egyptian peasant by a new standardized uniform in place of the gown worn traditionally, the fez for the turban, or the cap for the fez—by a much higher caloric intake of food and by a salary four times the average rate in Upper Egypt. In addition, the workers were to put their children into a boarding school arrangement, in some ways similar to the practice in the Israeli *Kibutzim,* which presumably would enable teachers to ensure a better and newer upbringing for the children. Moreover, like the rest of Egypt, "Liberation Province" was to become a mixed rural and industrial economy with factories interspersed throughout the agricultural area.

"Liberation Province" has had a stormy career, has certainly fallen short of its goals, and ultimately has affected very few people, but it may be regarded as a straw in the wind of changes which most Arab rulers expect to see. One may see this purpose, if less clearly specified, perhaps much more uniformly carried out in certain other ways. For example, as mentioned above, the army has long been regarded as a "school" in civic virtues. In addition, today the army has also become a school to impart modern skills, a hospital to cure the ills of society and turn out healthier men, and a source of discipline. Each year, approximately 20,000 Egyptians are inducted into the army for three-year enlistments; in Syria, about the same are called for a two-year period; and in Iraq, about 8,000 are called up for two years. From 1957 to 1963, perhaps as many as 130,000 Egyptians have passed out of the armed forces into civilian life. When one considers that larger scale, modern Egyptian industry in 1961 employed roughly a quarter of a million workers, the impact of this group of ex-soldiers can be appreciated.

Not very much is known about these "new men" when they return to civilian life. It is clear, however, that they are possessed of a rudimentary technical training, a sense of discipline, an indoctrination in nationalism and certainly a far higher standard of health than are those who have not had their army experience. All of these things are rare and prized possessions in a rapidly evolving and industrializing society.

At the upper echelons, the ex-Army officer is the "doer" of the new order. He may aspire to cabinet rank, or take a key managerial job in the apparatus of government-run industry or commerce. As a factory manager or a senior bureaucrat, he will play a crucial role in modernizing the country. In the middle levels, it is probable that the former non-commissioned army officer and junior officers have taken on lower level administrative and industrial functions and, former private soldiers have probably been readily absorbed into industry. It is doubtful that many have returned to village communities where their skills are not in demand and where the life they have learned to lead, or at least, aspire to, is impossible.

The fact is that as yet little is known in specific terms, but, in the round, it is possible to see that in the making is a multi-class, non-traditionalist, as yet politically or philosophically uncommitted, pragmatic, disciplined, privileged core of "new men." It would be of great interest to recalculate many of the sorts of changes—for example, per capita GNP—which have occurred in recent years from the perspective of this group, rather than from that of society as a whole, for upon their satisfaction or disaffection will depend much of the stability and progress of the area in years to come.

A. J. Meyer

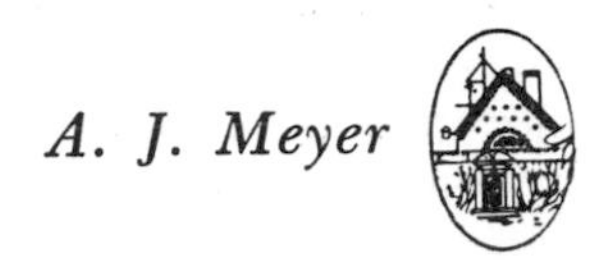

3

Economic Modernization

The Middle East Economy Before World War II

Economic historians debate constantly about the role played by the Middle East in the post-Byzantine era of early capitalism. Some interpret the continued life of entrepots such as Alexandria, Constantinople (now Istanbul), Beirut and Aleppo as indicating that an uninterrupted flow of goods, gold and men moved between East and West until the late nineteenth century. Others write of the disruptive effects of the breakup of the Eastern Roman Empire, the rise of Islam, Muslim-Christian tensions attendant upon the Crusades, and various aspects of Ottoman expansion. Whichever interpretation one accepts for the 700 years after 1200, one cannot but agree that the Middle East was an economic backwater for the half-century preceding World War II.

Many facts support the latter conclusion. No modern industry of any consequence was to be found anywhere in the area until textile and food processing began in Egypt in the 1930's. The operations of Levantine traders and bankers in Beirut, Aleppo and Haifa were inconsequential indeed when compared to those of the big firms of England and Western Europe—in the trade with India and the Far East. The Middle East's extractive industry—chromite

A. J. Meyer *is Associate Professor of Middle Eastern Studies, Lecturer in Economics and Associate Director of the Center for Middle Eastern Studies at Harvard University. He has been on the faculty of the American University of Beirut, Director of United Nations activities in the Gaza Strip and a member of the Harvard Pakistan Project. Among his writings are:* Middle Eastern Capitalism: Nine Essays, *and* The Economy of Cyprus.

in Turkey, copper and pyrites in Cyprus, gold in the Hejaz—was tiny compared to that elsewhere in the world. Only dates from Iraq and cotton from Egypt (after the mid-nineteenth century) played a major role in a phase of world trade. In the late nineteenth century the Suez Canal re-established the Middle East's position (lost since the decline of the Great Silk Way overland caravan routes) astride the international trading centers. But this, like the area's indigenous trade, industry and banking was inconsequential in world terms and meant little to the mass of Middle Easterners. Even the existence of oil in Khuzistan after 1912 was unimportant economically. It fueled the British navy and merchant marine in the East but had negligible effect on economic developments either in Western Europe or the Middle East itself.

The big political developments of the twentieth century—the forging of independent nations in Turkey and Iran, the stirrings of Arab nationalism, the consolidation of the Wahabi monarchy in the Arabian Peninsula, beginnings of Zionism and the mandate interlude—while they overshadowed economic events in importance, also brought powerful economic consequences. They led to forced draft schemes to catch up with the West, as in Atatürk's Turkey. They created attitudes of hostility and zenophobia toward the West which were to come out later. British and French control and rule in the mandates in Palestine, Syria and Lebanon, and in Egypt, created educated minorities which not only led the revolt against Britain and France, but which were later to turn their minds to economic pursuits. The first half of the nineteenth century was unquestionably a powerful incubator for later economic developments.

World War I and II were also of great indirect economic importance to the Middle East. Western armies left large amounts of money, improved public health conditions enormously (elimination of the Malaria mosquito in the Middle East, for example, was almost entirely a military undertaking), moved large numbers of people about, left more than a few demobilized Australian and British entrepreneurs to found enterprises in the area, and in World War II created the Middle East Supply Center—the first area-wide effort to manage and improve the region's productive base. All this set the stage for post World War II economic change.

Economic Expansion Since World War II

The Middle East since World War II has seen extraordinary economic change—inseparably linked to the area's even more remarkable political and social changes, described elsewhere in this volume. With it has come undreamed-of affluence for many people, modest betterment for far more, and perplexing and terrifying problems for all. Amidst the growth rates and problems are discernible several all-pervasive, catalytic influences. There are, *first,* the enormous and growing impact of oil shipments and earnings; *second,* the amazingly vast, and also growing, interdependence between the Middle East and the outer world, particularly the West; and *third,* the continuing joust between the West and the Soviet Union in the area. Linked to all these influences is the search, by Middle Easterners, for economic ideas and theories genuinely relevant to the decisions they face. A look at all this will preface an attempt, later in these pages, to speculate on future economic trends.

Most countries of the Middle East emerged from World War II with net per capita incomes of less than $100 per year—"underdeveloped" by the measuring rods of Western economists. In this category were Egypt, Saudi Arabia, Jordan, Iraq, Qatar, Iran, Yemen, Kuwait and a series of lesser shaikhdoms in the Persian Gulf and lower Arabia. Others, more fortunate and for widely variant reasons, lived on incomes ranging from $150 to $250. Here, one may point to Turkey, Syria, Lebanon, Mandate Palestine, and Cyprus. The low income states far outnumbered those with higher incomes—the first group contained over 50 million people, the second fewer than 25 million. All were well below the living standard of most European countries and far below those of the United States and the British Dominions.

In the decade and a half after 1945 a series of occurrences joined to give a dramatic upward boost to the Middle East's statistics of economic performance. One of these was oil. The incredible expansion of Western Europe's need for energy joined with equally unbelievable success in exploration in several Middle Eastern nations to create, by the early 1960's, a flow to Western Europe, Commonwealth countries and Japan of six million barrels daily and an eastward flow of more than $1.5 billion yearly to producing and transit countries. Another stimulus came from the opening up of new land for agricultural use in the Jezira in northeast Syria—which created, in Lebanon and Syria, a postwar wave of prosperity. Further thrust came from the creation of Israel, the resultant influx of more than a million new emigrants to the Jewish state, its rapid development, and the finances provided by more than three billion dollars from abroad—mostly from German reparations, international Jewry and United States aid.

Other elements also boosted the postwar Middle Eastern economy. Among them were the Korean War, which pushed up cereal and fibre prices to the great benefit of Egypt, Turkey, and Syria. Another was the growing intensity of the East-West Cold War which led to economic and military aid from the United States of more than $100 million yearly (in most years after 1948) each to Turkey and Iran, and $60 million yearly from Britain to Cyprus. Still further upward thrust came from investment financed by foreign borrowing. Turkey, Iran and Israel, for example, each pushed their foreign debts to over $500 million in the decade of the 1950's, adding to the advance of massive (and often controversial) investments under almost a dozen government development programs—in Israel, Egypt, Iraq, Iran, Turkey, Syria, Kuwait and elsewhere. The investment of public and private reserves accumulated during World War II also fed the advance, as did a growth in the flow of emigrants to Europe and America and a corresponding rise in their remittances home. The flow of Muslim pilgrims to Mecca likewise rose, and by the early 1960's Saudi Arabia was earning an estimated $90 million yearly from the Hajj. Finally, the Middle Eastern economy pushed ahead because a large portion of the citizenry responded to the economic challenges. Government officials and private investors put enormous sums of money to work, and people worked harder.

The result was a set of impressive rates of economic performance. Two shaikhdoms in the Persian Gulf, Kuwait and Qatar, although a bit irrelevant, hold the world's record. The former moved from a pastoral, bedouin economy with a net per capita income of no more than $35 to a completely urban, bustling, air-conditioned welfare state, virtually devoid of poverty and with a per capita income from oil of over $2,000. Qatar did the same, but because of its smaller population (20,000 against Kuwait's 250,000), its oil income averaged out to $3,000 per citizen. Other statistics rose also, to the highest rates in the world: investment as percentage of national income, increases in literacy rates and school attendance, hospital beds and doctors per capita and the rest.

Innocent of the awesome complexities of Western economic theory, the Shaikhs of Kuwait and Qatar evolved ingenious, and so far quite workable, concepts of public finance and expenditure. To spread money around, the ruler of Kuwait bought land at high prices from his constituents. The latter acquired the land, often a few days before its final sale, by the simple device of putting markers on bits of unclaimed desert and registering their claim in the title office. The Shaikh of Qatar proved even more imaginative. He offered a lifetime annuity of $900 monthly, payable to those male members of the ruling tribe, for each male child sired. As might be imagined, members of the "establishment" responded heroically to the challenge, and by the early 1960's outlays had grown to over $15 million yearly—out of a total oil income of $60 million. Kuwait and Qatar also offer incredibly generous subsidies to students of all kinds, at home and abroad, and the usual mass of housing developments, trips to Europe and other elements of the good life in the Persian Gulf.

Iraq offers a slightly less irrelevant example of extremely rapid economic growth. Owning much land, water, oil and only five million people, the Republic on the Tigris-Euphrates has, through massive public investment schemes, advanced its *net* per capita incomes at a rate in excess of five per cent yearly for most of the years since 1950. Despite disagreement (caused by lack of data and studies) over what the pre-1950 national income actually was, most economists agree that Iraq has, since 1950, almost doubled a per capita income that then stood at about $75. More important, the vehicle—water projects, schools and the rest—for sustained movement ahead is well under way toward assembly.

Further west, Syria and Jordan have likewise registered impressive income advances since World War II. Syria's net per capita income has expanded from about $120 to $160—an average of two to three per cent yearly. After 1959, Jordan claimed advances averaging five per cent net yearly, and by the early 1960's its per capita income was about $120. Syria did it by combining a vigorous entrepreneurial class with profits accumulated during World War II, and adding to this development of new land in the Jezira and inflated cotton and wheat prices during the Korean War. Jordan's later success came after ten years of stagnation following the Arab-Israeli War and was fueled by foreign aid, a rebirth of tourism in Arab Jerusalem, the development of mineral exports and a rising flow of remittances as a new generation of young Palestinians from Jordan left home to take lucrative posts in the Persian Gulf oil camps and elsewhere.

The three Levant countries—Cyprus, Lebanon and Israel—have likewise performed prodigious economic feats since 1945. In all three the formula has been pretty much the same—a well educated, vigorous populace combined with unusual, and extremely large, outside sources of funds for investment. Human ingenuity and money pushed these nations ahead during the decade of the 1950's at net per capita rates of three to six per cent despite substantial population upsurges (particularly in Israel, where a ten per cent increase per year was common) and inflation (especially in Israel and Cyprus, where price instability went on at five to ten per cent yearly).

The three heavily populated Muslim countries of the Middle East—Egypt, Iran and Turkey—likewise pressed ahead after World War II and in the fifties. Despite their well-known demographic burdens, Egypt and Iran added a few dollars during the decade after 1952 to a per capita income which in that year hovered about $100. The modest successes were largely attributable to determined efforts by new breeds of public officials in both countries. Blessed with greater resources, Turkey added about 25 per cent (two per cent a year) to its net per capita income between the late 1940's and the early 1960's. Most economists now place Turkey's net per capita income at between $200 and $250.

These same economists still despair of assessing Saudi Arabia's economic performance after World War II with accuracy. It is known that before oil, the Kingdom earned all of its foreign exchange from the pilgrimage, and that total per capita incomes could not have been higher than $35. By the early 1960's, oil and the pilgrimage together produced almost $500 million yearly. Yet the lack of population data persisted, with the result that per capita estimates ranged across an improbable spectrum of between $50 and $250, depending on whether one accepted stoutly defended population estimates of two million or ten million.

From the eastern Mediterranean to the frontiers of Baluchistan, therefore, one may point to a general economic expansion since World War II. Despite the only partial relevance of national and per capita income figures as indicators of human well-being, there is no denying that change has been vast: the villages of Lebanon, Cyprus, Turkey, Egypt and Iraq are infinitely better off (in terms of schools, water supplies etc.) than earlier; villagers in Iran have increased mobility, more access to schools, more bicycles, and are beginning to feel the wind of change; Israel has completely remade its inheritance from Mandate Palestine. Former market towns such as Kuwait, Dammam, Al Khobar, and Doha are now bustling, settled cities with pleasant streets and shops; enormous investments have been made in water projects and land reclamation, such as Wadi Tharthar and Habbaniya in Iraq, the Khuzistan Projects in Iran, Aswan in Egypt, the Negev in Israel; thousands of schools have been built and levels of education are rising. The Middle East's collective response to economic opportunity has indeed been remarkable.

Problems

Despite the rapid over-all expansion of the Middle East after World War II, by the mid-1960's the area faced a series of formidable economic problems. Some were inherited and had deep roots in the region's past. Others were partially creations of the new nations themselves and partially of the Western Alliance and the Soviet Bloc, both of whom came to play important roles in several countries.

Unequal distribution of income

One problem was that of unequal distribution of income. Although, as shown earlier, over-all national incomes advanced sharply in statistical terms in most Middle Eastern nations after World War II, only a few registered important shifts in allocation of funds among citizens. Surveys of income distribution in Iran, Iraq, Turkey, Egypt, Cyprus and Jordan, for example, showed (in the early 1960's) that, with few exceptions, rural villages had per capita incomes less than half those of town and city dwellers. Yet the peasantry made up 50-75 per cent of the population of these nations. Economically "locked-in," so to speak, the rural majority in much of the Middle East still cannot generate savings for investment on the land to improve yields. Nor can it offer a mass market for goods from city factories.

Only four countries, representing a combined population of well under four million people, really made sharp dents in the problem of income distribution. These were Kuwait and Qatar, whose soaring oil incomes financed welfare state policies which unquestionably advanced the lowest bedouin to undreamed-of opulence. Israel and Lebanon did the same, but along different paths. Israel achieved the most evenly distributed income in the world, by a combination of welfare state policies implemented through massive public investment schemes, coupled with very high, and progressive taxation. Lebanon saw its villagers' incomes advance rapidly, and in pace with over-all per capita income growth, because of its high levels of education, real estate boom, fluidity between city and village, sharp upswing in investment in fruit orchards in the mountains, and rising flow of emigrant remittances from overseas Lebanese.

Agriculture

The second problem is closely related to that of income distribution. Put simply, the Middle East had not, by the early 1960's

—despite its rapid national income expansion—come remotely near to solving its basic problems of agriculture. It was a fact, for example, that twenty years after World War II, no country in the Middle East could produce enough food grains, meat, fruits and vegetables to feed itself, year in and year out on a 2000-2500 calorie level. In good crop years a few countries (such as Syria and Turkey) produced surpluses for export. But in bad years even these nations joined Cyprus, Egypt, Israel (which by the early 1960's was producing about 75 per cent of its food requirements), Kuwait, Saudi Arabia, Iran, Jordan, and Lebanon as net food importers.

Further evidence of the agricultural problems facing the Middle East could be seen in the post-World War II record of monotonously regular crop failure due to capricious rainfall, inexplicable vitality of DDT-resistant cotton weevils (which in several years caused untold loss in Egypt), and the area's basic demographic imbalance, which left most countries with less than 1.5 cultivable acres per citizen—far too little by World Health Organization Standards. The land reform programs in Egypt, Syria, Iran and Iraq did *not* create a remotely viable rural peasantry; nor did they achieve any measurable redistribution of income. Accomplishments were measured largely in psychological, not in economic terms.

Even Israel, after investing massively in agriculture, and applying advanced technology and human ingenuity to its farmland, had reached chastening conclusions by the end of its first decade. Capitalization costs per acre and per farm were higher than anywhere in the world (including the United States), and costs of training agricultural workers proved far greater than in other fields. Yet Israel remained cursed with many of the same structural imbalances besetting her less developed neighbors.

The net result of postwar Middle Eastern efforts to solve farm problems was therefore discouraging—the area still could not feed itself. In structural terms, most nations kept upwards of 60 per cent of their bread-winners at work in the fields; yet in most countries agriculture produced less than 30 per cent of the national income. Rural underemployment was rife and farm incomes barely rose at all. In summary, the twenty postwar years taught the Middle East a great deal about its agricultural problems but *not* how to solve them.

Industry

Before 1945 only a handful of factories existed in the entire Middle East—mostly textile mills, food processing plants or bottling works succored by demand from Allied armies. With few exceptions, manufactured goods came from abroad. No commodity prominent in world trade was processed in the Middle East. Cotton from Egypt, copper and pyrites from Cyprus, and chromite from Turkey all went west to be made into final products. Turkey, under the *étatism* of Atatürk, built steel mills and aircraft engine factories, but these were more national monuments than creators of commodities in world trade.

After World War II, however, industry developed rapidly in several Middle Eastern nations. Israel put massive investment of public and quasi-public money into creating an industrial base. The Korean War created shortages of goods which gave a new lease on life to factories in Syria, Lebanon and Cyprus which had earlier thrived on serving Allied armies. Development plans in Turkey, Iran, Iraq and elsewhere helped create impressive industrial estates and plants, usually around national capitals. Prosperity in the Persian Gulf triggered construction of fruit and vegetable processing plants, and poultry and egg plants in Lebanon. Egypt's drive to broaden its industrial base after 1952 led to great expansion in industry.

But despite the claims of government propagandists, the record of expansion in industry in the Middle East since World War II has been sobering. All but a tiny percentage of industrial output has gone to import substitutes; little has flowed into international trade to earn foreign exchange and improve balances of payments. Most "industries" in the Middle East today still employ fewer than ten workers, and cannot be said to achieve real economies of scale. Most really successful industries are still extractive and are operated by foreigners—oil in several countries, shrimping in Egypt, copper and chromite in two others. Successful local "industries" are usually bottling works or assembly ventures operating under foreign patents and franchises and usually with foreign supervisory staffs. Industry in most Middle Eastern nations (Israel by the mid-1960's was becoming an exception) created well under 15 per cent of the national income and employed less than ten per cent of the available male labor force. In several countries—notably Cyprus and Israel—the "cost-push" of a well-organized trade union movement and high raw material and power costs, joined with narrow domestic markets, made it difficult to launch and sustain any export industry.

Lack of structural economic change

The three problems described above have combined to inhibit the structural economic changes that have distinguished most nations achieving sustained economic growth in the past. Put briefly, the United States, the nations of northern Europe, the British Dominions, and more recently Japan, have tended over time to increase the percentage of total national income created by services, government, and industry. In these advanced countries, as agriculture's role as earner of percentage of national income decreased, its over-all amount grew, and the number of agricultural workers dropped. While there is no ideal structural outline suitable for all nations, those achieving lasting growth have all undergone the shifts described.

Yet in the Middle East, these shifts have barely begun, and in no nation is wholesale structural change well under way. As mentioned, agriculture still employs 60-80 per cent of the labor force, yet it generates only 20-30 per cent of national income in most countries. Furthermore, throughout the region agriculture and industry together generate only 30-40 per cent of national income. In most advanced nations income from services of all kinds and from government—even from those governments employing relatively few workers—account for more than 50 per cent of national income. The broad changes in the base of the Middle Eastern economy, with improved agricultural and industrial efficiency, and with more workers being absorbed into service occupations, has yet to begin. The lack of structural change forces a more sober view of the extraordinary rates of income expansion.

The burden of armaments

Another problem besetting the Middle East since World War II has been the extraordinary growth in armaments expenditures. Before 1945 the only nations in the region owning armies were Turkey, Iran and Iraq, and even the latter was largely a British creation. After 1945 the emergence of new nations, the creation of Israel, military assistance from the West and the Soviet Union, and tension within the Middle East joined to trigger armaments outlays of alarming proportions.

Put in other terms, the percentages of national income and government expenditures devoted to military outlays by the nations of the Middle East came, after 1945, with few exceptions, to equal those of the nations of the Atlantic Alliance and probably the Soviet Union. Ten per cent of the national incomes and fifty per cent of the government budgets in Turkey, Iran, Iraq, Syria, Egypt, Jordan and Israel now go for military purposes. More than $1 billion of *local funds,* exclusive of Soviet, French, British and American aid, is now plowed into military expenditures each year in the region. Only Lebanon and Cyprus have shown restraint, and even the latter is now mounting an army.

On the positive side, military outlays in the Middle East have undeniably served, in some countries, to strengthen internal security and to provide education for civilian soldiers. But by the mid-1960's, the growing round of investments being made by Israel and Egypt in rocketry and nuclear capability—invariably for "defensive" purposes—bade fair to pose truly complicated and terrible problems for the future.

The urban explosion

Still another problem accompanying economic growth in the Middle East since 1945 was the rapid growth of cities and the emergence of a set of equally vast resultant economic and social problems. Begun by creation of military jobs during World War II, the flood of bedouins and peasants to Cairo, Alexandria, Istanbul, Ankara, Beirut, Baghdad, Damascus and Teheran has gone on with sustained momentum ever since. Cairo almost doubled, to over three million people in the generation after 1945; Teheran tripled, to 1.5 million; Beirut more than doubled, as did Nicosia, Ankara, Baghdad and Damascus; Kuwait, Doha and Riyadh multiplied populations many times.

As elsewhere in the world, urban growth in the Middle East was occasioned by city jobs, real or wished, for dissatisfied rural dwellers. The jobs often came from native development schemes heavily weighted on urban projects. Sometimes, as in Cyprus, they came from military expenditures by an outside power. In most countries the initial social disruption common to the Western city —delinquency, prostitution and the rest—were blunted by the social controls which were imported intact at least with the first generation to cities by villagers congregating together in specified districts. This situation unquestionably ameliorated conditions markedly in Cairo and Teheran, for example. In other communities such as Kuwait, Damascus and Tel Aviv, effective city and town planning prevented gross upheaval. But in most countries the urban explosion had reached gigantic proportions by the mid-1960's; slums expanded daily, and many thinking Middle Easterners wondered if their cities didn't beckon repetition of the Istanbul riots of 1955 or Cairo's "Black Friday" shortly earlier.

Distinguishing Features of Economic Development

Almost every aspect of Middle Eastern economic development in the post-World War II generation has been closely related to, and often dependent upon, events and forces *outside* the region—elements only rarely controllable by it. It is safe to speculate that at no time in the past has any nation or area, except perhaps nineteenth-century England, been so dependent on overseas developments and commitments. It also seems evident that patterns of growth so far forecast that the dependence will certainly not decrease, but will probably grow, in the next two decades. The relationship, as in the years after 1955, will probably also be punctuated by continuing jousts between the West and the Soviet Union in many countries.

Economic interdependence between the West and the Middle East

Petroleum—By the mid-1960's it had become evident that the economic relationship between the Middle East and the Western world had grown to incredible proportions—far exceeding the most optimistic post-World War II forecasts. A few examples are illustrative.

The most dramatic element in the economic interplay between the Middle East and the West was the already mentioned growth in petroleum exports to Western Europe and the Western Hemisphere. In large part it was an "accidental" development. Nobody in his right mind could have predicted, from the rubble of postwar Europe, that fifteen years later petroleum imports from the Middle East would exceed three million barrels daily. Nor did the most optimistic oil man predict, in 1945, that the Middle East contained sufficient reservoirs to permit such enormous exports. Climaxing the near comedy of poor forecasts was the fact that the companies which developed the Middle East oil fields did so not, at the beginning, to supply future European markets, but rather to gird for what they thought to be an inevitable shortage of petroleum in the Western Hemisphere!

Poor forecasts aside, the total production of six million barrels daily of which one half moved westward (most of it to Western Europe after the United States import controls checked trans-Atlantic shipments sharply after 1958) was earning over $1.5 billion yearly for Middle Eastern oil producing nations by the mid-1960's. Kuwait's revenues reached $500 million; Iraq's reached nearly $300 million; Saudi Arabia and Iran were earning $300-400 million each, and Qatar, Abu Dhabi and smaller shaikhdoms another $100 million.

Countries without oil, but located astride transit routes also profited from westward moving petroleum shipments. As transit countries, Syria, Jordan and Lebanon together came to earn a total of about $50 million yearly from pipeline fees earned from shipments of Iraq and Saudi Arabian crude. Egypt's net revenues from the Suez Canal likewise grew rapidly, to more than $60 million by the mid-1960's, as tankers came to account for three-quarters of canal tonnage.

Western Economic Aid and Military Assistance—Another large-scale stimulus to Middle Eastern economic growth came from transfers to the area of various kinds financed by Western governments —chiefly the United States, Great Britain and France. As shown below, United States economic and military aid alone to the Middle East totaled almost $7.5 billion between 1946 and 1963.

United States Economic and Military Assistance to the Middle East (1946-63) (in millions of dollars)

	Economic	*Military*
Cyprus	21	—
Iran	789	633
Iraq	22	46
Israel	957	5
Jordan	385	30
Lebanon	80	9
Saudi Arabia	46	n.a.
Syria	96	—
Turkey	1,761	2,403
UAR (Egypt)	807	—
Yemen	27	—
	4,991	3,126

British and French assistance, while more modest, limited largely to military commitments and harder to illuminate (because of governmental reticence) also added up to a substantial sum during the decade of the 1950's. Britain's treasury transfers to Cyprus grew to exceed $50 million yearly after 1954. U.K. aid to the armies of Jordan and Iraq totaled $30 million in many years during the 1950's. French military assistance to Israel, an unpublicized figure, probably hit about the same levels.

In aggregate, therefore, Western economic and military assistance to Middle Eastern nations came to a rough total of almost $7.5 billion between 1946 and 1963. Since most of the aid was packed into the period after 1948, an average reaching into the 1960's of about $600 million yearly emerges. Even after reducing the actual effect (because of "overvaluing" of equipment, purchases in America, Britain, etc.) the impact on the Middle East still may be said to have been in the magnitude of over $300 million yearly.

German Reparations and Gifts to Israel—During the ten years after 1952, German government reparations to Israel totaled roughly $800 million, and German private restitutions to Israeli citizens pushed the combined total of relatively "stringless" transfers to over $1 billion. During this same period overseas Jewry, mostly American Jews, made gifts to Israel of more than $1 billion. These monies played a prominent role in the high rates of investment maintained by the Jewish state during its early period of independence.

Additions to Public Debt—During the 1950's and early 1960's several Middle Eastern nations took extreme advantage of their international credit-worthiness. Iran pushed its foreign debt to over $600 million, Turkey's debt came to exceed $1 billion, Israel sold bonds abroad worth over $600 million, Egypt went through $1.5 billion of World War II accumulated reserves and piled up a debt of $300 million by the mid-1960's. Even Jordan and Syria, more conservative, accumulated foreign debts on the order of $40 million and $30 million respectively during the period. Only Kuwait, Lebanon and Saudi Arabia were free of debt by the early 1960's and the debtor nations of the Middle East faced combined debt service charges of about $300 million yearly.

Private Investment—By far the most important private investments in the Middle East after World War II were those made by Western oil companies. During the fifteen years after 1945, American, British, French and Dutch companies put over $3 billion into exploration, producing, gathering, refining and transporting facilities in more than seven Middle Eastern nations. By comparison, Western investments in non-oil facilities and ventures were small—probably no more than $200 million total in the Islamic countries and somewhat less in Israel.

During the period under scrutiny a less publicized, but nevertheless important, flow of funds moved out of the Middle Eastern capital forming nations into Western securities, real estate and other investments, and in lesser degree into urban real estate in Beirut and the mountains of Lebanon. By the mid-sixties, the Shaikh of Kuwait alone had accumulated foreign securities holdings in excess of $800 million—mostly in British debt and equity paper, with smaller amounts devoted to United States issues. The flow of funds out of Saudi Arabia into Western investments of many kinds—from Zurich to Wall Street to real estate loans in Athens and Miami—averaged $60-80 million yearly in most years after 1955. Lebanese investors bought substantial, if unknown, quantities of European and American securities and mutual fund shares in growing waves during the years after 1950. Several hundred million dollars of Kuwait and Qatar private holdings flowed into Lebanese apartment houses, hotels and office buildings, also in a rising tide after 1950. In aggregate, these capital movements westward probably averaged close to $200 million yearly after 1953 and by the mid-1960's totaled well over $2 billion. The Middle East's collective contribution to Lebanese and Western economic development was likewise substantial.

Non-oil Trade—Trade in commodities other than oil between the West and the Middle East also increased remarkably after 1950. Imports of merchandise items, for example, during the years 1953-61 rose each year at a rate in excess of 15 per cent for Saudi Arabia, Israel and Cyprus, at more than 11 per cent for Lebanon, Kuwait and Jordan, and at 6-9 per cent for Iraq, Syria and Egypt. Of these increases, all but a small part (which increasingly came from Japan, and to a much lesser extent from the Soviet Union) originated in the United States or Western Europe. Over the period most imports continued to be consumer goods, due in large part to demand generated by oil and pipeline developments. In Israel alone was the trend reversed substantially. There, by the early 1960's, most imports were in the form of producer's goods of various kinds—manufacturing machinery, pumps, metal pipe.

Exports from the Middle East to the West also grew during the years in question, but at a much more modest rate. Except for minerals from Cyprus and Turkey (such as copper and chrome ore and cupreous and iron pyrites), citrus fruits from Israel and Cyprus, industrial diamonds from Israel, cotton from Egypt and Syria and potash and phosphates from Israel and Jordan, the Middle East simply did not produce minerals, agricultural surpluses and manufactured products capable of competing in Western markets. By the early 1960's, Israel was exporting growing amounts of manufactured items, but the multiple exchange rate system made it virtually impossible to determine which of these were indeed competitive and which were financed by drawing on overseas grants.

The tremendous surplus of imports over exports in the non-oil countries naturally led to substantial trading deficits. In Cyprus these regularly exceeded $60 million after 1955, in Lebanon over $100 million, in Israel over $300 million—between $100 and $150 per capita! These were met in varying ways, but usually from Western sources and government transfers of various kinds, remittances from overseas emigrants, gifts by international Jewry, earnings from overseas banking and trade, and tourism.

An interesting aspect of Middle Eastern non-oil trading after 1950 was the fact that directions of trade changed relatively little. German and Japanese imports came to challenge United States, British, French, and Italian goods by the late 1950's; the Soviet Union took a large part of Egypt's cotton for several years after 1958 (even this shifted back after 1962), but basically the trading pattern remained intact. Eighty-five per cent of imports came from the West, with Japan and the Soviet Union and intra-regional trade dividing the rest in varying degrees. Exports worked out to about the same figures. At no point did intra-regional trade total more than ten per cent of the area's international trade. The Middle East's traders by the mid-1960's still looked westward for goods and markets.

Soviet aid and trade

Until the mid-1950's, the United States was by far the most important provider of economic and military assistance to the Middle East. British efforts in Cyprus and French help to Israel were significant in per capita terms to these nations, but the lion's share of public assistance came from America. After 1955, however, the Soviet Union elected to undertake aid of its own to several Middle Eastern nations. For the next decade the first serious aid competition, in a crucial area of great interest to both sides in the Cold War, took place between Russia and the West in the Middle East.

Russia's reasons for entering the aid competition were several. She had consolidated her hold in Eastern Europe, and the Iron Curtain was a generally accepted fact in European politics; relations between President Nasser and the administrations then governing France, Britain and the United States were sorely strained (over such matters as finance for the Aswan Dam, control of the Suez Canal and border incidents on the frontiers separating Israel and her Arab neighbors) and the time for entry seemed propitious; the Soviets at that time were electing to extend their propaganda and subversion efforts to the underdeveloped nations of South Asia and Latin America. The Middle East, with real troubles between it and the West, seemed a natural target.

The Soviet aid effort after 1955 took several directions. Loan credits, calling for interest payments at two and a half per cent yearly were offered in varying amounts to Syria, Iraq, Egypt and Yemen. Initial arrangements after 1956 forecast that as much as $800 million worth of credit might be extended in this fashion. Military aid, in the form of jet aircraft and technical instruction was also made available, chiefly to the first three nations. The Soviet

Union also undertook to provide most of the foreign finance required for the Aswan Dam.

Because of secrecy about the extent and value of Soviet military commitments after 1956, and the difficulty of separating these financially from economic and technical aid, it is difficult to arrive at accurate figures for the total. Most observers would agree, however, that by the early 1960's Egypt had taken on debts of over $300 million, Iraq about $200 million and Syria $40-50 million. While substantial, and calling for debt service charges of $20-25 million by 1970, the amounts were small indeed when compared to funds and equipment made available by Western nations.

Soviet trade with the Middle East also remained on a very modest basis prior to the mid-1960's. As mentioned earlier, more than half of Egypt's cotton crop went to the Soviet Union and satellite buyers for several years during the troubles after Suez. The Soviet Union on occasion bought "problem crops" (such as raisins from Cyprus or citrus fruits from several countries), but these purchases reached very small totals over the period after 1958. Soviet exports to the Middle East remained small, and consisted mainly of machinery for government projects. Few Soviet consumer goods were visible.

The failure of Soviet trade with the Middle East to expand, despite the area's disenchantment with the West over many incidents, probably was due to a combination of Soviet ineptness at trading (deliveries were slow, spare parts often non-existent), a shortage of goods for export, currency exchange difficulties, and the lack of willingness on behalf of the Soviet Union to pay high prices for cotton which it in fact did not need and often re-exported, via Finland, for prices below those offered earlier to Egypt by Lancashire weavers. In addition, the Middle Eastern trading community proved loath to abandon its long-established set of Western suppliers and purchasers in favor of the unknown abrasions of bloc trading.

Prospects for the Future

Enough has been said in the preceding paragraphs to make the point that Middle Eastern economic growth after World War II was in large part a response to tremendous, and quite unpredictable forces originating outside the area. Middle Easterners themselves responded—as private entrepreneurs in half a dozen countries, as public planners in nations such as Israel, Egypt and Iraq, and as consumers everywhere. Yet, as also made clear earlier, the strenuous efforts of large numbers of Middle Easterners were not sufficient, in view of geographic and demographic obstacles (and despite the enormous magnitude of outside economic stimuli) to change basically the region's economic structure. So by the mid-1960's, maintenance of upward statistical trends meant continuing reliance on forces abroad. It also depended on the search for an economic ideology suited to the region's peculiar conditions of time and space. And finally, it depended on what happened to the area's human resources—their quality, and their numbers.

Successful economic relations abroad

One of the more optimistic future trends visible in the Middle East during the mid-1960's was the outlook for petroleum exports. As noted earlier, Western Europe's intake of Middle Eastern oil rose to more than three million barrels daily by 1962, and for many years Europe's petroleum intake went up as high as 14 per cent a year. Fed by the growth of the mass market automobile, the shift from coal to oil in industry, alternative employment for coal miners in Germany, France and Belgium, and growing consumer preference for oil-fired central heating, imported oil came gradually to supply 36 per cent of Europe's energy requirements—a rise from about 14 per cent in 1945! Owning the world's largest proved reserves of cheap oil, and with no real competition yet practicable, the prospects for rising exports and earnings looked good. (Most forecasts held that nuclear power would not be really competitive before 1970, and United States coal shipped to Europe competed with oil only in England and a few Continental coastal areas.)

Yet oil exporting nations, and the Western oil companies producing, transporting and marketing their oil, faced real problems. Price was one. In August, 1960, the major international oil companies cut the posted prices of Middle East crude from $1.90 to $1.80. The cut came at the end of a decade of phenomenal growth in output and earnings for companies and producing governments. During the decade the 50/50 principle of division of net profits had applied. Although calling for equal division of profits, 50/50 had never meant exactly that. Early in the decade, for example, the oil companies took more than half of the profits, while by the end of the decade local governments enjoyed the larger share. Depending on whose figures one took, the split had become 55/45 or 60/40—meanwhile for practical reasons all concerned adhered to the fictions of "posted price" and 50/50 contracts.

The downward pressure on prices which occasioned the dramatic price cuts in 1960 was due to several forces. The major international oil companies themselves, spurred on by forecasts of petroleum shortages after the Suez affair in 1956, were simply too successful at finding enormous new fields in the Middle East and at Lake Maracaibo in Venezuela. And under pressure from Middle Eastern governments, they stepped up exports, causing European prices to falter. Another cause for lower prices was the growth in exports of oil in the hands of new international American oil companies lacking Eastern hemisphere transportation and marketing facilities and often with bank loans to meet. Further downward pressure came from the United States Fuels Import Control Program which, after 1958, effectively removed the United States market as the safety valve for surplus Middle East production. Next, Russian oil, flowing into Europe after 1959, sped the downward trend. So, too, did forecasts for North African production, then beginning in Algeria and soon to start in Libya.

To protect themselves from further price cuts, and to try to restore pre-August 1960 price levels, Middle Eastern producing governments (with Venezuela, and later Indonesia and Libya) formed the Organization of Petroleum Exporting Countries (OPEC). OPEC's demands called for restoration of pre-1960 prices, reaccounting of royalties, and elimination of various discounts. Operating from a headquarters in Geneva, OPEC arranged conferences of its parents, commissioned studies by outside consultants and pressed constantly for the three demands listed above.

Outside of OPEC, there were several evidences of harmonious arrangements between oil companies and producing governments during the early 1960's. One of these was the matter of relinquishment of undeveloped lease areas; agreements covering these matters were signed in Iraq, Kuwait, Qatar, Bahrein and Saudi Arabia. Another was the Aramco-Saudi Arabia agreement of April, 1963, which settled a myriad of disputed claims. Others involved new exploration contracts in which local governments, by agreeing for the first time to advance a share of development expense, received promise of proportionately greater shares of profits.

The above developments testified to a growth in sophistication within Middle Eastern producing governments as well as within oil company managements during the 1950's. That both sides were able to avoid, following the August 1960 price cut, the "eyeball to eyeball" confrontation which led the government of Iran and the Anglo-Iranian Oil Company to the mutually destructive shutdown of Iran's oil facilities in 1951, was evidence that both sides had learned much of each other's problems and were beginning to see that in many ways their interests were peculiarly parallel. Prices of Middle Eastern oil had, after all, held remarkably firm, and earnings of local governments continued to rise during the early 1960's, although at a less dramatic rate than during the 1950's. The task for the future obviously was for both sides to recognize more clearly their parallel interests.

In this same connection, the northward movement of loaded oil tankers and their southward transit under ballast through the Suez Canal came, by the early 1960's, to afford Egypt its most predictable, and in some years major (ahead of cotton), source of foreign exchange. Annual canal earnings exceeded $50 million net in many years, and these were more than two-thirds attributable to petroleum cargos. Egypt's plans, moreover, for widening and deepening the canal and generally improving its efficiency, envisioned earnings of nearly $100 million yearly from the waterway by the late 1960's. As with the oil producing nations, Egypt, too, had developed a substantial interest in oil trade.

Further interdependence between the Middle East and the West was in the matter of gifts, grants and loans to Israel. Most forecasts indicated that unless Israel cut its internal consumption or its high rate of investment, it would have to rely on finding financial coverage for import surpluses averaging $350 million yearly through the 1960's. Yet the first installments on its foreign bond issues of $600 million came due in mid-1963 with more to come at intervals thereafter. Reparations from the German government were tailing off, exports while rising were contributing only modestly to improved balances of payments because of the high cost of raw material imports, and the United States government (acting on recommendations of the Clay Committee in 1963) had signified its intention of cutting United States aid to Israel. So Israel faced the continuing need to raise $175 per citizen abroad each year—largely from gifts by American Jewry, and by increases in restitution by private German citizens. Its reliance on the West remained indeed high.

One aspect of interdependence which seemed virtually certain to diminish during the mid and late 1960's was that of United States foreign economic assistance. Fanned by growing concern over the United States gold stocks and balance of payments, inconclusive but acrimonious debate over whether United States aid should aim at promoting American strategic needs or local economic development, and the continued inability of foreign aid's supporters to offer quantitative evidence of the program's successes, sharp cuts were made in the early 1960's—with more forecast for later in the decade. Most reports and economy recommendations singled out Lebanon and Israel as among the nations which should be eliminated from further aid.

One striking opportunity for developing income from Western sources during the 1960's was through tourism. For fifteen years after World War II Middle Eastern nations did little—with two main exceptions, Lebanon and Israel—to promote the eastward flow of European and American tourists. Hotel facilities were inadequate, visa restrictions onerous, political conditions uncertain (such as revolutions in several countries, Suez, the Istanbul riots, British-EOKA troubles in Cyprus), and government promotion programs were feeble. But by the early 1960's several Middle Eastern nations began to wake up to what tourism had done to vitalize the economies of Italy and Greece and to capitalize on soaring European prosperity—and mobility. Jordan, Egypt, Cyprus, and Iran joined Lebanon and Israel as active promoters of tourist trade, with advertising programs, eased visa requirements, improved hotel facilities and the rest. By the mid-1960's the Middle East seemed in position to do well indeed from American and European tourists.

Emigrant remittances offered another prospectively lucrative source to Middle Eastern nations, and one which grew with Western prosperity. By the mid-1960's Lebanon had as many citizens abroad as at home, Cypriots were leaving Aphrodite's Isle at the rate of 3,000 to 12,000 yearly, growing numbers of refugee Palestinians and Egyptians were working in Persian Gulf oil camps. The flow of Egyptians and Israelis into Africa was growing. Together the movement of educated Middle Easterners abroad was yielding an estimated ten per cent of per capita income for Lebanon, Cyprus and Jordan and was serving both economic and political ends for Egypt and Israel.

The latter two nations were indeed engaged, by the mid-1960's, in parallel and increasingly competitive efforts in sub-Saharan Africa. Another aspect of the Middle East's growing interdependence with the outside world, Egypt and Israel offered education at home to Africans, sent technicians of all kinds to work in Black Africa and on occasion made capital grants for development projects. Egypt and Israel went to Black Africa for a variety of reasons. Both were buying votes in the U.N. and other international forums; both had concluded, by the mid-1960's, that their economic systems were so cleverly contrived that they deserved sharing with less privileged peoples; both had faced up, in varying degree, to surpluses of trained manpower at home during their early independence period; both sought captive markets, through bilateral technical assistance-trading agreements, for over-priced domestic manufactures from Israel and Egypt. Whatever their reasons for entering Black Africa (by the mid-1960's several thousand Israelis and Egyptians worked there), the work of Middle Easterners was heralded by their parent nations as a new form of international benevolence, free of the taint of imperialism.

The search for an economic ideology

By the mid-1960's it was evident that the nations of the Middle East were basically westward-looking in their search for economic ideology. Although several took assistance of various kinds from the Soviet Union, all had come to recognize that (up to that point, at least) their trading interests were with the West: the really massive source of gifts and loans was the West; their young men and women went West for education in a rising tide (as estimated 40,000-50,000 were studying in universities in the United States, France and Britain after 1960); those with funds to invest abroad bought shares in Wall Street, Zurich or London; and their economic advisers and technical assistance personnel came overwhelmingly from the West.

Yet despite the economic linkage, there was evident by the mid-1960's, a growing uneasiness about the universal validity of the Western economic experience and of the mass of theory which had grown up around it. This uneasiness afflicted large numbers of Western economists—called increasingly to offer advice—just as it struck Middle Eastern decision makers charged with implementing that advice. The common affliction helped create a rising new field of enquiry, "development economics," in Western universities. In the Middle East, it tended to promote a series of eclectic, often bizarre, experiments on the level of economic policy.

Development economics, unquestionably, drew part of its sustenance from some awesome conclusions drawn by its practitioners watching the Middle East. Several examples will suffice. Despite some impressive national and per capita income thrusts, there was little basic structural change in the seventeen years after World War II; despite squads of advisers and much investment of public money, the area's basic agricultural and industrial problems remained unsolved; coordinated economic planning, with the aid of Western advisers, remained very much an unproved process, and the rapid growth rates of Lebanon (for seventeen years after 1945), Jordan (for several years after 1959), and Syria before 1958—all with little or no planning—compared favorably indeed with the area's "planned" economies (i.e.) Israel, Egypt and Iraq. The Middle East, despite its high growth rates, remained *heavily* dependent on outside economic forces. Ideas advanced by Western economists—"balanced growth," "takeoff into sustained growth," capital output ratios, input-output accounting, theories of investment in "human resource" compared to that in physical plant and facilities, to mention a few—were probably more useful in training minds of young Westerners than in influencing Middle Eastern economic practices.

But despite the lag in formation by Westerners of economic concepts really useful to the underdeveloped Middle East, the West still held, by the mid-1960's, its monopoly on concepts and those who tried to put them to work. The Soviet Union had failed, despite several tries after 1956, to substitute latter-day Marxist ideas for those of the West in any Middle Eastern nation. Although Egypt called itself "socialist," its top economic advisers came exclusively from the West—Holland, Finland, the United States, for example. In no Middle Eastern nation by 1963 had Soviet advisers reached real positions of authority, and most got no higher than dam-building or jet engine maintenance. The West's position, while partially earned by default of its adversary, remained intact. The challenge lay in creating more exportable ideas with which to blunt the next attack in coming rounds.

Improvement of human resources

The significant growth in national incomes and economic activity in the Middle East after World War II was accompanied by some equally impressive advances in education. Percentages of eligible students in schools, literacy rates, numbers of students in colleges and professional schools (at home and abroad) rose sharply in most nations. Countries such as Israel, Cyprus, Iraq, Lebanon, and Kuwait launched programs forecasting that the new generations in these nations would completely escape the curse of illiteracy and that growing proportions of young men and women would have the background, and the financial resources to acquire advanced training in a dozen fields. By the mid-1960's Israel had already achieved one of the highest ratios of professionally trained manpower to population in the world; Lebanon (already with a very low illiteracy rate) was regularly exporting doctors, engineers (and even an occasional physicist!) to the industrial West; Jordan multiplied its school population at all levels; Cyprus had cut its illiteracy rate to a very low percentage; and Kuwait offered free primary and secondary education to all, and college fellowships abroad to virtually all takers. Iraq invested regularly enormous sums in schools, colleges and teachers. The advances scored by these nations in education led many observers to link their superior economic performance, and perhaps their apparent superior viability, to their strong base of human resources.

Yet other Middle Eastern nations still had a long way to go, as late as the mid-1960's, in developing human resources. Illiteracy rates in Turkey, Iran, Egypt and Saudi Arabia remained high. Only in Israel did levels of research and teaching in national universities approximate the generally high levels of better colleges and universities in the West—and too many national universities remained essentially political forums, with students "on strike" much of the time. Foreign institutions such as the American University of Beirut and the Université Saint Joseph in Beirut continued to offer Western-led instruction, but numerically at least their influence lagged behind that of the burgeoning national universities. Unquestionably, most Middle Eastern nations had come at least to recognize the role played in economic growth by healthy, educated citizens. Yet only those with small, and hence financially manageable, populations could afford investments creating dramatic results.

For several nations indeed, the *quantity* of population was as much a problem as its quality. For most years after 1945, the three big Muslim nations—Turkey, Egypt and Iran—grew at rates hovering about three per cent annually. At 1960 rates of climb, they stood to double their World War II populations before 1970. Turkey and Egypt, lacking oil, cursed with extreme demographic problems, and owning a most conservative peasantry, could hardly afford the enormous rates of increase—due partly to high fertility but largely to forward thrusts in life expectancy. By the early 1960's only one national leader, President Nasser of Egypt, had faced up publicly to the need for concerted action in population control.

Summary

In retrospect, one may point to a record of enormous post-World War II economic expansion in the Middle East. This expansion has not led to structural changes, widespread industrialization and universally dynamic agriculture, but instead has been largely a result of expanded commerce, services and government. The astounding advances have been accompanied by enormous problems. With it all, the intimacy of the economic relationship between the West and the Middle East has grown beyond all expectations, and the Soviet economic offensive had, by the mid-1960's, shown an equally unexpected lack of success. In view of the growth of common interests, the task facing the West and the Middle East in years to come is three-fold. First, both sides need to promote the flow of goods and services, public and private investment capital and payments, human beings, and ideas across one another's frontiers. Next, both sides must work to improve both the quality *and* quantity of Middle Eastern human resources—the area's citizens should be urged *not,* in short, to follow the West's post-World War II example of rapid population increase. Finally, Western nations must, hopefully with collaboration from the Soviet Bloc, join Middle Eastern nations in checking the potentially disastrous armaments race under way throughout the region at full tilt in the mid-1960's.

J. C. Hurewitz 

4

Regional and International Politics in the Middle East

The Middle East and North Africa may be seen from within as a geographic unit. Arabs look at the area from Morocco to Muscat as the Arab world, a sphere that the unity nationalists among them ardently hope will soon be fused into a single state. After 1945 they fought the Western powers tooth and nail for the liberation of Arab territories from imperial rule, and once Algeria became free, they could be expected to focus on the last surviving dependencies—the British protected shaikhdoms along the eastern and southern rim of the Arabian Peninsula. The Arab nationalists, particularly in Cairo, were also still beating the dead horse of imperialism, partly because of habit and partly because of lack of imagination. The Arab world forms part of a larger Muslim world, with Israel, Lebanon and Cyprus as exceptions. But this region of contiguous Muslim sovereignties was not fired by a unity of sentiment. Nor did the Turks, the Iranians, and the Afghans try to promote the independence of the Turkish and Iranian Muslim peoples whose territories, abutting theirs on the north, formed a part of the Russian empire ever since tsarist days.

J. C. Hurewitz *is Professor of Government at Columbia University. He has specialized on the politics of the Near and Middle East since the beginning of World War II and has traveled and lived for prolonged periods in the Middle East. He is the author of* Diplomacy in the Near and Middle East *(1956)*; The Struggle for Palestine: Middle East Dilemma *(1953); and numerous contributions to scholarly journals.*

Viewed from without, the belt of independent states from Morocco to Afghanistan still did not constitute a unified region in 1963. Under European imperialism, the Middle East had represented essentially a British preserve with only marginal French participation, in mandated Syria and Lebanon (1920-46); and North Africa, essentially a French preserve with only marginal Spanish participation, in Morocco, and international, in the city of Tangier. Libya, which fell between the two preserves in the interwar period, was for the most part assimilated, after the expulsion of Italy in 1942, into the British zone. Each of the two European imperial regimes, though part of larger global systems, nevertheless formed real unities. The British unified the region politically, militarily and economically as never before by developing in World War II a Middle East Command and a Supply Center. Both were responsible to a War Council which was headed by a Minister of the British War Cabinet resident in Cairo and comprised of the principal British political and military officers from all the participating countries. France also tended to treat its trio of North African possessions as interdependent and administered them accordingly, despite its governance of Algeria as an extension of the French mainland, and of Tunisia and Morocco as protectorates. In the postwar years, as the British and the French surrendered one dependency after another, the North African countries (the Maghrib) began to be drawn into the Arab League, the distinction between North Africa and the Middle East began to blur. But the process had not gone far enough to erase the lines of demarcation.

The Return of Regional Politics

The Middle East (including North Africa) is an area characterized by a bewildering interplay of domestic, regional, and international politics. This was not always so in the twentieth century. Until 1945, in fact, regional politics as such virtually did not exist, since the Middle East had been absorbed into European politics. The subjugation of the region, chiefly to Britain and France, took place step by step in the course of a century and a half and did not reach its widest scope until the years between 1918 and 1945. Following World War II, moreover, regional politics did not reappear all at once, but in successive stages. States began to be born, after a hiatus of nearly two decades, at a rate of almost one a year, so that between 1946 and 1962 their number had more than trebled from five to eighteen.

Controlled regionalism

When Britain and France between them ruled the Middle East, genuine regional politics was out of the question. Frictions springing from imperial rivalry or from differing imperial styles did not constitute true regional politics. The very essence of subjugation represented a mastery by the Europeans of the external affairs, including defense and finance, of their Middle East dependencies. Britain's preferential allies, Iraq and Egypt, conducted relations with the United Kingdom and neighboring independent states, but under the close surveillance of Whitehall. The region's sovereign lands, not necessarily Saudi Arabia and Yemen whose range of foreign activities hardly pushed out beyond the Arabian Peninsula, or Afghanistan, whose scope of external interests was comparably restricted, but even Turkey and Iran were inhibited by Europe from full liberty of action. The closest approximation to regional politics in the dependent Arab zone took the form of conspiratorial nationalist movements that occasionally crossed national frontiers, with the connivance at times of one European metropolitan power against another.

Middle East politics continued through World War II to be little more than a projection of European politics. The later French and British imperial retirement, however, did not take place all at once. The metropolitan powers resisted mounting nationalist pressures for independence and tried to hold on to their imperial positions for as long as possible. The most protracted withdrawals, the tedious negotiations (1946-54) for Britain's evacuation of its gigantic Suez Canal base in Egypt, and the bitter guerrilla warfare (1954-62) of the Algerian nationalists against France, together spanned more than a decade and a half. Copious bloodletting also attended Britain's laying down of imperial authority in Palestine and Cyprus, while more shouting than shooting accompanied the departure of Britain and France from such Arab dependencies as Sudan, Tunisia and Morocco.

Controlled regionalism in Britain's Arab zone began in the late 1930's with negotiations on Palestine and were resumed in 1943 when, with British encouragement and guidance, Arab political leaders in the Fertile Crescent, the Arabian Peninsula and Egypt launched negotiations that led to the creation of the Arab League two years later. Shaking itself free of imperial shackles almost from birth, the League provided a medium for independent regional politics, and as it accreted new states, swelling its membership from seven to thirteen, the geographic compass of the organization's activities spread from the Arab East to the Arab West.

The very banding together for regional and extraregional politics tended to separate the Arab states from the non-Arab. This helps explain why Iraq, though a founding member of the Baghdad Pact, was the first to leave it. The successor regional organization, known as CENTO, furnished an institutional framework for Turkey, Iran and Pakistan to meet together, especially for the coordination of their defense and foreign policies. The sponsorship of this regional organization by Britain and the United States converted it partly into an extraregional body and hardened Arab suspicions of its purposes. In regional affairs, Israel often found itself siding with Turkey and Iran because of their common isolation by the Arab states.

In international politics in the Middle East—that is, the political relations between the region's states and outside powers—it became customary to refer to geography, natural resources, communications and transportation, and military bases as the governing conditions. The proximity of the Middle East to the Soviet Union and the consequent fear of communist aggression, the need to safeguard the fabulous oil pools developed primarily since 1945 by Western enterprise and capital, the central importance of the Suez Canal and the region's air arteries for the NATO countries—have remained in the 1960's as in the earlier years premises of Western strategic thinking. However, the planning of the European powers and their allies for future security needs rested on past experience, and the memory of the value and versatility of the Middle East bases in World War II gained in nostalgia what it lost in clarity. The relatively slow-motion imperial withdrawals, moreover, kept old habits and old ideas from passing entirely out of existence.

Results of disimperialism

The postwar disimperialism in the Middle East has taken place wholly within the Arab (and Israel) area. In view of the weakness of the successor states, this represented a transfer from Europe to the Middle East of sovereignty but not of military and economic capability. The very uncertainties in the Arab area sharpened the rivalry throughout the Middle East between the Western powers, increasingly led by the United States, and the Soviet bloc (mainly the U.S.S.R.). The prevailing Cold War suspicions led the superpowers and their allies to engage in competition in many spheres —military, economic, and technical as well as political—thus giving the postwar period its unique stamp. Under the impact of the Cold

War the industrialized countries of the two rival blocs shared their largess with the underdeveloped states of the Middle East as never before, as they were also doing throughout Asia and Africa. Thus Gamal Abdel Nasser and Ahmad Ben Bella were receiving in 1963 amounts of material assistance that Kemal Atatürk and Reza Shah a generation earlier would not have believed possible, and might never have accepted.

In any study of the interplay of the domestic with regional and international politics, it seems logical to begin with the regional, and to start with the thirteen states among the region's eighteen that are Arab, and the problems that divide them in their dealings with one another.

Disunity in the Arab East

The overturn of the absolute monarchy in Yemen on September 26, 1962, by army officers, a week after the death of Imam Ahmad (1948-62), excited immediate repercussions throughout the Arab East. The United Arab Republic (U.A.R.) promptly went to the aid of the Yemeni rebels, while Saudi Arabia and Jordan took up the cause of the royalists. Within a few weeks rebel planes flown by Egyptian pilots attacked targets in the British-protected Federation of South Arabia and then in Saudi Arabia, which the Egyptians also assaulted from the sea. By June, 1963, the number of Egyptian troops deployed in Yemen had reached an estimated 28,000. The outbreak of civil war in the southwest corner of the Arabian Peninsula brought together strange bedfellows on the royalist side—the Zaydi Shiites of Yemen, the Wahhabis of Saudi Arabia, and the Hashimites of Jordan, all erstwhile enemies. It also threatened to spread into a wider regional war or even an international one, for the possibility could not be overlooked of Britain's involvement, in the event of sustained attack on its dependency, Aden. Moreover, the U.S.S.R. was already discreetly supplying the rebels with military equipment, including planes, some of them allegedly flown in combat by Soviet pilots. Faced with this evolving crisis the United States behaved in characteristic manner by attempting first to prevent the war from escalating beyond the frontiers of Yemen, then within the United Nations and outside it to arrange a disengagement of foreign troops and, hopefully, an eventual negotiated settlement.

Had the Imamate been overthrown in 1948, or even in 1955, when previous attempts were in fact made, repercussions of these dimensions would never have followed. Besides, although the U.A.R. had obviously helped the rebels plan the *coup d'état,* furnished them military equipment and technical advisers to develop the necessary administrative services for the districts that they held, and actually committed to the hostilities more troops than there probably were in the regular army of Saudi Arabia, still the tribal units of the royalists held out month after month, even after United Nations observers arrived in June 1963 to oversee the evacuation of foreign forces. The stamina of the royalists represented only one of the enigmas of the unfolding crisis. Another was the financial capacity of the U.A.R. to mount so elaborate an offensive, especially when its 1962 international payments balance showed a $300 million deficit, despite generous United States and Soviet aid. Most important for regional politics, however, the Yemeni crisis exposed to full view the persistent disunity that has characterized the Arab East in the postwar years.

Dynastic quarrels

This political discord passed through two phases. The first was essentially dynastic, centering around the rivalry between the Hashimites and the Saudis. It was a legacy of the consolidation in the 1920's of Saudi supremacy over most of the Arabian Peninsula, partly at the expense of the Hashimites and their decade-old kingdom of the Hejaz. In the ensuing political contest, which survived World War II, Saudi Arabia won to its side Egypt and Syria and occasionally even Yemen, while the two Hashimite kingdoms of Iraq and Jordan (Transjordan until 1949) were both underwritten by their patron, the United Kingdom. After the Palestine War of 1948-49, when it became clear that the Arab states had failed to pool their military resources and drive Israel into the sea, the Hashimites and their Arab rivals took to blaming one another for the debacle. Not until three years after the completion in 1949 of the Arab-Israel armistice system did the two Arab camps re-establish a united diplomatic front on the war's residual problems. In the interval Jordan had defied the anti-Hashimite coalition by annexing the Old City of Jerusalem and the east-central district of Palestine.

A subsidiary Arab quarrel of these years involved Syria and Lebanon. Many Syrians, particularly in the Sunni community, continued insisting on the "return" of Lebanon to "Greater Syria." This sentiment found supporters among Sunni Muslims in Lebanon, but the prevailing view there favored the retention of the sovereignty and political identity of the state. In the course of this quasidynastic dispute, Syria ended in 1950 the customs and currency unions, inherited from the French mandate.

Once the young army officers, under the leadership of Abdel

Nasser, reached in October 1954 a settlement with the United Kingdom for the evacuation of British forces from the Suez Canal Base, Egypt seized the initiative in Arab regional politics. To this end Abdel Nasser reactivated in 1955 the anti-Hashimite coalition, ostensibly to discourage Iraq from becoming a founding member of the Baghdad Pact, and to dissuade Jordan from joining it. The first move failed; the second succeeded. By the time of the Suez crisis in the fall of 1956, the cleavage between the Hashimites and their opponents under the new Egyptian management was deeper than ever. Thus the Syrian army in November 1956 blew up the Iraq Petroleum Company pipeline that conveyed oil from north Iraq through Syria to the Mediterranean. The damage to the pumps and lines, not fully repaired for almost a year, harmed Iraq even more than it did the foreign oil companies, which could temporarily tap other supplies. The assassination of Iraq's King Faisal in 1958 by his army officers brought an end to that Hashimite monarchy, the Hashimite coalition and Iraq's participation in the Baghdad Pact, but not to Iraqi rivalry with Egypt. General Abdel Karim Kassim, who soon established a personal dictatorship after eliminating his pro-Egyptian fellow conspirators, became as anti-Egyptian as the Hashimites had been before him.

Doctrinal divisions: Arab socialism

Syria's separation from the U.A.R. in September 1961 after less than four years of union, an act in part triggered by Cairo's attempted application to the northern region of a comprehensive program of socialism, ushered in the second or doctrinal phase of disunity. Socialism in Egypt, which Abdel Nasser ultimately labeled Arab socialism, was slow in building. In a sense it could be said to have begun with the nationalization of the Suez Canal Company in 1956 and the "Egyptianization" of British and French firms in 1957 and to have assumed major proportions in the summer of 1961. Abdel Nasser's nationalization at that time of banks and insurance companies contributed to Syria's secession, which in turn shocked the U.A.R. president into proclaiming a wholesale program of socialism for Egypt. The limit on private land ownership was cut back to 100 acres. To foreign trade, which had been nationalized earlier, and heavy industry which the state had organized, were now added some medium-sized industries. The government further restricted individual investment in others, arranged for labor representation in company directorates, and assured workers a 25 per cent share of profits. In addition, the property and assets of some 700-800 "capitalist reactionaries who had exploited the . . . people" and maintained "a monopoly of national income" were confiscated.

The military dictatorship in Egypt encountered recurrent difficulties in its efforts to organize popular support for the government programs. After originally outlawing all political parties, it announced in 1955 that a Liberation Rally would be created. Soon after this single party was brought into being the United Arab Republic itself was formed, and a new National Union projected for both regions. This in turn had barely gone into operation when Syria seceded, and once again the government set about organizing the successor Arab Socialist Union in April 1963. On each occasion the government pledged that the single party would form the basis for eventual popular rule and constitutional government. The earlier failures it ascribed to "reactionaries" and "capitalists." Membership in the Arab Socialist Union was limited exclusively to "progressive elements" and from it were expressly excluded the quondam owners of nationalized or sequestered land and property, all Egyptians convicted of subversion, and communists—altogether an estimated 77,000. Some 4.7 million men and women enrolled in the Union in 1963.

The doctrinal phase of Arab disunity commenced before the end of 1961 with Abdel Nasser's condemnation of King Saud and Imam Ahmad as "reactionaries" at the time that the U.A.R. president terminated the United Arab States, a nominal federation with Yemen conceived at the time of the union with Syria. In the months that followed, Egypt accused one Arab government after another of feudalism, corruption and greed, and called upon the Arab masses everywhere to rise up against their regimes and liberate their countries for Arab socialism. The campaign to line up countries on Egypt's side bore its first fruits in the summer of 1962, when Ahmad Ben Bella with U.A.R. blessing maneuvered himself into the premiership of newly independent Algeria and disclosed his adherence to the principles of Arab socialism. This was followed in September by the revolution in Yemen, and in February and March 1963 by pro-socialist *coups d'état* in Iraq and Syria. It was widely hoped in Egypt that the five "liberated" Arab countries would now form a coalition against the remaining conservatives.

But because of the peculiarities of Yemeni society, where the Imamate had preserved beyond the mid-twentieth century a patriarchal tribalism that kept the population at large at a very primitive level, the Yemeni republican leaders could scarcely claim to lead a liberated country. Religious and tribal conflicts took precedence over a sense of nationhood. Though led by a Shiite of the

Zaydi sect, the rebels established themselves where Sunni tribesmen predominated—in the coastal plain and the southeast mountain ranges—and in the major towns, including the capital, Sana. The rebels thus found themselves ranged, in essence, against the Zaydi Shiites, from whose ranks the Imam was chosen. The Egyptians and the republican rebels underestimated the determination of the Shiite tribesmen, concentrated in the mountain stronghold of the northeast, to uphold the Imam as the embodiment of their religious and temporal system. Indeed they viewed the Egyptian military units as foreign invaders, and declared a holy war in defense of the Shiite kingdom. Only fragments of those tribal groups that, for whatever private reasons, felt grievances against the late Imam Ahmad actually rallied to the republican banner. Nor could the insurgents effectively employ disciplined troops and superior armaments, including motorized equipment and air support, against guerrillas fighting in their own terrain in defense of their religious and political principles, and able to melt away at will among their fellow tribesmen. The resort of the republicans and their foreign supporters to terror tactics, such as dropping napalm bombs on villages and the dispersal of explosive cigarettes apparently did not destroy the morale of the royalists. The U.A.R. seemed in fact to be repeating, in fighting Muslim religious tribesmen, the military blunders of the Russians in their prolonged struggle against Shamil in Daghistan and Chechnia and of the French against 'Abd al-Sadir in Algeria, both more than a century earlier.

Separatism in the Arab West

In the prolonged struggle for Algerian independence (November 1, 1954-March 19, 1962) Egypt provided the nationalist rebels with greater assistance than did any other state. It gave asylum to Algerian leaders and counseled them in planning the revolt from the safety of Cairo, organized diplomatic and propaganda support among all the Arab League states for the nationalist cause in the United Nations and the world at large, and provided military and material aid to the insurgents. Little wonder that the leaders and the public in Algeria, after independence, were grateful to their sister Arab state. Moreover, Abdel Nasser himself became for many Algerians as he had for many Arab nationalists in other countries the symbol of political success. His defiance of the Great Powers had netted him bounteous military equipment from the Soviet bloc, ownership of the Suez Canal Company, the conversion of the military defeat at Sinai and Suez into a political victory, Soviet loans and technical assistance for the construction of the Aswan Dam, and renewed American aid on a scale unprecedented for Egypt. It would have been difficult indeed for the first leaders of Algeria to avoid emulating such a political Midas as Abdel Nasser.

Ben Bella and Socialism in Algeria

Indeed, Algeria's man of destiny in the first year of independence, Ahmad Ben Bella, had manifestly studied the techniques and policies of the Egyptian president and adopted many of them as his own. In the opening weeks of independence Ben Bella, who enjoyed the backing of the regular armed forces, took steps to eliminate Youssef Ben Khedda, the prime minister of the provisional government, who was supported by guerrilla units in the vicinity of the capital. Having accomplished this by the end of September without plunging the country into civil war, Ben Bella himself became prime minister after elections for the first National Assembly. As head of the government he turned to converting the National Liberation Front (FLN), the underground organization in the war for independence, into the only legitimate political party in the country. By early December as part of a "purification drive" the Communist and Social Revolutionary parties were banned and their principal leaders and members arrested because of their refusal to operate within the FLN. In January Ben Bella made the General Union of Algerian Workers subsidiary to the FLN, and by April he became secretary-general of the Political Bureau, the FLN's directorate, thus gaining uncontested control over the political apparatus of the country.

From Egypt, Ben Bella imported the principle of "positive neutralism" in the Cold War, which he preferred to call simply nonalignment. His record in applying this principle in the first year was impressive. On the eve of the United States-Cuban crisis in October 1962 he managed within a few days to visit Kennedy and Castro and not lose the support of either. Ben Bella, it was clear, weighed carefully the implications of offers of aid. Thus he welcomed a small contingent of American doctors sponsored by CARE but turned down much larger numbers of Soviet doctors, rejected Soviet schoolteachers in favor of French and then Egyptian ones, but accepted Soviet aid at no cost in clearing French minefields left in the country, after an Italian company had offered to do the job for the equivalent of $4 million. He also signed agreements with Bulgaria, Czechoslovakia and Yugoslavia for the construction of government-owned textile, clothing, and shoe industries. At the end of the war for independence, France had undertaken to finance

Algerian governmental operations through the end of 1962. Under a fresh agreement for 1963, the Ben Bella government succeeded in procuring the equivalent of $325 million in aid, and retained it even after outspokenly condemning France's atomic tests in the Sahara in March. At the same time, Algeria continued receiving from the United States afforestation aid as well as an estimated 20,000 tons of surplus food each month as part of the general relief program for sustaining the estimated 40 per cent of the population who were destitute.

In fact, Algeria's economy, seriously dislocated by the prolonged war, had been virtually knocked out by the mass exodus of the colons, or European settlers. From more than a million in June 1962 their number was reduced to about 130,000 in a single year. With their departure the expanding, modernizing sector of the Algerian economy ground to a halt, for in colon hands had been such agricultural enterprises as citriculture and viniculture for export, and the derivative wine industry (needed neither by Algeria nor by France), as well as most light industry, retail commerce, and the professional and technical services. The Muslim sector of the economy, on the other hand, chiefly agricultural, remained essentially primitive to the very end of French rule.

To meet this crisis, Ben Bella tore a leaf from Abdel Nasser's handbook in adopting pragmatic socialism. The first major step was the allocation of the 2.5 million acres of farmland abandoned by colons to peasant collectives under their own managing committees. Ben Bella took advantage of the atom-test crisis in March 1963 to seize the last remaining large private farms still in operation by colons, some of whom had been the most vocal advocates of *Algérie française*. Decisions were also taken for the ultimate transfer of all Muslim-owned farms larger than 125 acres to collective management. Indeed, the largest single sum of the development budget was assigned to government projects for housing, soil conservation, and electrification in rural areas. At the same time, the government nationalized hotels, movie theaters and other businesses that had been acquired by Muslim war profiteers. The budget also provided for full or limited state participation in light industry, and it was understood that the government would eventually nationalize public utilities, extractive industries, and firms engaged in foreign trade. The state would also be prepared to join private corporations as partner for any other suitable industrial ventures. On the other hand, the government hoped to attract foreign private capital for the expansion of manufacturing, still in its infancy. Specifically excluded from nationalization were the foreign-owned oil industry in the Sahara Desert and the related export of liquid gas.

In following in Abdel Nasser's footsteps, Ben Bella had manifestly to adapt to realities that differed measurably from those of Egypt. Scarred by war and immobilized by the departure of the colons, Algeria desperately needed outside aid, technical as well as material. No less significant was the inexperience of the fledgling state's leaders. The Algerian Muslims did not enjoy under French rule any real education in self-government, not even under the 1947 organic law, which divided the powers equally between the European settlers and the Muslims, who were nine times as numerous. The first real experience came in the war for independence, for more than five years of which Ben Bella himself languished in a French prison. Still he proceeded with his socialist program within a few months of independence while the situation was still malleable. Tolerating no opposition, he coerced the public through persuasion rather than by police-state methods.

What is more, the Algerian president's emulation of Abdel Nasser did not necessarily imply close political cooperation between the two men. For one thing, Egypt, before independence the principal source of outside aid, now trailed far behind other foreign benefactors, primarily France and the United States. For another, Ben Bella was emerging as a potential rival of his mentor in the fight against imperialism in Africa. This became clear at the Conference on African Unity in May 1963 in Addis Ababa, where all the delegates warmly received Ben Bella as the one African leader whose country had won its liberty by fighting for it. Besides, Ben Bella was too preoccupied at home to participate in adventurous foreign policies in the Arab area. Therefore although Abdel Nasser's doctrine of Arab socialist unity suddenly gained fresh momentum in 1963 following the tripartite decision in April of Egypt, Syria and Iraq to federate, and the Egyptian strong man made a visit to Algeria in May, Ben Bella did not commit himself to any scheme for creating an enlarged Arab state in the Arab East under Egyptian or any other auspices until the unity of the Arab West had first been realized. But Algeria's relations in its first year of sovereignty with the two other states of the Maghrib—Tunisia and Morocco—did not suggest early union of the three.

Moroccan and Tunisian gradualism

Tunisia and Morocco won their independence almost without a struggle in 1956. It was psychologically simpler for France to accede to the demands of the nationalists in the two protectorates, since their administrations had not been integrated with that of the metropolis. As Algeria was to do later, Tunisia and Morocco after independence created authoritarian regimes that leaned toward benevolence and away from repression, each dominated by a single individual.

The largest in population and the only one of the three with a long prior history of independence, Morocco reverted to the form of absolute monarchy that had prevailed before the loss of sovereignty in 1912. A full-scale revolt in 1958 of the Berber-speaking mountain tribesmen in the Rif area of the former Spanish zone was repressed and the district placed under military government for the next four years.

The political structure of Moroccan society underwent abundant change under French rule, when among the emergent urban middle class a nationalist movement had come into being to form the Istiqlal (Independence) Party, which had spearheaded the struggle for independence. King Muhammad V selected part of his cabinet ministers from Istiqlal ranks and gave effect to some of their policies. In the absence of elective offices and of legislature, however, the party's political role was severely limited. Under nationalist pressure, the king promised to promulgate a constitution by the end of 1962, and permitted in 1960 the first countrywide elections for local communal councils. By that time the leftist Istiqlal leaders had established their own National Union of Popular Forces (UNFP), which showed sufficient strength, particularly in industrial districts, to qualify for participation in the king's cabinets. Hasan II, who succeeded his father in February 1961, promulgated the constitution as promised, creating an elective legislature, but left the king's powers virtually intact. With this the Istiqlal and UNFP were dissatisfied, and formed an opposition to the king's newly founded Front for the Defense of Constitutional Institutions.

In the early years of independence the government cooperated closely with France, on which it depended for material and technical aid, and confirmed the base agreement with the United States, originally concluded with France in 1951. But Istiqlal leaders had worked closely with Egypt in conspiring for independence, and began to clamor for nonalignment. Thus the agreement with the United States was renegotiated in 1959 for the surrender of the bases by the end of 1963. A fresh accord with France, necessitated by differences over Algeria, foreshortened the date of the evacuation of all French troops, except those in a half dozen air-training bases, from December 1963 to March 1961.

After France granted independence to Mauritania, to which Morocco laid claim, Muhammad V responded to Abdel Nasser's overtures for sponsoring at Casablanca in January 1961 a conference for African countries which the heads of state of the United Arab Republic, Ghana, Guinea, and Mali attended. With the formation of the Casablanca bloc it was clear that Morocco had aligned itself with the African neutralist powers led by the U.A.R. However, Abdel Nasser's late doctrinal conflict with the conservative Arab regimes thrust Hasan II back toward a position of closer cooperation with the United States. On a visit to Washington in March 1963, he agreed to the continuation of the American naval base beyond the year's end. Istiqlal's irredentism, claiming the district of Tinduf in Algeria's western Sahara to provide a land bridge between Morocco and Mauritania, injected yet another irritant into Morocco's relations with other Arab governments.

Tunisia, the smallest in size and population of the states of the Maghrib, emerged as a constitutional kingdom in March 1956, but in less than a year and a half the National Assembly voted the monarchy out of existence and elected Prime Minister Habib Bourguiba president of the republic. Retaining both offices, Bourguiba established the exclusive rule of his Neo-Destour Party, which had played the leading role in the fight for political freedom, and absorbed into it the labor unions, the student union, and all other organizations of potential political importance. The party invited popular membership, recalling the practice of Atatürk and the Republican People's Party in Turkey in the interwar years. Bourguiba also agreed in mid-1963 to doubling the size of the Neo-Destour's fifteen-man Political Bureau to make it more representative.

Domestically, *Bourguibisme* developed as a form of gradual pragmatic socialism. The Tunisian president encouraged the quarter million colons to remain as long as possible, so as to ease the transition to Tunisian takeover. More urban colons left than did rural, so that although the number of Europeans was reduced by 80 per cent in seven years, they still owned 70 per cent of their original 1.25 million acres of land. While encouraging private investment, domestic or foreign, in the country's industries, Bourguiba nevertheless committed state funds, either in separate enterprises or jointly with private investors. The government also nationalized the country's transportation facilities, the phosphate industry, and the management of major exports (citrus and olive oil) and imports (tea and coffee). An omen for the future was the five-year limit on export-import licenses to private entrepreneurs.

Bourguiba first pursued a policy of close cooperation with

France and the West. But since he gave the fullest support possible to the Algerian revolutionaries, as had Muhammad V, the Tunisian president soon found himself in conflict with France. Tunisian curtailment of French military rights led to the sharp reduction of French aid, and having been denied military equipment by the United States and Britain, Bourguiba turned to the Soviet orbit. Nevertheless, on world issues he continued to endorse the Western position, even in the Belgian Congo, to which Tunisian troops were sent. In 1956 Tunisia like Morocco began receiving surplus food from the United States, which both used as a means of paying for part of the labor in public works projects.

A major reason for Bourguiba's Western leanings, despite his formal pursuance of noncommitment, was Egypt's promotion of his rival, Salah Ben Youssef, who had been ousted even before independence as the Neo-Destour secretary-general and later from Cairo plotted the overthrow of the Tunisian president. Although Ben Youssef was assassinated in West Germany in 1961, an attempt on Bourguiba's life as late as December 1962 was attributed to Ben Youssef's partisans, abetted by Egypt and Algeria. The continuing friction with Egypt, exacerbated after 1961 by Cairo's suggesting that Tunisia's government still awaited liberation, accounted for Bourguiba's lack of ardor for the Arab League. The feeling that Ben Bella was supporting Bourguiba's enemies led to the withdrawal in January 1963 of the Tunisian ambassador from Algeria, an act that was reciprocated. Hasan II tried to mediate the dispute. Meanwhile Algeria persuaded Egypt to reject Hasan's invitation to hold a meeting of the Casablanca powers in May. These stresses and strains in the former French dependencies did not augur well for the unity of the Maghrib. And in view of Abdel Nasser's opposition to the regimes of Tunisia and Morocco and the determination of Ben Bella to avoid entanglements in the internal problems of the Arab East, there was even less likelihood of Maghrib participation in any larger movement inspired by Egypt.

The Politics of Arab Unity

On April 17, 1963, the U.A.R., Syria and Iraq signed an agreement in principle to federate into a single state, to be known as the United Arab Republic. The three states, noted the agreement, were guided in their decision by "the popular will of the Arab people demanding unity, struggling to achieve it and sacrificing to protect it," and by the realization that "the nucleus of a strong unity" comprises "the unification of the parts of the homeland which have achieved their liberty" and where "nationalist progressive risings" have taken place, fired by the determination "to destroy the alliance between feudalism, capitalism, reaction and imperialism." The United Arab Republic would have Cairo as its capital and Islam as its established religion. The authority of the federal state would embrace foreign affairs, defense, national security, finance, economy (including planning and development), information, culture, education, justice and communications. The structure of the federal republic would remain essentially that of Egypt, with a president elected by a National Assembly and serving as supreme commander of the armed forces and head of a National Defense Council, with the right to issue, propose and object to laws, appoint the prime minister and all other cabinet members (who must enjoy the confidence of the president as well as the legislature), appoint, promote and dismiss all officers of the armed forces including the commanders, and appoint supreme court judges. The founding members of the proposed federal state would be designated the Egyptian Region, the Iraqi Region and the Syrian Region, and would have their own presidents, cabinets and legislatures.

The three governments agreed to elaborate the principles of the provisional federation agreement into a formal constitution, which was to be presented no later than September 17, 1963 to public referendums in Egypt, Syria and Iraq. If approved, the constitution was to go into probationary effect for a period of twenty months. The decision by the three countries to federate into a single republic, coming so soon after the overturn of regimes in Iraq and Syria in February and March, electrified the entire Arab world. During and after the negotiations the Egyptians attempted to oust the leaders of the doctrinaire socialist Baath (Resurrection) Party from the coalition governments in Syria and Iraq. But the Baath leaders, though favoring unity, were suspicious of Nasser's leadership and successfully resisted his efforts to dispose of them. Instead, Abdel Nasser's followers lost ground in the two revolutionary governments, which came under firmer Baathist control than before. The entire episode from the negotiations that preceded the agreement to the quarrel that burst into the open almost before its ink was dry typified the postwar behavior of the Arab unity nationalists and represented yet another manifestation of their endeavors to give concrete form to their political aspirations.

The Arab League: Limited unity

The origins of the Arab unity movement traced back to the peace settlement of World War I and to the Fertile Crescent, where the movement was largely confined until the mid-1930's. There the nationalists resented the replacement of Ottoman by European imperialism and the division of the zone by France and Britain into five separate countries, with provision in Palestine for a Jewish National Home, without first consulting the Arabs. The unity theorists held that all Arab lands would ultimately coalesce into a single state, but the first impulse of the movement derived from the practical desire to liberate and integrate the political fragments of the Fertile Crescent. British and French imperialism together with Zionism became the principal targets of Arab resentment and the principal stimuli for unity. It was the Arab-Zionist contest over Palestine, in fact, that led Egypt into the unity movement after 1936. In World War II, Britain's unification of the Middle East and its friendliness toward Arab unity nationalism as part of a policy of controlled Arab regionalism provided the kind of sponsorship that made possible the creation of the Arab League as early as March 1945 by the four Arab states in the Fertile Crescent (Iraq, Transjordan, Syria and Lebanon), the two patriarchal monarchies (Saudi Arabia and Yemen) and the kingdom of Egypt. In recognition of Egypt's cultural primacy and its large population, roughly equal to that of the other six founders combined, Cairo became the League's permanent seat and an Egyptian diplomat the first secretary general.

Arab disunity, which the nationalists ascribed to imperialism, hampered the League's performance as a regional organization. The League could never accomplish more than its members allowed it to, and their failure to cooperate brought them at times to frustration, as in the Palestine War of 1948-49, or to stillborn projects such as the decision in 1952 to integrate the armed forces of all the member states under a single command. Whenever members felt their interests threatened by actions of the League, they walked out of its Council and other organs. Tunisia did so almost immediately after joining the body because of Bourguiba's grievances against Egypt; Iraq when the League admitted Kuwait, which Kassim claimed as a part of his country; and Egypt itself in 1962, when the League Council placed on its agenda a Syrian complaint against Egypt for interfering in Syrian domestic affairs. Yet none of the walkouts was permanent, and the League itself grew steadily in size as more Arab states won their independence and joined the regional organization—Libya in 1953, Sudan in 1956, Tunisia and Morocco in 1958, Kuwait in 1961, and Algeria in 1962. More than that, it provided a forum for the discussion of common problems and a means for coordinating foreign policies and for settling disputes.

To the unity nationalists the League represented the first step toward the fulfilment of their dream of an Arab state stretching from the Atlantic to the Persian Gulf, or as they prefer to call it, the Arab Gulf.

To the Egyptians, who from the very beginning of their association with the unity movement had tended to act as if it were their destiny to lead Arab affairs, the League represented a means of organizing the support of the Arab states for the conduct of Egyptian foreign policy, while pursuing Arab unity ends. With the rise of Abdel Nasser to uncontested power in Egypt late in 1954, the Arab unity cause, which suffered from indecisiveness in the League, found purposive, flamboyant leadership in the person of the Egyptian president. Abdel Nasser galvanized the Arab masses into a crusade against imperialism behind the banner of "positive neutralism," a concept that he brought back to Egypt in April 1955 from the Bandung Conference where he met with Nehru of India, who had already established his mark as a practitioner of noncommitment in the Cold War. Positive neutralism fit well into the world outlook of Arab unity partisans, who were demanding the full and final eradication of the residual European controls in all Arab territories. They insisted that the Arab zone had to become wholly self-reliant in political and economic affairs, and that the defense of Arab countries had to rest upon an Arab collective security pact and unified command—any military association with an outside Great Power could only signify the continuance of imperialism in disguise.

Abdel Nasser: Unity leader

Abdel Nasser carried this message abroad through consummate use of the propaganda media. Through a press that already enjoyed wide popularity in Arab lands, a news agency, inherited from Britain, that had opened channels for disseminating news of Arab interest to all Arab lands, and especially the Voice of the Arabs radio station, devoted exclusively to Arab themes, Abdel Nasser's rallying cry reached the far corners of the Arab world. Egypt also encouraged teachers—an estimated 4,000 in 1956—to take jobs in other Arab countries, including Iraq, where they inculcated the liberation mystique in the minds of their students. Above all, Cairo became the haven par excellence for political refugees from all Arab lands, particularly those from countries still under alien domination. By marshaling all these techniques Abdel Nasser had found in the late 1950's a way of arousing the nationalist masses to topple their regimes that were under foreign rule or control. It was he who could claim a share of the kudos for Jordan's cashiering of the British commander of the Arab Legion in March 1956 as the first step in terminating that country's preferential alliance with the United Kingdom exactly a year later; in Morocco and Tunisia's wringing of independence from France; in the demise of the Hashimite monarchy that was working intimately with Britain in Iraq; in the expulsion of the French from Algeria.

Abdel Nasser's first opportunity to demonstrate an equal genius as unifier fell into his lap like a ripe plum early in 1958, when the Baath Party in Syria took the initiative, as a socialist Arab unity group, to lead its country into political union with Egypt. In the creation of a United Arab Republic representing the first concrete voluntary merger of two Arab countries into a single unitary state, and a United Arab States to which Yemen affiliated itself loosely a few weeks later, an ingenious device had been contrived to appeal to all Arab countries of whatever political stripe and social condition to join by either full or limited association. Egypt's opposition to any competitive scheme of Arab merger was shown by its hostility toward the reactive union in the same period of the two Hashimite kingdoms of Jordan and Iraq, which ended with the assassination of Faisal II in Baghdad. Despite the wide popularity of the U.A.R. among the unity nationalists, no other states joined either it or its federative appendage. Moreover, within the U.A.R. Abdel Nasser progressively eliminated from political office the original Baathist proponents of the unification and subordinated Syria to a highly centralized government run from Cairo. Syria had in fact been reduced by the summer of 1961 essentially to the status of an Egyptian protectorate with finance, foreign affairs and the military establishment directed by the central government and the truncated domestic autonomy in the hands of an army officer who patterned himself after Abdel Nasser. The introduction of socialism by decree coming on top of the subjection to Egypt and domestic suppression by police methods drove Syria to rebellion and withdrawal in September 1961.

The Egyptians viewed the Syrian act as one of secession and retained the name United Arab Republic as well as its flag with two stars. In terminating the United Arab States three months later, as the first blast against "reactionary" Arab governments in the new crusade for Arab socialist unity, Abdel Nasser seemed to be suggesting that in the future his device for achieving this goal would be solely one of full association. This kind of association, moreover, could be achieved only by states that had been "liberated," that is, remade in the Egyptian socialist image. The Egyptians helped in the liberating process by employing the same techniques they had used against imperialism. From that time on they had accumulated friendly army officers in various Arab lands, partly out of emulation and partly out of direct contact through military training missions that were furnished to Yemen and Saudi Arabia. More significant, Cairo continued to serve as a collecting center for disaffected politicians from the other Arab states. Indeed, a Free Yemen movement operating out of the Egyptian capital played a part in the rebellion of 1962. Army officers and politicians friendly to Abdel Nasser joined Baathists and others in toppling the regimes in Iraq and Syria early in 1963. The thinly disguised efforts by Abdel Nasser to get rid of his opponents in both these countries during and after the negotiations for the new federal union underscored the fact that the Egyptians were playing for keeps. In mid-1963 Abdel Nasser was still harboring opponents of the socialist regime in Tunisia and appealing to the masses for the overthrow of the remaining Arab monarchies—Saudi Arabia, Jordon, Libya, and Morocco. Omens for the future were the presence in Cairo of Syrian anti-secessionists who were not re-admitted to Damascus by the regime that negotiated the 1963 federal accord; and Saudi princes dissatisfied with the pace of modernization in their country.

In 1963 the image of Abdel Nasser as the great liberator had lost none of its brilliance for the Arab masses. His formula of socialism at home and positive neutralism abroad taught a lesson for success that no up-and-coming Arab head of state could afford to ignore. But Abdel Nasser had yet to demonstrate success or prowess as a unifier of Arab countries. He had changed the crusading slogan from anti-imperialism to Arab socialist unity, but not the preoccupation with techniques for smashing or helping to smash Arab regimes which Egypt did not favor. His integrative device, the U.A.R., which failed once because of rigidity, seemed to be growing increasingly inflexible.

The Uneasy Armistice

In January 1963 when the Egyptian-Syrian dispute over the consequences of the breakup of the U.A.R. was still raging, the Egyptian secretary-general of the Arab League appointed an Egyptian director of the League's Israel Boycott Office, replacing a Syrian. Syria accused the U.A.R. of "Egyptianizing" the League secretariat and, in withdrawing from the common boycott effort, won the applause of Jordan, Saudi Arabia and Iraq. Yet significantly Syria did not reduce its contribution to the Arab economic isolation of

Israel. In fact, despite institutional divisions and inter-state rivalries, the solidarity of view on Israel has remained one of the most potent unifiers in the Arab world. No Arab leader had to initiate a crusade for "liberating the Arab Nation from the peril of Zionism," or what Arab nationalists persisted in seeing as a surviving bastion of imperialism which intended to expand at Arab expense. This theme, so cardinal in Arab unity councils, automatically found its way into the declaration of union accord signed by Egypt, Syria, and Iraq in April 1963.

"This is, I believe," said Prime Minister David Ben-Gurion in the Israel *Knesset* (legislature) in May, "the first time that the destruction of Israel is laid down in a constitutional document of three Arab states as one of the principal aims, and perhaps the principal aim, of the unification of Arab armies." The Israelis had no doubts that "reconstitution of their ancestral homeland" was originally launched with international approval, first of the League of Nations and then of the United Nations, that they were prepared at any time to negotiate a formal peace, but that their repeated offers merely fell on deaf ears and were greeted with "unrelenting . . . belligerency." The repeated warnings by official Arab spokesmen that Israel would be destroyed worked as a powerful unifying agent in Israel, where the democratic system might otherwise have been hamstrung by the social divisions of a polyglot immigrant population and the political divisions of a multiple party system. The decisive leadership that Ben-Gurion provided from 1948 to 1963 might be attributed in no small measure to the general recognition by the Israel public that he in his capacity as defense minister understood better than any other Israeli the country's security problem and how to cope with it.

The fact that the Arabs insisted on viewing as a theory what the Israelis saw as a condition meant that fifteen years after the Palestine war no basic issue inherited from it had been resolved. Without a peace treaty, the parties had to rely on the increasingly inadequate armistice machinery structured in 1949 under United Nations auspices as a provisional and not a permanent arrangement. The displaced Arabs, for whose plight all parties to the Palestine dispute, the former mandatory government included, bore some measure of responsibility, were still for the most part confined to United Nations-financed refugee camps (in the Egyptian-administered Gaza Strip and in next-door Jordan, Syria and Lebanon) where their numbers were steadily multiplying. Israel's only clearly defined boundary was the Mediterranean. The Arab states still refused to recognize their unwanted neighbor and in other than the principal organs of the United Nations even to sit in the same conference chamber with it. In addition to the Arab economic boycott, Egypt continued the blockade of shipping to and from Israel at the Suez Canal.

Although the issues continued to bear the same labels, the problem itself had changed in character and dimension. The incipient, geographically limited and partly controlled Arab regionalism of the earlier period had given way to the genuine regional politics of sovereign states, which now reached into the Arab West. The dynastic regimes in Egypt and Iraq and the republican one in Syria were transformed into socialist governments by young army officers, while the surviving Jordanian monarchy became more and more militarized. The only Arab state bordering on Israel whose regime remained unchanged was democratic Lebanon. (It is noteworthy that the Lebanese segment of the armistice line has caused the least trouble.) Israel's socialist democracy, despite the ceaseless state of siege, managed to escape militarism by the device of a citizen army. The Arab boycott did not prevent Israel's economy from expanding and becoming progressively less dependent on outside aid, and the shipping blockade had lost much of its sting since the opening after the Sinai War of a passageway for Israel through the Gulf of Aqaba to the Red Sea. In the postwar years the Arab economies, particularly that of the U.A.R., also steadily expanded. Even Jordan's nonviable economy, after losing its original annual subsidy from Britain in 1957, almost immediately received a replacement from the United States.

The armed forces of the two disputants grew steadily larger as did also their stocks of modern weapons and their capacities to produce martial equipment. Israel's citizen army in Sinai in 1956 proved its ability to mobilize and demobilize swiftly and perform efficiently in the field. The U.A.R. six years later was able to mount an offensive in Yemen, more than a thousand miles distant, and commit close to 30,000 troops to sustained action. At the time of Israel's birth Britain's military presence still pervaded the Arab East; over the next decade and a half this restraint almost vanished. In its place the American military presence roved over the Mediterranean, with a limited anchorage in Turkey. That the Sixth Fleet was there for other than decorative purposes derived credibility from the memory of the unilateral American intervention in Lebanon in 1958.

The United States viewed its guardianship against hostilities in the Arab-Israel zone as complementing the efforts of the United Nations. There Israel's active persuit of a formal peace proved ineffective. The Arab states, on the other hand, convinced that the original resolution on the partition of Palestine by United Nations organs had been the manipulated result of Western imperialism, particularly that of the United States, sought to widen their support by courting delegations of states noncommitted in the Cold War. Out of this effort grew the Afro-Asian bloc.

Arab Israeli rivalry in Africa

Once Abdel Nasser appeared on the scene, he began to lay special stress on the assertion of Egyptian leadership in Africa, into which he extended his anti-imperialist crusade. Immediately after the Suez crisis of 1956 Cairo created the Voice of Free Africa radio station whose broadcasts expressly urged the peoples of colonial territories to rise up in revolt. At the same time Israel developed an elaborate program of technical assistance welcomed by an increasing number of African countries that were sensitive to the "neo-imperialism" of the Great Powers. This program, which reached out into many spheres, also promoted commerce with the recipient governments and brought large numbers of student technicians to Israel for special training. It was the very success of Israel's efforts that induced Egypt to intensify its own courtship of Africa, partly by denigrating Israel and classifying it as a tool of neocolonialism. In the projection of the Arab-Israel dispute into Africa, Egypt was generally more successful in organizing the African states for political action, even on occasion inducing recipients of Israel's technical assistance to endorse anti-Israel resolutions. Yet it should be noted that Egypt was unable at the constituent conference for the Organization of African Unity at Addis Abba in May 1963 to win approval for a resolution endorsing the Arab position on Palestine.

The most disquieting aspect of the uneasy Arab-Israel armistice, however, was the acceleration of the arms race. From the outset Israel was convinced that its security lay in the deterrent effect of its technical superiority, since it could never hope to achieve numerical superiority. The Arab signatories of the 1949 armistice, partly out of shame for past defeats and partly out of a desire to carry into effect their Palestine policy, were determined to overcome Israel's technical lead. By 1963 the U.A.R. was employing several hundred West German technicians in the development and production of ground-to-ground missiles and jet aircraft and had acquired jet bombers of recent design from the U.S.S.R; while Israel was producing jet trainers, acquiring jet interceptors from France, and had arranged for the import of Hawk ground-to-air missiles from the United States. Moreover, Israel and the U.A.R.

had nuclear reactors, although both insisted that these existed for peaceful purposes only. Israel had made it clear at Sinai in 1956 that it was willing, if in danger of losing its technical advantage, to mount a preemptive strike, while responsible Arab spokesmen have left no doubt that they would destroy Israel, once they felt certain of military superiority. The acquisition of more and more deadly weapons by disputants who had stated the conditions in which they would use them drained further vitality from the already debilitated armistice in the Arab-Israel zone and placed greater responsibility on the extra-United Nations guardianship of the peace.

The Aligned States

The preoccupation of the Arab states with their own quarrels and aspirations for unity created stresses and strains between them and the other Muslim lands in the postwar Middle East. For example, the U.A.R. severed diplomatic relations with Iran in 1960 over its recognition of Israel and with Turkey in 1961 over its recognition of secessionist Syria. In addition, divergent historical experiences accounted for the gulf that separated Turkey and Iran (and in a sense Afghanistan) from the Arab zone. For one thing, Turkey and Iran retained their sovereignty throughout modern times and participated in the European State System even before it was transformed by the League of Nations into a more universal one. For another, no Arab state ever lost territory to Russia or suffered occupation by it, whereas the tsars seized from Turkey and Iran many provinces which the U.S.S.R. did not later restore. In 1945, moreover, the Kremlin repudiated the treaty of neutrality with Turkey and laid claim to the northeastern Turkish districts of Kars and Ardahan, military and naval bases on the Turkish Straits, and the right for sharing with Turkey in the defense of the waterway. And in 1946 Moscow refused, even after the expiry of treaty rights, to withdraw Red Army units from northern Iran, where the Soviet puppet states of Azerbaidzhan and Mahabad announced their secession from Iran. Soviet policies at this time suggested that the U.S.S.R. was trying to convert Turkey and Iran into satellites on the Eastern European pattern that was then taking shape. Little wonder that in the postwar years Turkey and Iran were more sensitized to Soviet pressures and policies, real or imagined, than were the Arab states, which directed their external grievances against the paramount imperial powers in the Arab zone, Britain and France—and by extension, at times, the United States as well. Finally, the two

Middle East governments did not share the Arab antipathy toward Israel; indeed, their common separation from the Arab League tended to draw the three together. Thus Israel became the best client of the Iranian Government's oil company for the purchase of crude, and in 1963 Turkey and Israel were contemplating the opening of joint tourist offices in the United States.

Because of fidelity to Islam the largest independent Muslim state, Pakistan, which connects the Middle East with South Asia, supported the position of the Arab states on Palestine. At the same time Pakistan was annoyed over the failure of the Arabs to come to its side in the dispute with India over Kashmir and related issues, and was especially grieved over the growing intimacy of Egypt with India, a relationship that reached its fullest expression under Abdel Nasser. Afghanistan, which lies at the eastern extremity of the Middle East and is the most underdeveloped non-Arab Muslim state and in the postwar period, was more responsive to the activities of the superpowers than to those of her neighbors. The major exception was Pakistan, with which Afghanistan clashed over Pushtunistan, the districts occupied by Pathan tribesmen on both sides of the frontier between the two countries; this represented Afghanistan's irredentist claims to Pakistan's Northwest Frontier Province.

Turkey, Iran and Pakistan responded favorably to initiatives of the United States and Britain in 1954-55 for the creation of a regional defense organization that would be identified with and partly integrated into the Western collective security system. Turkey and Iran—the latter after an interlude of anti-Western excitement in the period of Muhammad Mosaddeq's premiership (1951-53)—were motivated by continuing fear and suspicion of the U.S.S.R., and Pakistan by its unabating desire to strengthen itself against India through regional and extra-regional alliances. These three were joined in the formation of the Baghdad Pact in 1955 by the Hashimite Kingdom of Iraq, which sought to terminate a preferential alliance with Britain and to shore up the Iraqi position within the Arab zone vis-à-vis Egypt. To all four the Western sponsors promised generous military, economic and technical assistance. The pact itself expressly ruled out the possibility of Israel's joining, but held the door open to Arab League members. In fact, Iraq tried to bring its fellow Hashimite Kingdom, Jordan, into the scheme, but countermeasures by Egypt foiled that move. In the end, no additional Arab states adhered to the new organization, and Iraq withdrew from it in 1959.

Iraq's defection necessitated the shift of the permanent secretariat from Baghdad to Ankara and the changing of the name to the Central Treaty Organization or CENTO. The Permanent Council, consisting of the ambassadors to Ankara from the member states and a representative of the Turkish Ministry of Foreign Affairs, sat in constant session, while a Council of Ministers, comprising the members' foreign ministers or their deputies, as a rule convened annually in the various capitals on a rotational basis. Four permanent committees were created: military, countersubversion, liaison and economic. The military committee was represented on a continuing basis by a permanent group of deputies and a combined planning staff, which organized joint air and naval maneuvers. The economic committee set up subcommittees, working parties and seminars on communications, trade, agriculture and health. With American and British financial help the regional members began the construction of interlocking railroad, highway and telecommunications systems, explored the creation of a free trade zone, and established in Tehran a nuclear training center.

The one extra-regional member of CENTO was the United Kingdom. The United States attended meetings as observer and participated in the financing but never formally joined, despite the fact that the arrangement was the brainchild of John Foster Dulles, during the period when he seemed to be trying to supplant the Pax Britannica with pacts Americana. The need for such a regional organization was indeed open to question: Turkey already participated actively in NATO; Iraq's shortlived membership merely served to antagonize Egypt and alarm Israel; the presence of Pakistan, which already belonged to SEATO, alienated Afghanistan and India; and in the wake of Iraq's withdrawl in 1959, the United States signed bilateral defensive alliances with the three remaining regional members. Nevertheless, the habit of consultation that Pakistan, Turkey and Iran were cultivating through CENTO on problems of common interest in the economic and military spheres proved useful in the coordination of foreign political policies. Thus in May 1963 Iran mediated the dispute between Afghanistan and Pakistan that had severed diplomatic and commercial relations two years earlier, and at that year's Ministerial Council meeting Secretary of State Dean Rusk and Foreign Minister Lord Home conferred on the ramifications of Soviet interest in Iraqi Kurdish separatism with Turkey and Iran, both having Kurdish populations.

CENTO

By 1962-63 evidence accumulated of some softening of the anti-Soviet shield among CENTO's Middle East members. Pakistan grew increasingly disturbed over the prompt American and British military aid to India after the outbreak of the border conflict between India and China late in 1962. Just before the 1963 Ministerial Council meeting the Pakistani press complained that the Western powers were giving India, which had opposed CENTO from the start, arms that might be used against Pakistan, a member of the organization, and urged their country to resign from it. President Ayub Khan absented himself from the meeting, although it was taking place in Karachi. Iran for its part after neogtiation lasting more than four years, concluded with the U.S.S.R. in October 1962 a transit agreement, that restored for the first time in more than two decades the right to send goods to Europe through the Soviet Union. Significantly, the instrument was signed shortly after Iran offered assurances that it would not permit foreign rocket bases on its soil. Even Turkey, the most outspoken postwar Middle East opponent of the U.S.S.R., entered into an agreement in the spring of 1963 to increase trade between the two countries by 30 per cent, launched discussions for joint construction of a dam and hydroelectric power scheme on the frontier with Soviet Armenia, and for the first time in thirty years sent to Russia a parliamentary delegation headed by the president of the Turkish Senate.

Meanwhile, Turkey had not yet recovered from the military intervention into politics in 1960. The army officers, it is true, after seventeen months of military government tried to restore civilian rule under a new constitution framed with their cooperation and approval. But in re-establishing a civilian regime the military retained ultimate power of veto and entrusted the civilianization to 77-year-old Ismet Inönü, the successor of Atatürk, and the man who made the original transition from one-party rule to the experiment in democracy. The elder army officers were determined to assure the success of the new constitution and thus backed Inönü in trying to avoid further military *coups d'etat* by young army officers (two abortive attempts occurred in February 1962 and May 1963, both involving the cadets of the Staff College) and the return to power of the successors of former Premier Adnan Menderes. Despite the internal uncertainty compounded by severe economic dislocation, Turkey nevertheless remained the most stable ally in CENTO.

More doubtful as a Western partner, however, was Iran, which in any case had traditionally pursued a policy of neutrality. In deciding to join the West in 1955, the Shah ignored the strong opposition of those who a few years earlier had followed Mosaddeq. The opposition included not only pro-Soviet Iranian groups but also many in the rapidly growing urban middle class who were denied participation in politics. The Shah's bold experiment in 1963 of wholesale land redistribution, under which the overwhelming majority of villages that had once been in the private ownership of individual families were to be given the peasantry without much prior preparation, won immediate popular approval. But such popularity was purchased at the expense of the immediate alienation of the large landowners, who still retained a virtual monopoly on public office, and of the religious leaders, who exercised considerable influence through the vast tracts of land in their custody under religious endowment. Moreover, the peasants were certain to require time and experience before they could effectively utilize their new properties so that their loyalty to the crown in the difficult period of transition could not be taken for granted. In staking his future on this scheme, the Shah in effect also staked the future of Iran's identification with CENTO.

Pakistan did not share with either Turkey or the Shah's supporters in Iran the fear of Soviet intentions as a motivation for aligning with the West in the Cold War. In any case, Pakistan is is not really a Middle East state and is preoccupied with India in calculations of security. Moreover, while Pakistan is a Sunni Muslim country, Iran is a Shiite one, and Turkey takes its Islam lightly; nor do the three share a common language or history or common aspirations for the future. Given the lack of any real common denominator among the three regional members, the string that tied CENTO together would seem to have been the special material benefits accruing from alliance with the United States. If in 1963 the United States was no longer equating neutrality with immorality, as it had done a decade earlier in the Dullesian period, or exacting alignment as the price for aid, what remained as the common denominator? In any case, CENTO was never an exclusively regional organization in the sense of the Arab League. The very participation of Western powers and the Western sponsorship tied CENTO securely to the West in the Cold War.

The Cold War

For at least a dozen years after World War II, many Western observers were convinced that once the British and French relaxed their grip on the Middle East it was in danger of falling behind the Iron Curtain country by country, unless the United States could formulate workable policies to safeguard the region. What was the picture in 1963? Not a single Middle East land had become a Soviet satellite. Communist parties were outlawed in all Middle East countries except Israel, the one country toward which the U.S.S.R. remained steadfast in its hostility. And even in Israel the communists represented an insignificant minority. On the other hand, the United States had proved far from successful in establishing meaningful foundations for mutual cooperation between the newly sovereign states—particularly in the Arab area—and the West. Simultaneously, the United States had managed to move step by step away from the principle of collective Western responsibility for maintaining regional peace to that of an almost wholly American responsibility.

Whenever possible, the United States tended to favor the settlement of Middle East disputes in the United Nations. From the Iranian complaint against the U.S.S.R. in 1946, the first issue that ever came before the Security Council, many disputes of the region occupied the principal organs of the international body—the Palestine problem alone took up one fifth of the Security Council's meetings. The record of United Nations accomplishment in the Middle East include: the withdrawal of Soviet troops from Iran in 1946, the Arab-Israel armistice regime, the care of the Arab refugees, the independence of Libya in 1951, the settlement of the Sinai-Suez crisis of 1956-57 and the stationing of a United Nations Emergency Force along the Egyptian sector of the armistice lines. The record might have been longer had it not been for the exercise of the veto by the U.S.S.R. in the Security Council and the fear thereof by the Western Powers, or for the changing voting patterns in the General Assembly as the world body doubled in size to admit newly independent countries from Asia and Africa. In the circumstances the United States was inclined in the intervening years to rely increasingly on actions taken outside the United Nations.

Even outside the United Nations the United States sought collective measures. This was well illustrated in 1950 when the United States joined France and Britain in issuing a Tripartite Declaration stating their unalterable opposition to an arms race in the Arab-Israel zone and to any forcible violation of frontiers or armistice lines; at the same time they offered the Arab states and Israel such military equipment as might be needed for self-defense or for participation in regional defense. The creation of the Baghdad Pact five years later was intended, in theory, to bring Middle East states into partnership with Western states in common responsibility for defense of the region. From the viewpoint of common action, however, the pact was ill-conceived on two grounds: it omitted France, thus breaking the Western unity established earlier, and it was open to interpretation by its manifold critics as an organizational disguise for Western military bases in the Middle East. What is more, the very formation of the pact pushed Egypt into Soviet arms, and Soviet arms into Egypt, thus vitiating the Tripartite Declaration. Since the three declarers did nothing in the fall of 1955 to prevent the unrestricted import of modern Soviet weapons into Egypt (and soon thereafter into Syria and Yemen), the remaining provisions of the 1950 statement also lost their plausibility. Thus even before the inaugural meeting of the new regional security system, the old collective principle had been destroyed, and the United States in the end never formally joined the new body.

The Eisenhower Doctrine of 1957, in stating that the United States armed forces would defend the sovereignty and territorial integrity of any Middle East country "requesting such aid against overt armed aggression from any nation controlled by international communism," was in essence reaffirming what had once been a tripartite guarantee as an exclusively American one, albeit in limited situations. But the American intervention in Lebanon in 1958, when the threat from international communism could not be proved, in effect widened the scope of the United States obligation to embrace any situation threatening the peace in the Middle East. As guardian of the peace, the United States had to demonstrate its willingness and its ability to apply force neutrally to situations demanding it, and to withdraw it as soon as the situation had been corrected. All these conditions the American intervention met: the United States was invited by a pro-American Lebanese president and his pro-American cabinet to help end a civil war in which the Lebanese executive had lost its popular mandate. Once in the country, our troops were employed to support political negotiations that led to the election as president of a man who had been opposed to the American landing and favored a neutral foreign policy for Lebanon. Peace was restored within four months, and the American forces left. All the states of the area and the U.S.S.R. carefully noted the American intervention and its implications: that the United States would henceforth serve as ultimate keeper of the peace in the Middle East until such time as it was challenged and failed to respond.

Residual British and French influence

This is not to suggest that by 1963 our trans-Atlantic allies were no longer participating in the defense of the Middle East. Quite apart from membership in CENTO, Britain sent troops to

Jordan in 1958 to synchronize with the American intervention in Lebanon. But Jordan was not then divided by civil strife, and King Hussain could be said to be in full command of the regime. The British presence in Jordan, however, signified close collaboration between the two Western allies. Britain's intervention in Kuwait in 1961 was of a different order, for the principality had just received its independence from the United Kingdom under an agreement that provided for British military assistance in the event of the shaikh's calling for it, which he did because of Iraq's claim to the oil-saturated shaikhdom. The only surviving British dependencies—the shaikhdoms in the Persian Gulf and along the southern Arabian coast—also engaged the United Kingdom in their defense and provided it with vantage points from which to support Western military operations in the area, as did Britain's base in Cyprus. By the same token, France continued to retain a defense interest in North Africa, by maintaining troops and enjoying access to bases in independent Tunisia and Morocco. But the prolonged Algerian war, to which the rest of the Maghrib was materially and emotionally committed, undermined the arrangements, first in Morocco and later in Tunisia, and in the latter, France announced in October 1963 the early surrender of its naval and air base at Bizerte. In Algeria, France was permitted to retain troops until 1965 primarily to protect the interests of the remaining colons. Since their number dwindled rapidly, however, the French military evacuation proceeded well ahead of schedule.

The Soviet challenge

The Cold War, it must be remembered, had come to the Middle East before the last shot was fired in World War II, when the Soviet Union late in 1944 began heaping abuse upon its wartime allies, the United States and Britain, for alleged encouragement of Iran in denying the U.S.S.R. an oil concession. The campaign crescendoed in 1945 when Russia demanded territory and bases from Turkey and in 1946 sought with the same heavy-handed diplomacy to dismember Iran. As a result of the campaign and the demands, the Western allies, principally the United States, came to believe that Stalin, Molotov and Company was planning to reduce Turkey and Iran to the status of satellites. This belief, once fashioned, grew into a fixed assumption on which the evolving postwar policies of the United States rested. Thus it soon became axiomatic that, even though France had already retired from Syria and Lebanon and Britain might have to retire from the rest of the region, the Russians had to be kept out of the Middle East at all costs. This was the meaning of the 1947 Truman Doctrine and its containment policy, which was first applied to Turkey (and Greece).

The U.S.S.R., meanwhile, regarded its Muslim republics and autonomous regions in the Caucasus and Central Asia not as dependencies but as integral parts of the Soviet state, exactly as France until 1962 regarded Algeria. The Kremlin, it is obvious, was far from happy over the pan-Turanist propaganda emanating from Turkey in World War II and especially disturbed over the friendliness toward the Nazis of a number of smaller Muslim peoples such as the Balkars, Chechens, Ingush and the Crimean Tatars during the German occupation of the North Caucasus and the Crimea. The determination to avoid a repetition of this experience must have weighed in the considerations leading to the attempted subordination of Turkey and Iran, the two non-Soviet Muslim states with potential irredentist grievances against the U.S.S.R. Because of the exposure of the Caucasus and Central Asia, the Russians were anxious to eliminate the existing bases of the European powers in the Middle East and therefore supported every development that would hasten the British departure and prevent the United States from shoring up existing positions of strength or establishing new ones. This aim after 1955 the U.S.S.R. was able to pursue by attracting a select clientele chiefly among the Arab states—Egypt, Syria, Yemen, Iraq and briefly Morocco and Tunisia—and Afghanistan for the sale of modern military equipment on easy terms. The Russians did not insist that their customers join the U.S.S.R. in alliance, but were wholly satisfied to have them adopt a position of neutrality which removed them from dependence on the West in the Cold War.

The defense of Western interests in the Cold War, even though it may take place in the Middle East, must be distinguished from the safeguard of peace within the region itself. The Truman Doctrine was an instrument of the Cold War, just as were the Strategic Air Command bases in Morocco, Libya and Saudi Arabia, the missile-launching sites and radar system in Turkey, and the U-2 base in Pakistan. Indeed, CENTO was from the American viewpoint more a Cold War than a regional arrangement. The Cold War positions of the United States, admittedly, reinforced the American capacity to carry out the Tripartite Declaration, the Eisenhower Doctrine and the Lebanese intervention as well as the American role of ultimate keeper of the peace. From the Russian standpoint, therefore, the lavish distribution of martial hardware to the Arabs could only stimulate the arms race in the Arab-Israel zone, almost assuring the renewal of hostilities there and thus embarrassing the United States in its self-appointed role.

Weapons and aid

The United States was the first to develop economic and technical assistance as a diplomatic weapon in the Cold War, in logical extension of wartime lendlease and postwar Marshall aid to Europe. American aid reached at one time or another every independent Middle East country, and while many received it only intermittently, such as Egypt, Syria, and Iraq, others including the CENTO countries and Jordan and Israel have received it steadily. The U.S.S.R., on the other hand, embarked upon its economic assistance program in the second postwar decade as an extension of the purveyance of military equipment and consequently tended to be more selective in its clientele. Just as the Western allies were complementing American aid, so too were the orbit lands of the Soviet program, although Communist China pursued a lone, if also limited, endeavor. One of the most ambitious Chinese projects in the Middle East, the construction of a highway in Yemen, was significantly carried out by the use, not of Yemeni, but of coolie labor.

A comparison of the styles of American and Soviet military aid would show that the United States was prone to favor complex bilateral and multilateral treaties for military cooperation with stipulated provisions on the use of the equipment. Thus the CENTO countries were required to pledge not to use their American arms except for defense. Most of the military equipment was given as grant aid, but small amounts were sold on a strictly controlled basis—the Hawk missiles to Israel, for example. The U.S.S.R. by contrast did not seek reciprocal assurances, and in such countries as Egypt, Syria and Iraq sold liberal quantities of arms for local currencies and agricultural commodities. When it came to economic aid, the United States in the earlier period proffered grant aid, later supplementing it increasingly with loans, and made available American agricultural surpluses. The Soviets offered credits only, at low rates of interest, with repayment starting at the time of project completion. The Americans publicized amounts allocated and spent each year; the Russians released cumulative figures of the credits offered each country from the start, whether or not these credits were actually taken up. At the beginning, the United States attempted to integrate its Middle East aid program with the purposes of the United Nations and the "free world," although after 1959 aid was extended to neutralist Middle East countries as well. The U.S.S.R. simply supported nationalist regimes wherever they proved receptive, so as to promote neutralism and cultivate anti-Western sentiment.

It should be noted that the two superpowers found themselves saddled with commitments of aid in countries that at times pursued policies inimical to the donors. Thus the U.S.S.R. continued aid to the U.A.R., Iraq, Syria, Tunisia and Algeria even after the suppression of their local communist parties. The first serious break in this policy came in June 1963 when the U.S.S.R. warned Iraq that it would suspend assistance unless the government changed its policy toward the Kurds, whom the Soviet Union supported. However, the Soviet threat, which was not carried out, seemed to reflect Moscow's desire at the time to refute China's charge that the U.S.S.R. had abandoned the communist cause by aiding countries such as Iraq that were suppressing their communist movements. The United States for its part, continued offering aid to Ben Bella even after he had embraced Fidel Castro, and to the U.A.R. despite its recurrent anti-American press and radio propaganda.

The lot of peace preserver in a fragmented, emotionally divided and unevenly modernizing Middle East was not a happy one. In helping Jordan, Lebanon, Libya and Saudi Arabia, for example, the United States was in effect supporting disunity in Arab regional politics; in assisting Egypt, the United States was promoting Arab unity. Since the two sides were in constant conflict, the American taxpayer was contributing to the financial costs of the squabbling, and the fighting too, whenever the parties resorted to arms, as Egypt and Saudi Arabia did in Yemen. Nor was the problem eased by our uninterrupted experience of having to play both ends against the middle in the Arab-Israel contest after 1948. Regionalism was thus coming between the United States and the individual Middle East countries to frustrate the development of an integrated policy for the area as a whole. Among the few comforts that the United States could enjoy in the evolving Middle East situation was the comparable frustration of the U.S.S.R.

Regional and international politics in the Middle East cannot escape stubborn domestic realities: the condition of fragmented societies that attract external entanglements, the prevailing instability of governing systems which are sensitized to outside pressures, and the universal commitment of the governments to modernization while all are at differing stages of achieving it. The third reality is, in many respects, the most important. The modernization effort becomes transmogrified, as it spills over from the domestic to the regional and international levels. When the governments of Egypt, Algeria, Syria or Iraq appeal directly to the citizens of other Arab lands to overthrow their regimes in the name of Arab socialism, the politics of modernization becomes the politics of subversion. When the United States and the U.S.S.R. compete in the offer of economic, technical and military aid to Middle East countries, the politics of modernization becomes the politics of the Cold War.

Harry B. Ellis

5

The Arab-Israeli Conflict Today

En route to the African chiefs of state conference at Addis Ababa in May, 1963, President Ahmadou Ahidjo of Cameroon flew directly to Ethiopia from Israel, where he had been paying an official visit. Also participating at Addis Ababa was President Nasser of the United Arab Republic. Despite Mr. Nasser's influential presence, the final communique of the conference contained no criticism of Israel for what the Arabs call Israel's economic and cultural penetration of Africa.

These two events—the arrival of President Ahidjo directly from Israel and the exclusion of the Palestine problem from the Addis communique—in a sense were linked. During the conference President Nasser has been bluntly warned by several Negro leaders not to press for an anti-Israel resolution.

"We are friendly with Israel," the Negro presidents had told him in effect. "You are not. That is your business, but do not inject a personal note into Addis. If you do, you will split Africa in two. You will carry white (Arab) Africa and we will carry black Africa. We would never forgive you for splitting Africa this way."

A policy triumph

This outcome at Addis was a triumph for an Israeli policy which had begun to take shape in the late 1950s. Disturbed by the

Harry B. Ellis *is currently Paris Bureau Chief of* The Christian Science Monitor. *For ten years he was Middle East and Mediterranean correspondent for that paper and wrote several books on Middle Eastern affairs. Among them are:* Heritage of the Desert; the Arabs and the Middle East (*1956*); Israel and the Middle East (*1957*); The Arabs (*1958*), *for children;* Challenge in the Middle East (*1960*).

ease with which Mr. Nasser had obtained an anti-Israel statement at the Bandung conference in Indonesia, Israeli leaders placed the blame on the almost total ignorance about Israel shared by Africans and Asians. Foreseeing the coming independence of Africa, and foreseeing also that Cairo would do its best to freeze Israel out of the continent, the Israeli Government determined to move first.

In 1956 Israel began by opening a consulate at Accra, capital of the Gold Coast, raising this to an Embassy when Ghana became independent. There followed the flood of African nations racing into independence and the Israeli program mushroomed. Today the Jewish state enjoys diplomatic relations with every state south of the Sahara except Mauritania and Somalia.

Often these relations are very special, involving the presence of Israeli technical missions in Africa and the dispatch of African students, thousands of them over the years, to learn farming and other techniques in Israel. As a result of this thickening network of cooperation, roughly half the chiefs of state of Negro Africa—many of them Moslem—have been to Israel. These men, gathered at Addis, knew more about the Jewish state at first-hand than did Mr. Nasser and the other Arab leaders at the table.

Maturing of the problem

This expansion of Israel into Africa marked not so much a change in the Arab-Israel conflict, as a maturing of it. Denied the use of the Suez Canal by Egypt, blocked from full international trade by the Arab economic boycott, Israel nonetheless had found a way to make friends in Africa—President Nasser's own continent—to a greater extent than had the Egyptian leader himself.

In other ways the Palestine problem has matured. In April, 1963, France restored diplomatic relations with the United Arab Republic, thus completing a process of French *rapprochement* with the Arabs that had begun with the end of the Algerian war. Egypt was Israel's chief enemy and France was the closest friend of the Jewish state in the Western world. Indeed, during the process of diplomatic renewal, Paris had informed Cairo that its special friendship with Israel in no way was subject to negotiation. This condition Egypt had accepted, just as Israel had been forced to accept a deliberate French effort to regain its influence among the Arabs.

WITHIN THE MIDDLE EAST ITSELF

This external evolution of the Arab-Israel quarrel, as reflected in the changing relationship of both sides to the outside world, cannot cloak the fact that, within the Middle East itself, there has been no easing of friction. Fixed Arab-Jewish positions have hardened and been overlain by an arms race which makes it even more difficult for either side to back away. Viewed in the context of direct relations between Israel and the Arabs, the Palestine problem remains as intractable today as when Senator J. William Fulbright called it in 1960 "probably the most delicate international situation which exists in the world."

Unfoldment of Middle Eastern scene

The unfoldment of Middle Eastern events discloses this continued corrosion of Arab-Israel enmity. In April, 1963, Egypt, Syria, and Iraq signed a manifesto in Cairo, calling for an expanded United Arab Republic among the three. The peoples of the three nations would become citizens of one U.A.R., which would have a national president and a federal government seated in Cairo. Predictably, the manifesto called for the liberation of Palestine as an Arab national duty.

Israeli Premier David Ben-Gurion demanded in response a Soviet-American guarantee of Israel's frontiers. The two great powers, he declared, should warn President Nasser that refusal to make peace with Israel would mean the cutting off of all military and economic aid to the U.A.R. Alternatively, Mr. Ben-Gurion sought a mutual defense pact between Israel and the United States. Explaining this plea, the premier told the *Knesset* (Israel's Parliament) that his government had "sufficient grounds to believe without a shadow of a doubt" that the Arab states were contemplating an attack. Mr. Ben-Gurion found it inconceivable that the United States would not take seriously the threat contained in the Cairo manifesto.

Despite the vigor of Mr. Ben-Gurion's words, had Israel truly found in the announcement of an expanded U.A.R. a fundamental change in the Arab-Israel conflict? Privately, Israeli officials admitted that the possibility of a larger U.A.R. remained only a paper threat to Israel, so long as the merger was confined to Egypt, Syria, and Iraq. This was particularly true, they said, in view of the vitiating struggle for control between President Nasser and the Baath parties of Syria and Iraq, which might frustrate the union altogether.

Role of Jordan

Very likely Mr. Ben-Gurion had sought to put on record Israel's opposition to the engulfment of Jordan by the new Arab movement and, should that event occur, the retention of Israel's freedom to act—possibly by sending its troops east to the Jordan River, thereby thickening Israel's vulnerable waist. Sensing this, the United States Government warned Israel against making any preventive move into Jordan.

A familiar circle had come full round. The Arabs had made a new spasm toward unity, accompanied by a reflex threat against Israel. The latter had renewed its demand for a big power guarantee of the Jewish state. To this the Soviet Union had responded not at all, while the United States had rejected a unilateral pledge to Israel, beyond the promise to defend any victim of aggression in the Middle East, including Jordan. Thus the situation remained essentially as it had before.

Cold War entanglement

At least the episode had thrown light on Israel's current assessment of the Palestine problem. Despite the warmth of French-Israeli relations, Premier Ben-Gurion had not appealed for help to France, knowing that President de Gaulle had little leverage with Mr. Nasser. Only the United States and the Soviets, as the chief suppliers to Egypt of economic and military aid, could, in the Israeli view, force President Nasser to come to terms. This reflected Israel's conviction that the Arab-Israel quarrel, like Cuba and Laos, had become entangled in the Cold War and probably could not be solved, so long as East-West tension continued.

Precisely because the Arab-Israel dispute had been caught up in the Cold War, nothing too serious was likely to happen, since President Nasser would need the support either of Washington or Moscow, before taking military action against Israel. Such support he would not get from the United States, and almost certainly not from the other wary giant.

But the status of uneasy Jordan troubled Israel. Iraq and Syria were established nations, with histories of their own, and presumably could carry their own weight within an Arab federation. Jordan, on the other hand, was an artificial creation and its submergence might place Egyptian commanders on Israel's eastern frontier. This Israel could not tolerate.

Fallacy claimed

The Israeli Government made no secret of its disagreement with American policy in this regard. For the United States to supply Egypt with massive economic aid, Israel argued, in effect released Egyptian funds for new arms purchases from the Soviets. This showed the fallacy of Washington's efforts to limit the Middle Eastern arms race. These efforts could be exerted only on Israel, but not on Egypt, which received all its weapons from the Soviet Union.

Israeli officials cited the visit to Moscow in June, 1963, by Field Marshal Abdel Hakim Amer, commander of U.A.R. forces. Reportedly the Egyptian military chief had secured from the Soviets additional quantities of conventional arms, including tanks, transport aircraft, and spare parts, to build up U.A.R. forces after their losses in Yemen. President Nasser would have found it harder to restock his arsenal, the Israelis claimed, had American economic aid not been flowing.

The Israeli Government did not doubt the pledge by President Kennedy that the United States would come immediately to the Jewish state's defense in the event of Arab attack. But such a pledge was insufficient, Mr. Ben-Gurion declared. Suppose President Nasser were to unleash his air force for a lightning attack on Israeli cities? In a matter of hours, almost minutes, Tel Aviv, Haifa, and Jerusalem could be devastated. What good would be American help after the fact? Hence the need for utmost preventive pressure on Mr. Nasser from the United States, preferably in the form of a mutual defense pact with Israel.

To this Washington would not subscribe. It did agree to sell Israel a battalion of Hawk antiaircraft ground-to-air missiles, to counter Egypt's advantage in jet aircraft. Sale price of the Hawk missiles, whose numbers were undisclosed, was about $25,000,000. These would provide Israel with a supersonic "homing" missile, designed to knock down invading aircraft from treetop level to higher than 38,000 feet.

United States Position

While acknowledging Israel's concern, President Kennedy's Administration continued to measure American Middle Eastern policy against another yardstick—that of essential United States interests. Before Mr. Kennedy came into office, American policy in the Middle East had evolved through two phases, neither of which had been found satisfactory to over-all United States interests—the Truman policy of open partiality for Israel, followed by the Dulles effort to punish Nasser for having accepted Soviet arms.

By 1958 Washington had become convinced that the containment of communism in the Middle East required an even-handed approach toward Arabs and Israelis, favoring neither but supporting the integrity of both. This policy line included several complex strands—recognition of Mr. Nasser as the dominant Arab leader, maintenance of King Hussein on his Jordanian throne, the securing of American oil interests in Saudi Arabia and the Persian Gulf Shaikhdoms, a guarantee of Iran against Soviet aggression, and the continuance of America's traditional friendship with and protection of Israel.

In particular the United States sought to avoid an imbalance in the Middle Eastern arms race. Thus it cut off the sale of American arms to the Jewish state, except when a specific weapon was needed to balance a break-through by the United Arab Republic. The sale of Hawk missiles to Israel fell within this context. The United States also worked to keep the Arab kings on their thrones, conscious that the overthrow of Hussein, in particular, would react immediately upon the Arab-Israel dispute.

Aid to U.A.R. and Israel

A conspicuous feature of this developing United States policy was the resumption of large-scale economic aid to Cairo. In 1963, the United States gave the United Arab Republic about $220,000,000 worth of aid, principally in food, compared with approximately $80,000,000 to Israel. (Apart from this, American Jewry made substantial contributions to Israel through the United Jewish Appeal and the purchase of State of Israel bonds.) Jordan, by contrast, received about $53,000,000 worth of American aid in 1963.

Since 1960 Egypt has been by far the largest single recipient of United States government aid in the Middle East, excluding Turkey and Iran, which lie somewhat outside the focus of the Arab-Israel conflict. Until 1959 Israel had received each year from the United States more aid than all the Arab states put together. Washington's decision to support President Nasser's economic development programs tipped the balance in favor of the Arabs, and especially in favor of Egypt.

Improvement in the Israeli economy at the same time caused United States development aid to Israel to shrink. Even in 1963, however, when United States Government aid to Israel dipped, the Jewish state still received more on a *per capita* basis than did the U.A.R.

Policy roots

The roots of American policy lay in the determination of the United States to deny the Middle East to the Communists. This presupposed strong and independent governments in the area, able and willing to resist Soviet encroachment. To have bolstered other Middle Eastern governments while ignoring that of Egypt, it was felt, would have been self-defeating, for nothing was likely to force President Nasser more quickly into external adventure than frustration at home. Stability in Egypt could only be secured through an attack upon the nation's overwhelming social and economic problems, bred in part by Egypt's runaway population growth. A cooperative response on the part of Mr. Nasser would also ease the American path elsewhere in the Arab world. Finally, on humanitarian grounds no Middle Eastern people needed economic betterment more than the teeming millions along the Nile.

Source of oil

Dictating the various threads of United States policy was the primacy of the Middle East as a source of free world oil and the strategic position of the area as a crossroads of sea, air, and land routes leading between Europe and Asia. Britain and Western Europe must have access to Middle Eastern petroleum. Otherwise their oil thirst would force their reliance on Western hemisphere supplies. This in turn would dangerously drain hard currency from Europe and sap United States and South American oil reserves. Middle Eastern pipelines and the Suez Canal, as well as the Arab oil fields themselves, must be kept out of Communist hands.

Important in itself, the Middle East was also the land link through which the Soviets might turn the flank of India and Pakistan and penetrate the emergent lands of Africa. Washington's bilateral treaty with Iran was an anchor to the east. Maintenance of a non-Communist Egypt was regarded as a less tangible, but equally essential, buffer against the spread of Soviet influence in Africa.

Soviet head start

In one sense the Soviets had a huge head start, through their monopoly of military aid to the U.A.R. and through their contract to build the High Aswan Dam. But the lead was not as one-sided as it appeared. Throughout the three Arab lands where the Soviets had probed the furthest—Egypt, Syria, and Iraq—there was mounting disillusionment over the quality of Communist bloc goods and, equally important, with the hidden aspects of Soviet aid. These aspects included the resale of Egyptian cotton at discounts on the Western European market, manipulation of the Egyptian cotton market through careful timing of Communist bloc purchases, and the delivery of Soviet bloc goods long after the Arabs had paid for them in commodities.

Additionally in favor of the West was the preference of the Egyptian, Syrian, and Iraqi governments for Western machinery—American, British, and West German—to tool the vast industrialization programs on which the Arab governments had embarked. In Syria, particularly, development projects which had been surveyed by Soviet technicians often were awarded for construction to non-Communist firms. This official preference for Western technology was matched by the desire of Arab consumers to continue buying the Western consumer goods to which they had long been accustomed. Finally, Soviet assistance in no way had influenced Egyptian, Syrian, and post-Kassim Iraqi authorities to lift their ban on Arab Communists.

The armed forces of Egypt and Syria remained cast in a Soviet mold, those of Iraq to a lesser extent. The High Aswan Dam, the single most prestigious project in the Middle East (as well as the most exacting), had been won by Moscow. These were manifest gains for Soviet diplomacy. But Arab exposure to a wide range of Soviet bloc manufactures had enhanced the competitive position of Western goods. The Middle Eastern market appeared open to Western traders, to the degree that Arab capital could be shaken loose to buy.

Communism checked

Those observers, American and Israeli, who saw in the strengthening of Mr. Nasser a deepening threat to Israel, decried Washington's generosity to the U.A.R. The Egyptian leader, it was said, successfully had played off East against West. But the State Department, under President Kennedy as under General Eisenhower at the last, pointed to a Middle East in which the Soviets had been checked.

Nor had Israel's insecurity been heightened, in Washington's view. The American pledge to defend the Jewish state against aggression was as explicit as before. President Nasser had shown his awareness and even tacit acceptance of this pledge, renewed by President Kennedy in May, 1963. He had, as one ranking United States official put it, accepted "like a gentleman" Washington's sale of Hawk missiles to Israel. By this was meant that Mr. Nasser had indulged in no public polemics, as he had done so often in the past.

Crucial difference

The crucial difference between the United States and Israel lay in their assessment of Mr. Nasser's rationality. Both governments agreed the Egyptian leader was unlikely to attack Israel with ground troops, through fear of the Israeli Army and because the Soviets would oppose such a move, as involving the United States. But Israel could not exclude from its planning the possibility of an irrational air attack from Cairo. To the United States this possibility seemed too slight to warrant a policy shift that would undercut American interests in the Arab world.

This general framework of American policy in the Middle East did not contribute directly to a solution of the Arab-Israel conflict. Meanwhile Soviet policy, for its part, was one-sided, Moscow having chosen the Arabs over Israel as an instrument of attempted Communist expansion.

British Role

At one time Britain's role in the Palestine problem had been fundamental. The British Government's Balfour Declaration of November 2, 1917, promising British help in the establishment of a Jewish national home in Palestine, had laid a juridical floor beneath Zionist efforts to return to the Promised Land. This British commitment had been furthered, though seldom to Jewish satisfaction, during the period of British mandate over Palestine, between the two world wars.

Earlier the British Government had contracted two other engagements, apparently incompatible with the Balfour Declaration. To secure a revolt of the Arabs against Turkey during World War I, Britain had promised the Arabs an independent kingdom after the war, with its capital in Damascus and including, as the Arabs saw it, Palestine. This promise had induced the Arabs to launch their revolt against the Turks on June 5, 1916.

Simultaneously, Britain had entered into a secret compact with France (the Sykes-Picot Agreement of 1916) to divide the Middle East into British and French spheres of influence after the war. France would receive mandates over Syria and Lebanon, while Britain was to govern Palestine and Iraq. Britain subsequently created the Amirate of Transjordan, east of the River Jordan, as a separate new state within its mandate area.

Within Palestine the British mandate power was caught in the middle of a sharpening struggle between the Arabs and Jews for control of Palestine. This struggle was interrupted by the outbreak of World War II, whose completion found a depleted Britain in process of slow withdrawal from the Middle East.

The mandate over Palestine was terminated May 14, 1948, following the earlier partial relinquishment of British control over

Iraq and Transjordan. In the years following—except for a brief flareup during the Suez campaign of 1956—Britain's direct involvement in the Arab-Israel quarrel became less important than that of the United States and the United Nations.

France and Israel

The relationship between France and Israel deserves a special word. The ties between these two powers had been publicly exposed during the Anglo-French-Israeli attack against Egypt in 1956, when military cooperation between France and Israel was close. This tight coordination was continued, with France remaining the chief foreign supplier to Israel of military equipment, including jet aircraft.

Much that goes on between France and Israel is secret. Israel, for example, is the only foreign power which maintains a permanent mission attached to the French atomic energy commission. The Israeli Army is the only foreign army with a mission attached to the French ministry of defense, quite apart from the functions of embassy attachés. Intelligence and military officials of the two countries exchange visits under the de Gaulle Fifth Republic, as they did in Fourth Republic days.

Atomic reactors

French-Israeli collaboration in atomic developments in the Negev has raised questions as to the potentialities and aims of these efforts at a time of increasing anxiety over the possible proliferation of nuclear arms. The United States, which had helped Israel develop a small 1,000-kilowatt atomic reactor near Tel Aviv, was disturbed to discover in 1960, through its own sources, that France and Israel were constructing a 24,000-kilowatt reactor outside Dimona, in the Negev. Neither government had informed the United States of this collaboration. There was concern in Washington that Israel, with French help, was preparing to add atomic weapons to its arsenal, a suspicion which caused President Nasser to observe that if Israel obtained the bomb, so would the U.A.R.

Washington's concern was only partly eased by Mr. Ben-Gurion's assurance that the reactor was intended exclusively for peaceful purposes and that scientists of friendly countries would be invited to visit the Negev plant. No visits have been announced and the French and Israeli Governments remain as close-mouthed as before about the reactor.

It is known that Israel and France have conducted "highly

sophisticated" atomic experiments in the Negev. How far this co-operation may be carried in the future is unclear, since France—fast becoming an independent nuclear power—shows increasing reluctance to permit the further spread of nuclear weapons, at least outside Europe.

Following the initialing of a partial nuclear test ban treaty by the United States, Britain and the U.S.S.R., both Egypt and Israel —Egypt immediately, Israel three days later—announced they also would sign the treaty when it was opened to other nations.

France and Israel founded their close working relationship on common hostility to President Nasser, whom the French regarded as a major source of aid to the Algerian nationalists during the long Algerian war. This common factor is receding, now that Algeria is independent and Paris and Cairo have resumed diplomatic relations. But the bonds uniting France and Israel appear as strong as ever and the friendship between the two countries remains an element of importance, however the Arab-Israel conflict may unfold.

Concentric Circle

The separate relationships of Israel and the Arabs to the outside world, and the relationship of the major powers to either side, have been seen to act as concentric circles, enclosing but not touching directly on the core of the Arab-Israel dispute. Next to be considered are those internal aspects of the conflict which make the Palestine problem so difficult to solve.

On the fundamental question of making peace the Arabs and Israelis remain as far apart as ever. Israel demands a roundtable conference between the two sides, without prior conditions. The Arabs insist that Israel, as a precondition to talks, must accept in principle all United Nations resolutions bearing on Palestine, including the key measure of December, 1948, which called for the return to Palestine of all Arab refugees who wished to go back and the payment of compensation to those who chose to settle outside. (Paragraph 11 of General Assembly resolution 194 (III) of December, 1948).

Other United Nations resolutions on which the Arabs now base their stand are those relating to border rectification, including the contested demilitarized zones adjacent to the Sea of Galilee and around El Auja in Sinai; and, at least for bargaining purposes, that calling for permanent internationalization of Jerusalem.

Israel stands on the proposition that the borders won by fighting in 1949 are not negotiable and that an international regime for

Jerusalem should include only the Holy Places sacred to all faiths, but not the New City, which Israel, without United Nations sanction, made its capital in 1950. Israel also insists on implementation of a later United Nations resolution, calling for free passage of Israeli shipping through the Suez Canal.

Essentially these opposing positions have remained the same since the shooting war in Palestine ended on January 7, 1949. (See map.)

Border raids

For several years in the mid-1950s armed clashes between Israel and its Arab neighbors kept the world on tenterhooks. These border raids began in earnest in 1953, when Israel, stung by months of petty depredations by Arab refugees from Jordan, decided on a policy of massive retaliation.

On the night of October 14, 1953, a battalion of the Israeli Army swept across the Jordanian border and killed more than fifty Arab men, women, and children in the village of Qibya. Israel was condemned for this raid by the Security Council of the United Nations. Israel claimed in defense that the number of Arabs killed at Qibya was smaller than the number of Israelis who had been killed over the period of months by infiltrators from Jordan. Only by a sound thrashing, the Israelis argued, could the Jordanian Government be compelled to curb its restless refugees.

Endangered politically by its inability to protect its villages along the border, the Jordanian Government cracked down sharply on Arab marauders, arresting many and ordering the Arab Legion to shoot refugees attempting to slip across into Israel. But the infiltration continued and so did Israeli raids, notably an attack on the Jordanian village of Nahhalin (March, 1954), to revenge an earlier Arab assault on an Israeli bus at Scorpion Pass. The final major Israeli attack against Jordan occurred at Qalqilya during the night of October 11, 1956, when approximately 25 Arabs were killed.

Sea of Galilee—To the north, Syrian gun positions above the Sea of Galilee persistently sniped down on Israeli fishing boats working their nets in the eastern part of the lake. At least twenty-five times, Israel claimed, its boats had been molested by the Syrians during 1955. On December 11 of that year the Israeli Army launched an attack on these gun positions and nearby Syrian settlements, killing forty-nine Syrians. Again Israel was condemned by the Security Council.

The reason for repeated condemnation of Israel by the Security

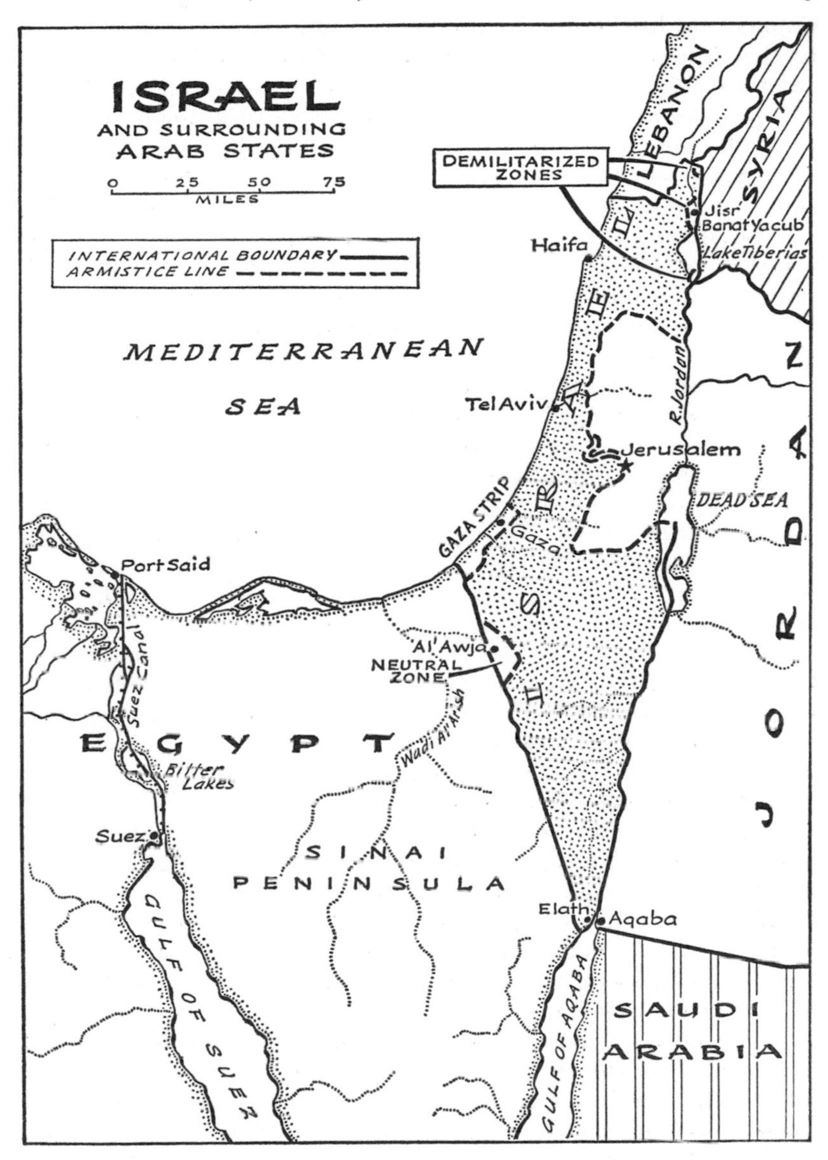
ISRAEL
AND SURROUNDING
ARAB STATES
0 25 50 75
MILES
INTERNATIONAL BOUNDARY
ARMISTICE LINE
DEMILITARIZED ZONES
LEBANON
SYRIA
Jisr Banat Yacub
Lake Tiberias
Haifa
MEDITERRANEAN
SEA
Tel Aviv
R. Jordan
Jerusalem
DEAD SEA
GAZA STRIP
Gaza
Port Said
ISRAEL
JORDAN
Al Awja
NEUTRAL ZONE
Suez Canal
Wadi Al Arish
EGYPT
Bitter Lakes
Suez
SINAI
PENINSULA
Elath
Aqaba
GULF OF SUEZ
GULF OF AQABA
SAUDI
ARABIA

Council was fundamentally the same in most cases. It was a protest by the United Nations authority against Israel's policy of direct retaliation without recourse to the established peacekeeping machinery set up under the armistice agreements. Israel's unwillingness to rely on the findings of United Nations Truce Supervision observers and the decisions of the Mixed Armistice Commissions put the Israeli Government in the position of ignoring United Nations authority.

In August, 1963, following the slaying of two Israeli farmers near the Syrian frontier, Israel did appeal to the Security Council, rather than retaliate massively on its own. The United States and Britain introduced a resolution condemning the "wanton murder" of the two Israelis and implying that Syria was to blame. The Soviet Union killed this resolution by veto.

Border with Egypt—Meanwhile, Israel's desert border with Egypt in the south had become disturbed. Arab infiltrators from Gaza had begun to mine Israeli roads and blow up water pipelines and bridges—a campaign military in nature, as opposed to the thievery and individual murder acts of marauders from Jordan. In February, 1955, Israel struck back against the Egyptian Army in Gaza, killing thirty-eight Egyptian soldiers. It was this raid, President Nasser later said, that finally convinced him of Israel's aggressive intentions and sent him in search of foreign arms, first to the United States, then to the Soviet Union. A second Israeli attack drove Egyptian units from occupation of the El Auja demilitarized zone, a particularly important outpost enroute to Sinai which none but United Nations patrols were entitled to occupy.

Fedayeen raids—Far from being intimidated by these Israeli attacks, the Egyptian Army in 1955 organized selected Arab refugees into squads of fedayeen, or commandos, and sent them into Israel to create terror, through sabotage and killing. These fedayeen, under the over-all direction of Col. Mustapha Hafiz of the Egyptian Army, operated from Gaza and Sinai and later from Syria and Jordan. It was this extension of the fedayeen attacks that spurred Israel's raid on Qalqilya in October, 1956.

The stage was now set for the climactic act in this tragedy of border clashes. On October 29, 1956, thirty-two thousand Israeli soldiers stormed into the Sinai Peninsula, under orders to destroy the nests of fedayeen, clear the Egyptian Army from Sinai, and once and for all pacify the southern frontier. In seven days the Israeli forces had cleared the peninsula and reached the Suez Canal.

On October 31 Britain and France began to bomb Egypt as a prelude to invasion of the Suez Canal Zone. Their action was designed to recapture control of the Canal after its abrupt nationalization by President Nasser. The United Nations moved swiftly to achieve a cease-fire and to force the evacuation of the invading troops. Under intense pressure from the United Nations and the United States, Britain and France withdrew their last forces from Egypt in December, 1956.

A reluctant Israel likewise bowed before the threat of economic sanctions from the United States, though the Israeli retreat from Sinai was not completed until the following March. Meanwhile, a hastily assembled United Nations Emergency Force (UNEF), made up of troops from neutral and small countries, had begun arriving in November, 1956, to police the Egyptian-Israeli borders. The appearance of these blue-helmeted guardians along the Gaza frontier and at Sharm el-Shaikh at the tip of the Sinai Peninsula marked a new stage in the peacekeeping responsibilities of the UN in this troubled area. By UNEF's appearance, Israel, which had been denied the fruits of its military victory in Sinai, gained an important advantage in the Red Sea passage. No longer was the Israeli port of Elath barred to shipping by Egyptian guns, planted at Sharm el-Shaikh and on the tiny islands of Tiran and Sanafir. The Gulf of Aqaba was open under UNEF surveillance and the port of Elath began to boom as an outlet for Israeli exports to East Africa and the Far East, and as a port of entry for oil from Iran.

Border raids ceased to be a major manifestation of the Arab-Israel conflict, though short-lived shooting matches occasionally still break out, particularly along the Syrian frontier. In the south UNEF acts as a plate glass window which neither side could break without affronting the United Nations. The Egyptian Army again having tasted defeat at Israeli hands, Cairo showed no desire to renew the fray.

Military buildup

Though the danger from border clashes has receded, the same is not true of the Middle Eastern arms race, which tends increasingly toward the development of ground-to-ground rockets and air power. There seems little reason to doubt that the Israeli Army, capable of mobilizing more than 200,000 highly-trained soldiers in a few days, remains more than a match for any combination of ground troops the Arabs could put into the field.

The Egyptian Army (total effectives, perhaps 160,000 men), while improved since 1956, still is hampered by lack of an adequate officer corps and by generally mediocre foot troops. Jordan's Army (about 30,000 men) retains enough British elan to muster the best-disciplined force in the Arab world. But Jordanian troops are inadequately equipped by modern standards. Syrian forces, totalling perhaps 150,000 line and reserve troops, are Russian-equipped, but held to be relatively poor in training and morale. Iraq's Army of 70,000 men, heterogenously-equipped with Soviet, British, and American weapons, looks primarily toward its Kurdish problem in the north.

German scientists in Egypt—Israel's confidence in the ability of its army to turn back any attack by Arab tanks and infantry remains unshaken. But a different kind of threat caused the Israeli Government to increase its 1963-64 defense budget by 17.4 per cent. Cairo, with the technical help of West German and Austrian scientists, had developed two types of ground-to-ground missiles, or rockets—the "Conqueror," with a range of nearly 400 miles, and the "Victorious," with a 200-mile range. Launching sites for these rockets, each capable of delivering about one ton of conventional explosives, were being spotted throughout the Sinai Peninsula. President Nasser had claimed these rockets were in "mass production."

The guidance system for these rockets is believed still to be faulty. But the presence of these missiles in Sinai causes great uneasiness in Israel, since the possession of rockets, coupled with air power, to some extent liberates the Egyptians from dependence on unreliable foot troops. Israel claims to have no comparable ground-to-ground bombardment missiles, though its defense ministry is known to be working on their development. This is one weapon the Israelis cannot obtain from France, which lacks them also.

There is no solid evidence that the U.A.R. is trying to tip its rockets with atomic or nuclear warheads, though Israeli intelligence claims West German scientists in Egypt are working on some kind of radio-active warhead, not necessarily dependent on fission or fusion.

More than 200 West German and Austrian scientists are in Egypt, according to Israel, some of them receiving salaries far higher than could be offered by the West German Government or by German industry. A number of these men are said to be working with the Spanish branch of Messerschmitt and with Swiss firms to develop jet airplane frames and engines for the U.A.R.

Concern over these activities prompted the Israeli Government to demand in March, 1963, that West Germany bar its nationals from working on armaments in Egypt. This was not legally possible, Bonn replied, under the Federal Republic Constitution. Nonetheless, parliamentary representatives of major West German political parties indicated they would seek restrictive legislation.

Quietly the West German Government sought to persuade some of its nationals to quit the U.A.R. by offering them jobs at home.

Former West German Defense Minister Franz-Josef Strauss was known to have found new work for at least one top-ranking scientist who had been employed in Egypt.

The visit to Israel by Herr Strauss in May, 1963, disclosed, however, that West Germany, like France, was contributing to Israel's defense needs, though details remained secret. Bonn's contributions to Israel's "vital" security interests were no less important than those of France, according to Shimon Peress, deputy minister of Israel. In Bonn, a West German member of Parliament confirmed that Israeli soldiers were being trained in West Germany, though he denied that weapons were being sent from Germany to the Jewish state. This aid program was apart from the $823,000,000 being paid to Israel by the West German Government over a 12-year period, as reparation for Nazi crimes against Jews.

Soviet military aid—Of separate concern to Israel was the rapid buildup of the U.A.R. Air Force and Navy by virtue of their Soviet acquisitions. Israel had only two outmoded submarines, two destroyers, and a flotilla of smaller craft to match the U.A.R.'s 10 Russian W-class submarines, seven destroyers, and fleet of motor torpedo boats equipped with guided missiles.

The U.A.R. Air Force boasted approximately twenty squadrons of Soviet MIG-19 and MIG-21 jet fighters, equipped with air-to-air guided missiles. Soviet TU-16 medium bombers were replacing older IL-28 light bombers. Against these Israel had obtained from France several hundred advanced jet fighters and bombers, including Mystéres, Super Mystéres, Mirages, and Vautours.

Through its purchase of Hawk missiles from the United States, Israel was acquiring a ground-to-air weapon to counter the U.A.R. air threat and to match the Soviet SAM-II (surface-to-air) missiles protecting Cairo, Aswan, and the Suez Canal. Israeli forces already possessed French air-to-air and anti-tank guided missiles. Israel's great lack was in ground-to-ground rockets to balance those being emplaced in Sinai by the U.A.R.

Economic Warfare: the Arab Boycott

The economic boycott of Israel was instituted by the Arab League as a device for strangling the Jewish state economically. This the boycott device has failed to do, though it has forced Israel to develop its trade in awkward directions. A country's natural trading partners are its neighbors, particularly if their economies—as in the case of Israel and the Arab states—are complementary. With Arab import and export markets cut off, Israel has been thrust into expensive trading patterns, as when motor cars assembled in Israel were being sold in Uruguay and Finland, because they could not find sufficient markets closer at home.

The boycott is administered through a central office in Damascus, with branches in other Arab lands. Operation of the boycott is two-fold—to prevent any trade between Israel and the Arab world and to blacklist foreign firms and ships doing business with the Jewish state. Faced with the loss of their Arab markets, dozens of Western firms and shipping companies have capitulated to the boycott and severed trade ties with Israel. Arab smugglers—as, for example, farmers in south Lebanon looking toward their traditional outlets in Palestine—risk both public opprobrium and sanctions levied by the Boycott of Israel Office.

Israel and Common Market

As a result of the boycott Israel's need to reach some kind of accommodation with the European Economic Community (EEC), or Common Market, has become urgent. Western Europe as a whole is Israel's largest customer and the diminution of this market would deal a grave blow to the Jewish state. Two rounds of negotiations, so far inconclusive, have sought to conclude an arrangement whereby Israeli products would retain some form of preferential treatment, after the imposition of the EEC's common external tariff, due as early as 1967.

The Arab boycott has been hailed as an instance of Arab cooperation, one of the few subjects on which their quarreling governments have agreed. Even here, however, basic rivalries show through. The economic boycott has dealt special damage to Jordan, by excluding Jordanian trade from its natural port of Haifa, and forcing Jordan to use expensive rail and road transport links through Lebanon and Syria. The latter governments derive important income from this transit trade. The opening of Haifa to Jordan might cause the Lebanese port of Beirut to lose more than twenty per cent of its entire transit trade, with the Syrian state railroad suffering even greater loss.

Nor is the boycott office exempt from the traditional rivalry between Egypt and the eastern Arab lands. When, in January, 1963, the Arab League appointed an Egyptian, Mohammed Maghub, as the new Commissioner General of the Boycott of Israel Office, Syria refused to receive the new commissioner and transferred responsibility for the boycott office in Damascus from the Arab League to the Syrian foreign ministry.

Repercussions in the United States

In January, 1960, it was disclosed that the United States Navy in effect was respecting the Arab boycott of Israel, by inserting an option clause in its contracts with oil tanker companies. Under this option the Navy was authorized to cancel its charter if a vessel were denied access to an Arab port because of previous trade with Israel. This option had sprung from an incident in 1957, when the tanker "National Peace" had been forbidden by the Saudi Arabian Government to pick up an Aramco oil cargo at Ras Tanura. When the U. S. Military Sea Transport Service canceled its charter and chose another ship, owners of the "National Peace" sued the Navy for breach of contract and $160,000 damages.

This led Navy authorities to introduce the option, as a protection to American taxpayers. Its effect, however, was to discriminate against those American-owned tankers which had done, or were doing, business with Israel. Disclosure of the "Haifa clause," as the option became known, roused a Congressional inquiry and the Navy agreed to eliminate the clause from future contracts.

Similarly charged with discrimination in this respect were the United States Department of Agriculture and the Commodity Credit Corporation, engaged in shipping surplus American farm products to the U.A.R. under Public Law 480. Rather than risk the loss of large sums of money through the choice of blacklisted ships, all three U. S. government agencies very likely continue to examine carefully the past shipping records of vessels to which contracts are awarded.

Suez Canal

Following the Palestine war of 1948, the Egyptian Government, adhering to the general Arab economic boycott of the Jewish state, barred the Suez Canal to Israeli shipping, causing the awkward routing of much Israeli commerce around Africa. This situation was somewhat improved from Israel's point of view after the Suez campaign of 1956, when the Jewish state gained unrestricted use of the Gulf of Aqaba, opening Israel's southern port of Elath.

For a time after the clearing of the blockaded canal in 1957, it appeared that this improvement might extend to the Suez Canal. Through the strenuous efforts of U. N. Secretary General Dag Hammarskjold, Israeli cargoes carried in non-Israeli ships were quietly allowed to transit the canal. This silent agreement on Egypt's part had followed concerted pressure by Western governments, warning

President Nasser that world opinion was against his continued flouting of three international agreements pertaining to the waterway.

These were the Constantinople Convention of 1888, guaranteeing freedom of passage through the Suez Canal; a Security Council resolution of September 1, 1951, urging Egypt to stop interfering with the canal; and Mr. Nasser's own declaration of April 24, 1957, promising to respect the terms of the Constantinople Convention. It was on the basis of this latter promise that at least forty Israeli cargoes in non-Israeli ships passed through the canal.

Early in 1959 Egypt blocked even this limited form of transport beneficial to Israel. In May of that year the Danish freighter "Inge Toft," bound for the Far East with an Israeli cargo, was stopped by the Egyptians at Port Said, northern terminus of the Suez Canal. In separate and laborious talks with Israelis and Egyptians, Mr. Hammarskjold finally won agreement for the following formula:

1. Israeli cargoes would be permitted through the Suez Canal, if:
   a. Israel did not publish their movement in advance.
   b. The cargoes were carried in non-Israeli flag ships, though Israel might charter the vessels.
2. Cairo also required that cargoes outbound from Israel must be F.O.B. (free on board), meaning that ownership of the cargoes had passed to the purchaser by the time the ship reached the Suez Canal.
3. Cargoes inbound for Israel must be carried C.I.F. (cost, freight, insurance), meaning that the cargo, at the time of its passage through the canal, still was owned by the non-Israeli exporter.

In December, 1959, the Greek ship "Astypalea"—the first vessel to run the gauntlet since the "Inge Toft"—headed for the canal with a cargo of Israeli cement, bound for Djibouti, French Somaliland. The "Astypalea" was stopped by Egypt at Port Said. Finally both the "Inge Toft" and "Astypalea" unloaded their cargoes at Port Said and sailed away empty. The Hammarskjold formula had not worked and since that time no Israeli cargo is known to have transited the Suez Canal.

This whole issue had repercussions in the United States, when both Houses of Congress, before approving the administration's foreign aid bill for 1960-61, added an amendment permitting the President to withhold American aid from any nation engaged in economic warfare against any other country receiving United States aid. Senate sponsors of the amendment made clear the move was aimed at the U.A.R.'s denial of the Suez Canal to Israel.

A second incident occurred on April 13, 1960, in New York harbor, when the Seafarers International Union threw a picket line around the Egyptian ship "Cleopatra." The union said it was protesting loss of American sailors' jobs caused by the Arab econnomic boycott of Israel and also for what was termed harassment of United States seamen in Arab ports. Paul Hall, head of the S.I.U., said some American ship owners refused to trade with Israel, while others, whose vessels already were blacklisted by the Arabs, declined to enter the Suez Canal.

Arab trade unions from Morocco to the Persian Gulf retaliated by boycotting American flag ships in all Arab ports. Anti-American feeling throughout the Arab world threatened to erode the posture of United States neutrality between Arabs and Israelis, so carefully nurtured by the Eisenhower Administration.

On May 6 the S.I.U. withdrew its pickets from the "Cleopatra," after the State Department had promised to investigate the union's complaints and to renew diplomatic efforts to "assure freedom of the seas and to protect the interests of our shipping and seamen now being discriminated against by the Arab boycott and blacklisting policy."

Whatever the State Department may have done to implement this promise, no visible change has occurred. The Suez Canal remains tightly closed to all Israeli commerce and the Arab economic boycott remains in effect.

Jordan River Waters

Still mounting toward possible crisis is the complex question of sharing the waters of the Jordan River. This problem arose from Israel's need to bring water to its barren Negev southland, where most of its immigrant settlement is taking place. With this end in view, the Israeli Government began work in September, 1953, on a water diversion canal at the B'not Yaakov bridge on the Jordan River, between Lake Huleh and the Sea of Galilee.

This work fell within a demilitarized zone established between Israel and Syria. The latter government, complaining to the United Nations, obtained a U.N. stop work order against Israel. The United States gave force to this order by cutting off American aid to Israel until Israeli technicians left the B'not Yaakov site.

But the U.N. order had no effect on work within Israel itself. There the Israeli Government showed both its determination and the fundamental importance of the project by constructing a 108-pipeline system to carry Jordan River water southward. More than ten billion cubic feet of water yearly were scheduled to be pumped from the Jordan down to the thirsty Negev. This pipeline system has been nearly completed, lacking only the final link-up with the Jordan.

To avoid the issue with Syria, Israel switched its link-up point south from B'not Yaakov to a place just north of the Sea of Galilee and wholly within Israel. This complicated the engineering problem by forcing Israel to lift its water uphill from the Jordan to a reservoir at Sahl Batouf, near Nazareth, whence the water would flow into the 108-inch concrete pipeline leading south.

Meanwhile, the political problem was growing more complex. The Jordan is an international river, rising in the Hasbani River of Lebanon, the Dan River of Israel, and the Banias River of Syria. These three streams merge in the Huleh valley to become the Jordan, whose riparian rights are shared by Syria, the Hashimite Kingdom of Jordan, and Israel. All the Arab states concerned expressed fear that diversion of the Jordan River by Israel would deprive the Arabs of their rightful share of water and also would increase the salinity of the river south of the Sea of Galilee.

United States role

In an effort to resolve the conflicting claims, President Eisenhower in 1953 sent Eric Johnston as his personal representative to the Middle East. In four trips to the area, extending to 1955, Mr. Johnston hammered out a compromise plan which won the approval of Arab and Israeli engineers.

This plan would allocate to Lebanon, Syria, and Jordan a total of 60 per cent of Jordan River waters and 40 per cent to Israel. Specifically Lebanon would receive 35 million cubic meters (mcm.) from the Hasbani; Syria's share would be 132 mcm. along the Yarmuk and Jordan rivers; the Hashimite Kingdom of Jordan would be allocated 480 mcm., and Israel would receive 400 mcm. Israel's original demand was thus scaled down from 550 million cubic meters to 400 mcm. The plan represented vital compromise for both sides. Israel's acceptance of reduced allocations of Jordan water meant revisions of long-standing development plans. The Arab's technical acceptance of the sharing of riparian rights represented their first tacit recognition of Israel's existence. Yet neither side wholly accepted the implementation of the plan.

The idea of a U.N. authority over Jordan water distribution seemed to Israel an invasion of its sovereignty. The idea of cooperating in a water scheme which would benefit Israel was politically unacceptable to the Arabs. Furthermore, the Lebanese and Syrian governments threatened to divert their sources of the Jordan River, to prevent Israel from carrying out its diversion plans. So far as is known, neither Arab government has allocated money to carry out its diversion threat, which also might injure the Hashimite Kingdom of Jordan.

At the U.N. the United States, Britain, and France submitted a resolution favoring continuation of the diversion project, if the rights of all parties could be safeguarded. This resolution was vetoed by the Soviet Union on January 22, 1954, and since that time the diversion issue has hung fire at the United Nations, as in the Middle East.

Water Table Dropping—In 1959 the Israeli finance minister declared that diversion of the Jordan River had become a matter of top priority to Israel, whose water table was falling dangerously from overuse. Israeli Government sources since have indicated that, as soon as the Sahl Batouf works are completed at the end of 1963, the Jewish state intends to fill its waiting 108-inch pipeline. A political problem no longer exists, in the Israeli view, since its diversion would take place entirely within Israeli territory and only the amount allocated under the Johnston Plan would be taken. (There is concern among some engineers in Israel that water from the Sea of Galilee, fed by underwater salt springs, may prove too saline for Israel's orange groves.)

Israel points to the Jordan Government's continuing diversion of the Yarmuk River to create new farmlands by irrigating portions of the eastern Jordan valley. In June, 1963, the United States Government agreed to provide $2,500,000 to complete the last phase of this East Ghor Canal project. The Hashimite Kingdom of Jordan also adheres to the allocations of the Johnston Plan and Israel regards the East Ghor Canal as a precedent for the completion of its own diversion plans.

Arab Refugee Problem

At the very heart of the Arab-Israel conflict, lies the problem of Palestine Arab refugees. The more than 700,000 persons who fled their homes in 1948 have become, through natural increase, a refugee population of 1,210,170, at the latest official count. Some 654,092 of these refugees live in Jordan, according to registration figures of the United Nations Relief and Works Agency for Palestine Refugees in the Near East (UNRWA); 279,156 reside in Gaza;

149,983 are in Lebanon; and 126,939 live in Syria. Put another way, refugees comprise more than two-thirds of the total population of the Gaza Strip (administration by Egypt), more than fifty per cent of Jordan's population, and nearly ten per cent of the population of Lebanon.

Undetected false registrations and the tendency of refugees not to report family deaths make exact totals tentative. Also, a fraction of those listed are self-supporting. Substantially, however, the bulk of refugees listed above drag out a sterile existence, preoccupied with their longing to return to Palestine.

This longing has not decreased over the years, despite the fact that only two out of every five adults now dependent on UNRWA actually lived in Palestine as adults. Every year the proportion shifts more heavily toward those who grew up outside their homeland as refugees.

Over-all Arab view

In his 1962 annual report to the General Assembly, Dr. John H. Davis, then Commissioner-General of UNRWA, declared his conviction that it was "the Arab people as a whole, and not just the million-odd displaced refugees, who feel deeply that an injustice has been committed against the Arabs in Palestine. As they view the situation, they see a country obliterated and a people uprooted and dispossessed, a majority of whom have been subjected to conditions which have deprived them of their means of livelihood and left them dependent for fourteen years on international charity."

The strength of this feeling—"as deep today as at any time in the past," is due, in Dr. Davis' opinion, to the fact that there has been little progress to date toward implementation of paragraph II of General Assembly resolution 194 (III), calling for the return to Palestine of those refugees who wished to go back there. Accepting this analysis, the General Assembly in December, 1962, extended the life of UNRWA by two years, to June 30, 1965.

Experience had shown, Dr. Davis said, that general Arab refusal to settle the newcomers permanently outside Palestine had frustrated UNRWA's earlier efforts to launch works projects designed to rehabilitate the refugees. Such efforts would not be repeated. Rather Dr. Davis drew the attention of the General Assembly to the critical need of refugee youth and to UNRWA's role in satisfying those needs.

Lack of skills

Half the refugees on UNRWA's rolls were children under seventeen years of age and these boys and girls, maturing at the rate of thirty thousand a year, were growing up almost completely deficient in work skills. Their parents for the most part had been Palestinian farmers, small businessmen, or unskilled workers, who had been unable to find work in the host countries to which they had fled. Traditionally in the Middle East, Arab young people acquired their skills by working with their parents or other adults. Along with this training came the inculcation of habits of self-discipline, essential to a working life. As children of parents who had not been working, the young refugees had acquired no skills and, beyond this, had not mastered the basic self-discipline which would make them employable, even if job opportunities could be found.

"Therefore it would seem," Dr. Davis wrote, "that a high percentage of the young refugees who have grown to adulthood during the past fourteen years are destined to be handicapped for life, even when they have placed before them what to persons with normal backgrounds would be challenging opportunities."

Dr. Davis further concluded that the host countries—Egypt, Jordan, Lebanon, and Syria—each grappling in varying degree with rapidly-growing populations of their own, could absorb permanently large numbers of refugees only by making large-scale and often uneconomic investments. Therefore a major proportion of the Palestine Arab refugees eventually would have to cross some international boundary to find work. A prerequisite for this was the possession of needed work skills.

Education and vocational training

To this end UNRWA was concentrating on the general education and vocational training of refugee boys and girls. Seven new vocational and teacher training centers had been added to four already established. More refugee children were being enrolled in primary and secondary schools and the period of schooling offered by UNRWA had been extended by one year. About five hundred university scholarships were being given each year to worthy refugee students.

All this required holding to a minimum—about $30 per capita annually—the direct relief assistance granted by UNWRA to the great mass of refugees through the provision of basic food, health services, and camp shelter. Even at this minimum level, direct relief consumed each year more than $25,000,000 of UNRWA's total income of about $38,000,000 (all of it obtained by voluntary subscriptions from United Nations member countries). Most of the approximately $13,000,000 remaining was being spent on the education and training of youth, in an effort to slow down the tide of unemployable young adults swelling UNRWA's relief rolls.

UNRWA was not a vehicle for over-all settlement of the Arab-Israel conflict and, in Dr. Davis' view, the agency must concentrate on administering relief, education, and vocational training, while other parties worked toward a solution of the fundamental problem.

Financial aspects

In 1959 Secretary General Hammarskjold was asked by the General Assembly to make recommendations for the "reintegration of the refugees into the economic life of the Near East, either by repatriation or resettlement." Mr. Hammarskjold then set forth the results of a careful estimate of the actual costs of such reintegration in terms of manpower and money. In essence he found that reintegration of Palestine refugees would be possible only "within the context of general economic development."

Given the low per capita income of the populations of the four Arab host countries, ranging from $128 a year in Egypt to $364 yearly in Lebanon, and the rapid population increase in all Arab nations, he foresaw a need for outside capital assistance to these countries of some one and one-half billion dollars between 1960 and 1965, if per capita incomes of the indigenous populations were to be raised at all. The cost of providing jobs for an additional refugee labor force of some 380,000 persons (as of 1959) would require a further one and one-half billion dollars of external capital investment.

This order of magnitude of the cost of reintegration was established as a basis for any future political efforts toward either repatriation or resettlement. All such efforts to date have had to take these high costs into account.

Other Arab demands

Status of the refugees is only one aspect of the conflict on which Israel and the Arabs do not agree. The Arabs demand that Israel give up all lands in excess of the territory assigned to the Jewish state by the United Nations partition plan of 1947. This excess, about 30 per cent of the present territory of Israel, was won by the Israeli Army during the Palestine war. These lands Israel refuses to cede, on the grounds they were won in a war in which Israel was the victim and not the aggressor. In May, 1948, it had been Arab armies which had invaded Israel and not the other way around.

Similarly the Arabs require, before the conclusion of a peace treaty, that Israel agree to the United Nations resolution of December 9, 1949, calling for the administration of Jerusalem under a separate international regime. Since the Palestine war Jerusalem has been a divided city, with a no man's land lying between the New City (the Israeli sector), and the Jordanian sectors comprising the Old City and the hillside areas to the east. Government House, in the demilitarized area overlooking the divided city, retains a symbol of United Nations authority as the headquarters of United Nations offices, including the Truce Supervision Organization and the Palestine Conciliation Commission. (See map.)

Refugees are root problem

Far more basic than these demands, however, is Arab insistence that the more than one million refugees be given a free choice to return to their homes in Palestine or receive compensation for their losses. While this insistence is rooted in general Arab conviction, a grain of politics also runs through Arab attitudes. World sympathy is with the refugees and their unsettled status provides an effective propaganda weapon against Israel. Also, having trumpeted so long for the return of the refugees to Palestine, no Arab government could rationally discuss any other solution without risking the anger of its people.

Lebanon—The Lebanese Government has practical reasons for refusing to settle permanently its 144,774 refugees within Lebanon. With a population half Moslem and half Christian, and with a governmental structure geared to that delicate balance, Lebanon could not give citizenship to its refugees, part of whom are Moslem, without profoundly altering the political, social, and religious foundations of the state.

Jordan—Jordan is the only Arab country to have given citizenship to its refugees. This followed the unilateral annexation to the Hashimite Kingdom of Jordan in 1949 of those parts of Palestine not occupied by Israel. Despite their new citizenship, most of Jordan's refugees remain dependent on UNRWA, because of the general poverty of the Hashimite land.

Egypt—At one point Egypt agreed to settle 50,000 of its Gaza refugees in Sinai, if UNRWA engineers could find water in the peninsula. Looking ahead, the Egyptian Government may have foreseen an outlet in Sinai for some of its own surplus population along the Nile. Failure to find water caused the abandonment of this scheme. A plan to siphon water from the Nile-fed Sweet Water Canal into Sinai was similarly dropped, when the Egyptian Government claimed Nile water was insufficient to meet home needs. Completion of the High Aswan Dam, it was said, might bring a revival of this plan.

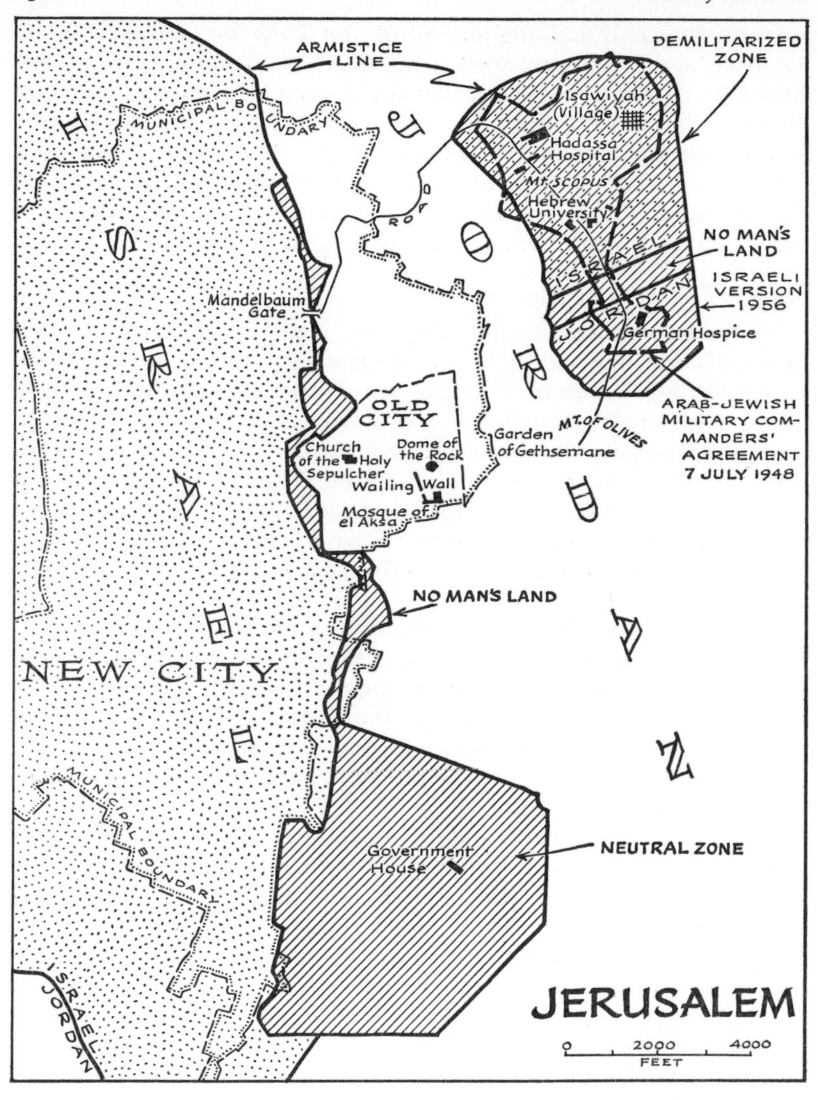
ARMISTICE LINE
DEMILITARIZED ZONE
MUNICIPAL BOUNDARY
ISRAEL
JORDAN
ROAD
Isawiyah (Village)
Hadassa Hospital
Mt. SCOPUS
Hebrew University
NO MAN'S LAND
ISRAELI VERSION 1956
German Hospice
Mandelbaum Gate
ARAB-JEWISH MILITARY COMMANDERS' AGREEMENT 7 JULY 1948
OLD CITY
Church of the Holy Sepulcher
Dome of the Rock
Wailing Wall
Mosque of el Aksa
Garden of Gethsemane
MT. OF OLIVES
NO MAN'S LAND
NEW CITY
Government House
NEUTRAL ZONE
MUNICIPAL BOUNDARY
ISRAEL
JORDAN
JERUSALEM
0 2000 4000
FEET

Meanwhile, some qualified Gaza refugees are beginning to find opportunities in specialized categories of technical employment in Egypt. Students from Gaza are being admitted to Egyptian universities, thus emphasizing the trend toward making Gaza a part of Egypt and reducing the explosive potential of the crowded strip.

Syria and Iraq—Syria, whose undeveloped lands potentially could settle all its refugees and more, illustrates the internal tensions springing from the Arab refugee problem. Officially, Syria offers equal job opportunity to Syrians and Palestinians alike. Yet Syrian workers protest that refugee laborers can underbid them, because they are bolstered by a monthly food ration from UNRWA.

This line of argument was used by the Syrian Government to refuse early UNRWA rehabilitation projects, on the grounds that Syria's depressed citizenry would be discriminated against by the settlement among them of refugees financed, trained, and equipped by UNRWA. Similar arguments have been used by Iraq, which has welcomed only a few thousand skilled Palestine refugees. The Syrian and Iraqi governments also declare that settlement of the refugees in Arab lands would imply acceptance of Israel's presence in the Middle East.

Under these circumstances many refugees feel themselves strangers in their host lands. In Lebanon they are denied citizenship and also work opportunity, because of local unemployment. In Syria they have no citizenship and sometimes meet discrimination in seeking jobs and university scholarships. (Conversely, all refugee children in Syria are guaranteed UNRWA lower schooling, a privilege denied to some Syrian children through lack of facilities.) In Jordan refugees have become citizens, but cannot be given jobs, because of prevailing unemployment throughout the kingdom.

Inter-Arab tensions

Apart from these internal tensions, some aspects of the Palestine conflict have caused strains in the relationship of various Arab states to each other. Note has been made of the transit trade advantages enjoyed by Lebanon and Syria from the economic boycott of Israel and the equivalent damage suffered by Jordan through inability to use its natural port of Haifa.

The partiality of many West Bank Jordanians—that is, new citizens from Palestine—for President Nasser is a source of political concern and sometimes crisis for King Hussein and the Government of Jordan.

Jordan also bears a disproportionate burden of border tensions, because of the way the 1949 armistice line sliced through Jordanian villages, in some cases giving Arab farmlands to Israel while leaving their houses in Jordan. Dispossessed farmers naturally took to raiding across the border, a root cause of the frontier violence which flared between Israel and Jordan in the mid-1950s.

In 1952 Israel offered to give back to Jordan some farmlands of the village of Qalqilya, in return for an uncultivable area near the Dead Sea, which Israel could exploit in connection with its Dead Sea potash works. Such a trade would have benefited the people of Qalqilya, deprived of their primary source of income, and would have reduced a point of acute border tension. Yet the Jordanian Government refused the transfer, unwilling, or unable, to bring itself to break the monolithic Arab refusal to do business with the Jewish state.

Israel's contention

Faced with this obstinacy on the part of its neighbors, Israel is equally adamant in its refusal to implement General Assembly resolution 194/III concerning the Arab refugees. This resolution declares "that refugees wishing to return to their homes and live at peace with their neighbors should be permitted to do so at the earliest practicable date, and that compensation should be paid for property of those choosing not to return . . ."

Israel points to the phrase "live at peace with their neighbors," as operative. How could Israel be assured of the peaceful intentions of returning refugees, when the Arab states that house them refuse to make peace with the Jewish state and continually incite their peoples against Israel?

Beyond this, Israel denies responsibility for the initial flight of the refugees, claiming that the bulk of the Palestinians fled at the urging of their own leaders. Finally, it is said, Israel's own massive program of Jewish immigration forbids her to reintegrate large numbers of Palestine Arabs.

Johnson mission

In an effort to break this stalemate, the Palestine Conciliation Commission (a United Nations body composed of the United States, France, and Turkey) in 1961 engaged Dr. Joseph E. Johnson, president of the Carnegie Endowment for International Peace, to make a fresh study of the refugee problem. Dr. Johnson found, as had others before him, that the intransigence of both sides ruled out any formal agreement on the number of refugees who might be permitted to return to Israel.

To Israel the security problem precluded an accord on any

large number of returnees. The Arabs, on the other hand, refused to proceed to details until Israel had accepted in principle the provisions of paragraph 11 of General Assembly resolution 194/III.

As a basis for his discussion, Dr. Johnson sought to define the intentions of the General Assembly when it had passed this basic resolution in 1948. Certainly the primary consideration had been the human welfare and wishes of the refugees themselves. But this welfare could not be allowed to conflict with the legitimate interests of the states concerned. Specifically, the General Assembly had not intended a solution that would threaten either the existence or security of Israel, a nation brought into being by the United Nations itself.

Solution proposed—A solution along the following lines thus seemed in order. Refugee heads of families, insulated by the United Nations from pressure from any source, should be allowed to choose voluntarily between a return to Palestine and compensation. These choices must be made specific—that is, each refugee should know exactly what opportunities for resettlement existed in Israel and what amounts of compensation would be made available as an alternative. Compension should be based on 1947-1948 values of property in Palestine, plus accrued interest. The United States and other members of the United Nations, including Israel, would contribute to this compensation. Israel would have the right to run a security check on each refuge opting for return.

Those refugees who had lacked property in Palestine would receive a reintegration allowance, wherever they might choose to go. Such allowances would be administered through the United Nations, which also would act as a cushion between the two sides during the long process of settlement.

Demands on Arabs and Israel—Such a settlement scheme demanded compromise from Arabs and Israel alike, including a willingness not to intimidate the hapless refugees during their process of choice. Some United Nations agency would need to operate freely on both sides of the armistice lines. Any government would have the right to withdraw from the plan, if it considered its basic interests threatened. The entire operation would need to be gradual and of a type which, if abandoned along the way, would not leave the refugees worse off than they had been before.

Dr. Johnson's proposals in effect were rejected by Israel in November, 1962. Without referring to the plan as such, Foreign Minister Golda Meir recalled a *Knesset* resolution of November, 1961, which stated there could be no returning of the Arab refugees to Israel and that the only solution to the problem was their settlement in the Arab states. Since that time, Mrs. Meir told the *Knesset,* there had been no change in the fundamental issues.

The Arab governments, while not rejecting Dr. Johnson's proposals openly, continued to insist that Israel first must accept in principle the pertinent United Nations resolution. In January, 1963, Dr. Johnson resigned from his United Nations work. Since that time the United States Government has been quietly exploring among Middle Eastern governments the possibilities of some accommodation along the lines suggested by Dr. Johnson. No visible sign of progress has emerged.

United Nations Role

The United Nations directly entered the arena of the Arab-Israel conflict in the spring of 1947, when Britain, as the mandate power in Palestine, called for a special session of the General Assembly to consider the problem. An eleven-member United Nations Special Committee on Palestine (UNSCOP) was established, with instructions to report the results of its investigations to the fall session of the General Assembly.

UNSCOP's report called for an independent Palestine, economically unified, with the United Nations to play a supervisory and interim role over the proposed state. The report then broke down into specific majority and minority recommendations.

The majority report (Canada, Czechoslovakia, Guatemala, The Netherlands, Peru, Sweden, and Uruguay) suggested the partition of Palestine into a Jewish state, an Arab state, and an internationalized Jerusalem. A minority report (India, Iran, and Yugoslavia) recommended a federated Palestine, with Arab and Jewish communities possessing local autonomy, and with Jewish immigration to be allowed for three years up to the absorptive capacity of the Jewish canton.

Partition voted

The majority report, recommending an independent Jewish state, was warmly supported by the Zionists and as ardently opposed by the Arabs. An historic vote of the General Assembly on November 29, 1947, approved the partition of Palestine into separate Jewish and Arab states, linked by an economic union, with Jerusalem to become an international city. The partition plan first was rejected by Arab governments, but now is accepted by them as a basis for peace talks with Israel. (As already noted, Israel's present territory exceeds by about thirty per cent the limits assigned to the

Jewish state by the 1947 partition plan, because of its gains made during the Palestine war.)

On May 14, 1948, the day Britain relinquished its Palestine mandate, the Zionists proclaimed the State of Israel. Swiftly recognized by the United States and the United Nations, Israel also was invaded on May 15 by the armies of Lebanon, Syria, Transjordan, Iraq, and Egypt. In an effort to halt the fighting, the United Nations Security Council on May 20 appointed Swedish Count Folke Bernadotte United Nations Mediator for Palestine. Count Bernadotte secured two inconclusive truces (June 11 to July 9 and July 18 to October 14), but was himself assassinated by Jewish terrorists in Jerusalem on September 17.

His place as United Nations mediator was taken by Dr. Ralph Bunche, who, from January to July, 1949, engineered a series of separate armistices between Israel and Egypt, Lebanon, Jordan, and Syria. Iraq refused to sign an armistice and all the Arab states, even those which concluded armistices, consider themselves still technically at war with Israel.

New tasks for the United Nations

The shaky peace brought new tasks to the United Nations, including the provision of relief assistance to the Palestine Arab refugees through UNRWA, as recounted above. Equally important was the formation of a United Nations Truce Supervision Organization (UNTSO) to act as a buffer along the sensitive borders.

This organization comprises separate teams of military observers or Mixed Armistice Commissions, whose task is to mediate frontier disputes and report their findings to the United Nations in New York. During the troubled years of the mid-1950s, when border fighting flared, UNTSO was the focal point of the United Nations effort to keep peace in the Middle East. Today UNTSO numbers about 700 men and, in 1963, cost the United Nations $1,633,000 to maintain.

United Nations Emergency Force—An extension of this type of work was the creation, after the Suez fighting in 1956, of the United Nations Emergency Force (UNEF) to patrol the borders between Israel and Egypt and to prevent the rearming of Egyptian shore batteries at the entrance of the Gulf of Aqaba. UNEF operates on the Egyptian side of the frontier as Israel has refused to allow UNEF patrols within Israel on grounds of sovereignty. This extremely important peacekeeping force totals about 5,000 men, whose 1963 budget was $19,256,870.

Palestine Conciliation Commission—The same United Nations

resolution of December 11, 1948, which dealt with the status of the refugees also created a three-nation Conciliation Commission for Palestine (PCC), charged with continuing the functions of the United Nations Mediator in Palestine and with undertaking whatever tasks might be assigned to it by the General Assembly. One of the most recent such tasks was the engagement of Dr. Johnson to make a fresh study of the refugee problem.

Through its technical office the PCC, whose members are the United States, France, and Turkey, also is completing the immensely complicated identification and valuation of all immovable property owned by Palestine Arabs who abandoned their homes in 1948. This work, against the day when an over-all settlement may permit the payment of compensation, has entailed the valuation of 453,000 separate parcels of land, many of which were owned jointly by more than one refugee.

Another task accomplished by the PCC is the progressive release of Arab bank accounts in Palestine banks, initially frozen after the Arab-Jewish war. Beginning in 1953 until July 31, 1962, the Israeli Government had authorized the release of blocked accounts totaling 3,532,088 pounds sterling. Also in process of release, through the medium of PCC, are the refugee-owned contents of safe deposit boxes in Israeli banks.

The 1960 budget of the PCC was $32,400, a sharp reduction from the 1962 budget of $154,260, when Dr. Johnson's survey was being conducted in the Middle East.

Special Representative of Secretary-General—In Amman, capital of Jordan, the United Nations maintains a Special Representative of the Secretary-General as a kind of watchdog over inter-Arab relations. An explosion of Arab rivalries in Lebanon in 1958, with threatening repercussions in Jordan, caused the United Nations to establish its Amman office as a calming influence and as an observation post. This office cost the United Nations $45,800, in 1963.

In ways not central to the Arab-Israel dispute, such United Nations agencies as the United Nations Technical Assistance Board (TAB), the United Nations International Children's Emergency Fund (UNICEF), and the United Nations Educational, Scientific and Cultural Organization (UNESCO) operate in the Middle East, as elsewhere in the world. At least eleven Middle Eastern countries, for example, have requested and received various kinds of technical assistance from the United Nations.

Over-all United Nations role—Relief and peacekeeping functions of the United Nations in the Middle East run up bills totaling $57,000,000 to $59,000,000 yearly, with about $36,000,000 of that amount eaten up by UNRWA and much of the rest by UNEF. This network of United Nations activities would seem of particular importance to the United States; not from a financial point of view, since the United States Government already pays about 70 per cent of United Nations expenditures in the Middle East, but from the standpoint of providing a neutral buffer between Arabs and Israelis as the long stalemate drags on.

Israel and the Arabs cannot be trusted to keep the peace by themselves. Some moral authority has to be imposed between them and, in the absence of the United Nations, it is difficult to see who but the United States could perform such a function. This would involve Washington in a maze of conflicting rivalries, including a direct policy confrontation with the Soviet Union. Seen in this light, the activities of UNRWA and UNEF have significance beyond their everyday tasks.

Richard H. Nolte

6
United States Policy and the Middle East

John Morley has referred to "that shifting, intractable, and interwoven tangle of conflicting interests, rival peoples, and antagonistic faiths that is veiled under the easy name of the Eastern Question." For Lord Morley and the statesmen of nineteenth-century Europe, the area primarily involved was the Balkan Peninsula, but the description applies accurately enough to the contemporary Middle East. The problem of the Balkans was mainly a matter of "filling up the vacuum created by the gradual disappearance of the Turkish Empire"; and for Britain, France, the Dual Monarchy, Russia, and Germany, the region thus became an arena of contention and conflict, the "powder keg of Europe." For the emerging peoples themselves, using and being used by the rival powers, the important thing of course was the assertion of nationalist pride and the competitive struggle for independence.

The parallels between the Eastern Question before World War I and the problem of the Middle East since then are striking. Or perhaps "continuities" is the better word: the ground has shifted; the emerging peoples are Turks, Persians, Israelis, and Arabs instead; the major protagonists have grown or dwindled in the scale; modern technology has introduced new magnitudes of power; but the "vacuum" and zone of conflict left by the decline of imperial control, the rise of new nationalisms, and the internecine competition

RICHARD H. NOLTE *is Executive Director of the Institute of Current World Affairs. A student of Islamic jurisprudence, Arabic languages, history and literature, Mr. Nolte has contributed many articles on the Middle East to scholarly publications. His most recent book is* The Modern Middle East.

of great power systems have all continued as before. And if half a century ago the Balkan powder keg could explode into a major world war, the Middle East in recent years has held a similar threat.

As was true of the Balkans, Great Power concern about the Middle East has been motivated mainly by considerations external to the area itself, or external at least to its inhabitants. Control was sought in order to establish bases of military strength or secure lines of communication against rival powers, or to establish outlets for goods or capital investment or secure raw materials, or to deny all these to others. And not the least of the objectives in an age of empire was to gain prestige. The inhabitants themselves, if thought of at all, tended to be regarded as instruments for or at worst obstacles to the achievement of such ends.

Thus Napoleon, with his eye on India: "Really to conquer England," he said "we must make ourselves masters of Egypt." His success in 1798 was soon thwarted by Lord Nelson, but the importance of Egypt to England was clear. "The Englishman," prophesied Kinglake in 1844," straining far over to hold his loved India, will plant a firm foot on the banks of the Nile"; and the British occupation in 1882 proved him right. Similarly, before World War I, it was necessary to support Ottoman Turkey, the "Sick Man of Europe," not for the sake of the Turks but to oppose the Russian thrust, four centuries long, toward an outlet on the Mediterranean, or (for the Germans after Bismarck) to facilitate the *Drang nach Osten* or (for the French) to safeguard long-standing commercial and Christian privileges in the Levant. Again, the British interest in Persia and Afghanistan was to counter the Russians and so protect India.

During most of the 19th century the four or five Powers competed in the Middle East on more or less equal terms in a shifting pattern of alliance and opposition, with the rivalry between Britain and France in Egypt and Syria and between Britain and Russia at the Straits and in Persia providing the dominant theme. Occasionally this led to direct confrontations. But for the most part, the Powers preferred to act indirectly, utilizing and inflating the passions and rivalries of local leaders, factions, and religious communities, and making them all the more intransigent and dangerous by the promise of external support. Herein lies a major clue to local uprisings and conflicts in the Middle East no less than in the Balkans —the civil war in Lebanon, for example, in 1860; the Armenian revolt; the war of Greeks and Turks after World War I; the struggle between Arabs and Israelis; and once again, in 1958, the civil strife in Lebanon. It is wholly natural that Middle Easterners should have come to view themselves, like their Balkan counterparts, as pawns in a Great Power game.

Having gradually gained the ascendancy over all rivals in the Middle East after 1882, Great Britain emerged from World War I as virtual master of the area. The new Turkey under Atatürk, it is true, soon asserted and thereafter maintained its independence of British and other influence, but the revolutionary preoccupations of the Russians at home made Turkey and the Straits seem less important. Again France was present in mandated Lebanon and Syria, but here—in contrast to North Africa where French control after nearly a century of intermittent conquest and colonization was all but complete—France was weak and in no position to challenge the British lead. All during the interwar decades, in Egypt and the Sudan, in Palestine, Transjordan and Iraq, in the Persian Gulf and along the southern rim of Arabia, even to an extent in Arabia and in Persia, Britain enjoyed paramount power. The Ottoman vacuum had been filled.

British hegemony was secured by a variety of arrangements with local ruling groups—protectorate or mandate, treaty or alliance, agreement with local parties or sheikhs, financial and commercial suasion and influence—in which the interests of Great Britain were reconciled as much as possible with the desires of local populations. But underpinning it all was the reality of British power. Retaining essential positions of strength in her own hands, Britain could deal, with her own forces alone if necessary, with any threat, external or internal, that might arise. The value of this network of control was amply proved when the great test came. Britain easily displaced Vichy France from Syria and Lebanon in 1941, put down with Arab cooperation the brief Rashid Ali revolt in Iraq in the same year, and thereafter controlled the communications and managed the resources of the whole area practically undisturbed. Meanwhile, from the great base complex in the Canal Zone, Britain was able to muster the strength to turn back the Italian and then the German drive into Egypt, and to mount the decisive counter thrust of her own.

At the moment of victory in 1945, with an overwhelming preponderance of military power in Egypt, the Levant, Iraq and southern Iran, and undisputed mastery of the surrounding seas, Great Britain may have hoped for an enduring sway in the Middle East with stability and profit for all. Instead, in hardly more than a decade—half the span of a Cromer or a Glubb—British control would dwindle away. The Middle East would lie revealed once again as a "shifting, intractable, and interwoven tangle of conflicting interests, rival peoples, and antagonistic faiths," but on a vastly more dangerous scale. And into the new "vacuum," having shouldered the responsibilities of global power, the United States would inescapably be drawn.

Groping for a Policy

A successful Middle Eastern policy for the United States, according to Professor E. A. Speiser's prescription in 1946, would involve certain basic principles. It would have to be independent of British or other domination and reflect a clear understanding of America's own long-range interest in the area. It would have to be consistent within the area, and integrated with United States foreign policy in general. It would have to be based on a clear and up-to-date understanding of the changing social and political realities and trends in the area. And it would have to be carried out by able, conscientious and experienced personnel. Such a policy in the world's "global center of gravity" would hold great promise for the future of the United States and the world; failure might well lead to Armageddon.

As it turned out, United States policy efforts in the Middle East after World War II violated these principles repeatedly, in general and in detail, perhaps unavoidably so. The cost has been heavy, the lessons painful. But from the vantage point of the present, one can assert that particularly in the last four or five years, there has been substantial progress toward filling the prescription for success. So much so, indeed, that in the long perspective of history the American response to sudden challenge in the Middle East, mistakes and setbacks notwithstanding, seem impressively swift and effective. A 20th century Armageddon is still possible of course; but it is a measure, at least in part, of American policy success in the Middle East that the threat has now receded, leaving instead reasonable hope for the future.

But this deserves a closer look. The growing American involvement in the Middle East during the past two decades or so seems to lend itself to a synopsis by episodes, each of which has its lessons, and all of which are part of the general theme: groping for a policy.

Friendly non-involvement

During the century preceding World War II, while numerous American individuals and groups were patiently devoting themselves to educational, medical, and spiritual welfare all over the Middle East—and building a fund of admiration and good will in the process—the United States had no particular policy objectives in the area. On the official level, it remained well-disposed but uninvolved.

It is true that President Wilson's twelfth point in 1918 had urged "a secure sovereignty" for the Turks and self determination for other nationalities in the Ottoman Empire, and that in 1919 the King-Crane Commission had been sent over British, French, and Zionist objections to ascertain the wishes of the Arabs in Palestine, Syria (including Lebanon) and Mesopotamia (Iraq). It is also true that diplomatic efforts were made during the interwar period to secure access for American interests to the new oil fields in Iran and Iraq. But the King-Crane recommendations were totally ignored by an America turned isolationist, and the discovery of new oil reserves at home reduced governmental concern about the Middle East. The rule holds: lacking policy objectives, the United States remained uninvolved.

During World War II, new air bases and American forces in Libya, Egypt, Saudi Arabia, and Iran; lend-lease agreements with Turkey, Iran, Iraq, Saudi Arabia, and Egypt; economic and technical assistance to Iran and Saudi Arabia, a constant traffic of American ships and cargoes, visitations by high level Americans including President Roosevelt—all these things brought the United States into the Middle East suddenly, and on a very large scale. Strategically, although American air forces were in action from 1942 onwards, the main function of the United States was the vital one of supply. For the most part too, the United States was content to leave diplomatic initiatives to the British. But the beginnings of American policy interests were observable in a renewed concern about oil supplies, which led to friction with the British and to a plan for a trans-Arabian pipeline; in a concern about the Palestine problem which had become a factor in the 1944 elections; in a concern to continue the air base agreement with Saudi Arabia; in American support for Lebanese and Syrian independence after 1943; and in President Roosevelt's "anti-imperialist" line with Middle Eastern rulers. But it remains generally true that American activity during the war was innocent of policy objectives with respect to the Middle Eastern countries themselves. All the potential leverage for postwar advantage remained unused; the whole American purpose was to help win the war and withdraw. The United States thus continued to be friendly—in very tangible ways—but essentially uninvolved, and its prestige among local populations rose to an all time high.

The Truman Doctrine 1946-1947

Turning its attention elsewhere after the armistice in Europe and dismantling its war effort in the Middle East, the United States seemed disposed to leave matters in that area under British direction as before. But, drained by the war, Britain was no longer equal to the task either in resources or resolution, and under the pressure of local nationalisms the decline of British control was swift indeed. Having presided at the final liberation of Syria and Lebanon from the French in 1946, Britain in a single decade had itself to quit Palestine (1948), Iran (1951), Sudan (1953), Egypt (1954-6), Jordan (1957), and Iraq (1958), leaving the Middle East empty of all but peripheral vestiges of its former sway. The perennial Eastern Question came alive again, and the grand theme of the postwar Middle East has been the competitive struggle by the United States, the Soviet Union, and the Middle Eastern nations themselves to fill the new "power vacuum."

American intervention in the Middle East, responding to the threat of Soviet encroachment and control, first became specific in Greece, Turkey, and Iran under the so-called Truman Doctrine. For centuries the Russians had sought by war and diplomacy to gain control of the Straits and to expand southward to the Persian Gulf. In 1940 Molotov had been explicit that "the center of the aspirations of the Soviet Union" was "the area south of Batum and Baku in the general direction of the Persian Gulf." In the months following the armistice, the Communist Civil War in Greece, Soviet pressure on Turkey to cede two northeastern provinces and share control of the Straits, the movement of Soviet troops into Iran after the evacuation deadline early in 1946 (American and British forces having departed), together with the establishment of Communist puppet regimes in northwestern Iran—all this seemed evidence of Soviet intentions; the old Tzarist drive was very much alive.

As was traditional, Great Britain took up the financial and diplomatic burden of support in Greece and Turkey, while the United States, as was traditional, was not disposed to intervene. But, in March 1946, shocked by the events in Iran, the United States rose to the challenge during the historic first session of the Security Council and demanded that Soviet troops be withdrawn. After three weeks of crisis, the Soviet Union agreed. The collapse of the puppet republics duly followed, and the Soviet oil concession extracted during the occupation was later repudiated by the Iranian Parliament.

Meanwhile Soviet pressure on Turkey mounted. Fearing invasion, Turkey kept its army mobilized, causing inflation and raising the spectre of bankruptcy. In Greece at the same time, Soviet-sponsored guerrillas controlled 75 per cent of the country and were gaining ground in their war against the government. At this point, the British government informed Washington that its military and economic support to Greece and Turkey would have to be discontinued.

The American response to Greek and Turkish need was immediate and vigorous. The Truman Doctrine of 1947, involving an initial sum of $400 million in economic and military assistance and a total outlay of assistance in all categories through June, 1962, of over $7 billion has been successful in helping to eliminate the Communist threat in Greece, in building up the economic and military strength of both Greece and Turkey, and in enlisting both nations as willing participants in the Western system of defense. Similarly, economic and military support totalling $28 million was extended to Iran in 1948, which has since risen to a total through June, 1962, of $1.3 billion. Except for the Mosaddeq interregnum 1951-53, the Iranian government has been eager to maintain an alignment with the West ever since.

Thus, by the end of 1947, the United States had suddenly become a major participant in the affairs of the Middle East. With respect to Greece, Turkey, and Iran, the American response to the Soviet challenge in 1946-47 appeared to be successful; and success in the north seemed to have established a pattern for effective resistance to the Soviet Union elsewhere in the area.

Intervention in Palestine 1947-50

Later on, when the need for incorporating or keeping the Arab countries in Western defense arrangements came to seem urgent, this pattern might have been applied with good effect. Meanwhile, however, American involvement in the Palestine dispute was to make the task all but impossible.

When the Balfour Declaration of 1917 made its celebrated pronouncement in favor of a Jewish National Home in Palestine, President Wilson endorsed it and resolutions of support passed both Houses of Congress. Then, and since, the idea had enjoyed a general sympathy in the United States, the more so as Jews in Germany began to flee Nazi persecution en masse during the 1930's. The British White Paper of 1939 limiting Jewish immigration into Palestine came as a shock, and as news of extermination began to seep out of Europe in 1942, the Zionist Movement overwhelmingly adopted the "Biltmore Program" for the conversion of the whole of Palestine into a Jewish State. The quest for an alleged "Jewish vote" in the United States led both political parties to endorse Zionist aims in the 1944 elections and again in 1946, while President Truman in 1945 and again in 1946 appealed to Prime Minister Attlee for the immediate admission to Palestine of 100,000 Jewish refugees left over from the war in Europe—without, however, offering to assume any responsibility for getting the Arabs to agree. The British role in Palestine soon became untenable in the face of American pressure, vehement Zionist attack and the growing Arab and Jewish violence in Palestine. In 1947, Britain put the problem in the lap of the United Nations and prepared to vacate the Palestine mandate the following year.

In November 1947, seemingly through the activity of influential private citizens behind the scenes rather more than by the efforts of a lukewarm State Department, the United States played a major role in securing the necessary two-thirds recommendation of support in the General Assembly for the most recent United Nations partition plan in Palestine. The United States government was still unprepared, however, to supply the force which might have made partition possible without war. When the new state of Israel was proclaimed five months later, President Truman extended immediate United States recognition with Russia close behind. In 1950, underwriting Israel's wartime gains, the United States joined Britain and France in the Tri-Partite Declaration on the Security of Middle Eastern Frontiers—which did not prevent the invasion of Egypt in 1956 but which still remains in effect. Since the beginning, American economic, technical, and financial support for Israel, public and private, has been impressive. From 1948 through June 1962, quite apart from the high level of direct private investment, government grants and loans totalling $880 million and private gifts (tax free) and bond purchases totalling approximately $1.5 billion have flowed into that small country. Given a population of some two million people, this represents something like $1,200 for every Israeli man, woman and child.

Wholehearted and openhanded American backing for the establishment and growth of Israel represents the first substantial political involvement of the United States in the Arab part of the Middle East. It was not undertaken for reasons of national security as in Greece, Turkey and Iran, but, as events were to show, in spite of them. Some of those concerned with American security, Secretary of Defense Forrestal for one, were indeed aware of the hazards involved (many Jewish citizens were concerned also with the potential dangers of a double loyalty), but such views were castigated as "anti-semitic" or as oil-mongering and had little effect. In essence, the pro-Zionist policy was in part a projection of domestic politics, with political leaders and parties competing with pro-Zionist attitudes and promises for the so-called "Jewish vote"; but more fundamentally it was an expression of the humanitarian good will and sympathy of the American people at large—who have only slowly become aware that "righting the wrongs of Europe" and "making the desert bloom" in Palestine were not done in a vacuum and that other wrongs were committed in the process.

The history of Palestine etched on the consciousness of every Arab who has reached political awareness, one-sided and incomplete as it may be, is that it began after World War I with a broken British promise of independence and the imposition of Balfour Plan immigration over the protest of the ten-to-one Arab majority of that country; that as a result of Jewish immigration during the following quarter-century while the Arabs continued to lack any organ of self-government through which to protect themselves, the ratio shrank to two-to-one; that with the approval and support of the Western (but not the Asian) countries, the process culminated after 1947 in dismemberment, defeat, and the forcible displacement of a whole nation to make room for another.

This was and is viewed by Arabs as a monstrous injustice, and that it should have been so enthusiastically supported by the outspoken champion of "inalienable rights" and equal treatment for all men added the bitterness of an ideal betrayed. The high regard so long enjoyed by the United States in the Arab world was thus converted almost overnight to suspicion and hostility. The policy of supporting Israel for domestic reasons was not incompatible with supporting Greece, Turkey and Iran for reasons of defense; the latter nations had little interest in the Palestine dispute. But as the United States acquired security objectives in the Arab world, it proved a handicap indeed.

WOOING THE ARABS 1950-1962

Phase I: Egypt 1950-51. The Middle East Defense Command—By 1950, evidence of Communist determination and success in the Cold War had steadily mounted: the Czechoslovakian takeover in 1948, the Chinese Communist victory in 1949, the Berlin blockade in 1948-49, the first Soviet atomic bomb in 1949, and then in 1950, the Korean invasion. As alarm in the West grew, the importance to Europe and Western defense of Middle Eastern oil—estimated at that time to include two-thirds of the free world's reserves—and the strategic value of the Canal and the British bases in Egypt and other Arab states seemed ever more apparent. But both the oil and the bases were increasingly threatened by nationalist defiance, in Iran against the British-controlled oil industry, in Egypt against British forces, and in Iraq against both.

Reminiscent in a way of Victorian England and its concern for Ottoman Turkey, the whole instinct of the United States in this situation was to support the British in their military positions of strength, and most of all in Egypt which was clearly the strategic center of the whole Middle East. The first effort (apart from the five year renewal of Dhahran air base lease and the military training agreement with Saudi Arabia in mid-1951) was to devise with Britain a Middle East Defense Command linking the United States, U.K., France, Turkey and the Arab states in a defense system based on the Canal Zone bases, the Arabs to supply the facilities and the Western powers the command. But the Four Power Proposal, notably mistimed, was presented to Egypt only five days after that nation with wild enthusiasm had abrogated its 1936 Treaty with Britain and demanded the immediate evacuation of British troops. The Egyptian Government rejected the proposal out of hand, and the other Arab states followed suit. Secretary of State Acheson then stated stiffly that "the United States government considers the action of the Egyptian government (abrogation) to be without validity." But this hardly brought the Arabs any closer to a defense arrangement. In the Arab view, the United States was not only the champion of Israel, but was seen to be fully in league with the hated imperialist powers of Europe as well.

Phase II: Egypt 1952-54. The Military Regime—A new "go it alone" phase free of the embarrassments of British leadership was made possible by the Egyptian Revolution of July, 1952. The new government of General Neguib and Col. Nasser, pragmatic and honestly concerned with reform in Egypt, enjoyed American approval from the beginning. United States diplomatic support helped the new regime to achieve its overriding political objectives: British agreement in 1953 to withdraw from the Sudan and in 1954 to evacuate its Canal Zone bases (except for brief periods 1948-49 and 1955-56, Israel has not been Egypt's primary external concern). Honoring a promise contingent on the evacuation agreement, the United States supplemented its Point IV aid with $40 million in economic assistance, and a similar promise of military aid remained to be negotiated. The clear hope was, if Egypt was not to be coerced, its cooperation in Western defense arrangements might nevertheless be won once the British were out of the way. If so, with its traditional role of leadership enhanced by the new Revolutionary management, Egypt could be expected to exert a favorable leverage in other parts of the Arab world. Up until the events of 1955, the prognosis was favorable.

The American second phase in Egypt coincided with the emergence of the Point IV approach to the problem of American security. The idea was that by giving substantial economic and technical assistance to the so-called underdeveloped nations of the world, the United States would help to raise standards of living, provide new jobs, foster development. This would, it was assumed, stabilize local politics, give local populations an interest in the political status quo and in a friendly association with the United States. Communism and the Soviet Union would lose their appeal, and the threat to American security would correspondingly diminish. For most Americans, to be sure, humanitarian concern for less fortunate people was a major motivation in their support for Point IV and similar aid programs, but for a tax-conscious government and Congress the reasons were primarily those of Cold War defense. As a part of the Mutual Security Program, Point IV agreements were made in 1951, and subsequently with Egypt, Lebanon, Jordan, Saudi Arabia, Libya and Iraq as well as with Turkey, Iran and Israel. Syria continued to reject the program as a new form of imperialism, but elsewhere the initial reception was not unfavorable, not least in Egypt, the one country where the government's investments in the program were consistently larger than the American. Before long, however, and especially after 1955, Arab sentiment began to crystalize against the aid program. To some extent this may have been a result of the inevitable mistakes and failures that attend large ventures in unfamiliar areas, but mainly it was for reasons unrelated to the program itself—giving rise to an American Ambassador's rueful remark that economic and military assistance could be an excellent adjunct, but not an alternative, to sound policy.

The second phase of the American effort to enlist Arab cooperation continued into 1955, but ended abruptly with President Nasser's simple statement in September that "we have bought arms from Czechoslovakia for cotton and rice."

Phase III: Iraq 1954-58. The Baghdad Pact—Meanwhile, a third phase in the American effort to enlist Arab cooperation in defense arrangements began to center around Iraq. In 1953, Secretary of State Dulles made a visit to the Middle East, and found that while most of the Arab states, fearing Israel instead of Communism, were not ready for a Middle Eastern NATO, there was more awareness of the real danger in the "northern tier of nations" along the Soviet frontier. Stimulated by renewed Russian pressure on Turkey, the United States granted that country, Greece and Iran a further $396 million in military aid, and soon began planning a military assistance pact with Pakistan. This materialized in the spring of 1954; and in the fall, Pakistan joined the Southeast Asian Treaty Organization (SEATO). By the end of 1954, the United States, with pacts of military assistance and cooperation, had created an unbroken defensive zone all along the southern border of the Soviet Union, linked via Turkey with NATO in the west and via Pakistan with SEATO in the east.

Iraq was now to be incorporated in this grouping. Back in 1953, Secretary Dulles had raised the old Middle East Defense Command idea with Col. Nasser. The latter's answer was unequivocal: No external defense alliances. They would be political suicide for the new regime, and for the sponsors, self-defeating. The only real danger in the Middle East was from Communism inside the region, and the only real defense was internal strength and unity. Alliances ("divide and rule") would create the opposite. "What use will 'linear strategy' be, if the attack comes from inside?"

But if Nasser was not willing, Nuri al-Said, strong man of Iraq, staunch ally of the British, was. In April 1954, he accepted United States military assistance. During the summer, with Iraq under firm military control, he was negotiating with the British even as the Anglo-Egyptian evacuation agreement was being worked out in Cairo. In the fall he went to London, and in January 1955, he announced the Iraqi-Turkish Treaty. The British adhered in April and the so-called Baghdad Pact was in being. Iran and Pakistan joined before the end of the year.

Having sponsored the Pact in the first place and supported it financially and militarily, having subsequently attended the meetings and successively joined the various subcommittees set up by the Pact, the United States nevertheless never formally joined it. Ostensibly, this was to avoid offending Arab public opinion in general, the numerous protagonists of Israel in the United States, the anti-Hashimite King Saud, and above all, President Nasser. Not many were fooled, however, least of all Nasser, and the United States was roundly criticized both by opponents of the Pact for supporting it, and proponents for not supporting it fully and openly.

But Iraq, or at least its ruling triumvirate, had been incorporated into Northern Tier defense. During the next four years, United States economic and military aid to Iraq totalled $58.6 million, and perhaps this contributed to Western security during that period.

Iraq's participation in the Pact ended with the murderous revolt of July 1958, a whirlwind stimulated in part by the Pact itself. But even if seemingly successful for a time in Iraq, the Pact was a disaster in Egypt. It signaled the end of the Western beginning with Nasser, and led instead to the deal for Soviet arms.

Phase IV: Egypt 1954-55. Soviet Arms—To Nasser, the Baghdad Pact represented betrayal by Nuri al-Said and by the British, and it was the beginning of disillusionment with the United States. In September 1954, Nasser and Nuri al-Said had failed to reach agreement on how best to deal with the great powers, Nasser still insisting on no external alliances for any member of the 1950 Arab League Collective Security Pact, and on a building up of independent united Arab strength instead. Nuri, more concerned about the Soviet threat, less concerned about Arab public opinion, and above all eager for the benefits of alliance with the West, nevertheless promised not to make any external agreement without the approval of other members of the Arab Pact. Then he went off to London. The promise by the Iraqi Foreign Minister was repeated in Cairo in December 1954, and by Nuri to the Chamber of Deputies in Baghdad. Then came the January announcement of the Turkish Treaty, a clear violation of the promise, and of the policy of united non-alignment Nasser felt to be vital.

As for the British, the Canal Zone agreement after tough negotiation had been reached in July 1954 and signed in October. A turning point, said Nasser. "With this agreement a new era of friendly relations based on mutual trust now opens between Egypt and Britain and the Western countries." The agreement provided for evacuation of British forces from the Suez bases within two years in exchange for a 7-year agreement to British use of the bases in the event of an attack on any Arab country or Turkey by an outside power, i.e., the Soviet Union (even this small departure from the no-alliance, no strings, principle earned Nasser the angry label of "Western stooge" from Egyptian patriots and resulted in an assassination attempt one week after signing). Foreign Minister Eden looked forward to "a new understanding and friendship between our two countries." But all the while plans were going forward to bypass Nasser through his archrival in Iraq. Nasser's reaction to the Pact, characteristically, was immediate and violent: four days later his radio began a vitriolic and sustained assault on Nuri al-Said, his traitorous Pact, and everything it stood for.

A few weeks later, at the end of February, Israeli forces destroyed an Egyptian military post in Gaza, killing 38 and wounding 31. Although there had been a series of military reprisals against villages in Jordan, beginning in Qibya in 1953, this was the first against Egyptian forces and the first into Egyptian controlled territory since 1949. Why, after the long period of relative calm? The sequence of events in a period when Nasser appeared to enjoy the favor of the United States and might join, as was hoped, in a defense agreement with the West from which Israel would be excluded, is suggestive: the Anglo-Egyptian Agreement in July, 1954 which would soon remove the British military buffer between Egypt and Israel, the only force-in-being able to support the 1950 Tripartite agreement guaranteeing frontiers; the capture in Egypt of Israeli *agents provacateurs* assigned to arrange the destruction "by Egyptians" of American and British buildings (the Lavon affair); and the unscheduled return early in 1955 after 22 months of desert retirement of David Ben-Gurion to the Israeli Ministry of Defense. Eleven days later, the Gaza raid, as if to emphasize to the Egyptians that even without the British garrisons in between and notwithstanding Nasser's new friendship with the United States, Israel was ready and able to defend itself under any circumstances.

But whatever the Israeli motive, the effect on Nasser of the Gaza raid and similar blows during the following months was clear: Egyptian forces were no match for the Israelis. Arms to match the new Israeli weapons became an immediate necessity, not least because of angry pressure from the young military officers upon whose support the regime depended. The two-year-old search for arms in the West was intensified. The British sent forty tanks but withheld ammunition, the French made aid conditional upon withdrawing support from the Algerian "rebels," and the United States, arms "promise" notwithstanding, would supply arms only on the basis of a Mutual Security agreement or in token amounts for cash in dollars—which Egypt lacked. In April Nasser attended the Bandung Conference where Chou En-Lai is said to have suggested an approach to the Soviet Union. Negotiations with the Soviets began in June, and after a final effort to impress the United States with his need and the imminent alternative, Nasser made his historic decision. Meanwhile violence continued along the Sinai-Gaza frontier.

Thus did American policies in 1954-55, in supporting the Baghdad Pact, in condoning the repeated military jabs of Israel, and perhaps above all in declining to implement its arms promise on terms acceptable to Nasser ("no pacts, no missions"), help to estrange the man already looming as an Arab Bismarck and to produce precisely the result most feared: the emergence for the first time of Soviet power and influence in the heart of the Middle East.

Phase V: Egypt 1955-56. The Suez Crisis—The effect of the arms announcement was spectacular: shock and outrage in the United States and Europe (as if, being denied in the West, Egypt was not entitled to look elsewhere); and in the Arab world after decades of humiliation, a universal jubilation at Nasser's master stroke. A champion against the imperialists at last; and Nasser's star soared as the scale of the arms agreement became known. Syria and Yemen soon applied for arms on the same favorable terms. The reaction in Washington was to send at once an Assistant Secretary of State to see what might be retrieved. Next day in Cairo he was made to wait, and if as generally believed he carried a revised offer of arms, he was unsuccessful. But for Nasser, the arms agreement and the strong reaction in the West were confirmation that his new system for utilizing the Cold War, "positive neutralism"—which meant in essence "balanced exploitation" of both sides—could be made to bear fruit.

The next step was to let it be known that the Russians had shown an interest in the projected High Dam, which would add a third to Egypt's agricultural wealth and which had become a revolutionary symbol of hope in the struggle against a runaway growth of population and mass hunger. As if to prove Nasser's diagnosis correct, the United States and Britain in the fall of 1955 offered to help finance the Dam instead, and the World Bank made a contingent offer of support. Negotiations began, but when it became clear in 1956 that the Russians had not been and were not interested, after all, it became possible in the Cold War logic of Secretary Dulles to withdraw the offer, the British and the World Bank following suit.

There were many persuasive reasons for withdrawing it, once it became possible; perhaps the main ones being Nasser's continuous radio slandering of the Baghdad Pact effort and his sudden recognition of Communist China in May (itself a reaction to American approval of the sale of NATO Mystére jet aircraft by France to Israel, and twenty Sabre jets by Canada). But when the moment came in mid-July, the withdrawal was made in such a way as to be a deliberate, public, and inescapable insult to the Egyptian President and his people. The upstart Nasser was to be taught a lesson. But the angry riposte, nationalization of the British and French-owned Suez Canal Company, sent Nasser truly into orbit as the deliriously acclaimed hero and vindicator of all the Arabs.

The United States withdrawal of the High Dam offer proceeded from a decision to have done with Nasser, marking the end of the fifth phase in the continuing American attempt to incorporate the Arabs in the Western system of defense. There is some irony in the fact that, the decision having been made, the first action taken should have established Nasser as the idol of the Arabs, including fully, for the first time, the mass of the Egyptians as well. Irony too, that as a result of the ensuing crisis and war, the Soviet Union would emerge as the high-minded and steady champion of the Arab underdog, the French and British allies would be forced to retire in utter discredit, and Nasser himself, surviving military defeat, would reap a political harvest of impressive size.

Phase VI: Saudi Arabia, Jordan, Syria, Lebanon 1957-58. The Eisenhower Doctrine—The Israeli invasion of Sinai began on October 29, 1956. British and French ultimatums the following day transformed what seemed at first a local conflict into an unmistakable Western attack on Egypt. The General Assembly with unprecedented speed and rare unanimity demanded an immediate end to the fighting and a withdrawal of foreign forces. On November 6, Britain and France were forced to agree, having achieved nothing; and Israel, having secured its military aims, was willing to agree too. A central factor in the General Assembly's success in stopping the invasion was the vigorous and determined leadership of the United States.

The fact that Britain and France were its two chief allies; the inhibitions imposed by a presidential electoral campaign in its final stages, including a reluctance to alienate an alleged bloc of Jewish voters for whom Israel could do no wrong; a willingness to see Nasser removed—all of these factors might have argued for a different course. But, just as in Korea, here was a case of open aggression, and the United States had to support principle for very practical as well as moral reasons. Emotional reasons were involved too: anger at the deliberate deception practiced by Britain, France and Israel. But failure to support principle would have meant the probable collapse of the United Nations and the hope of an international security system it represented; it would have meant the alienation, possibly permanent, of most of the nations of Asia and Africa, from which the Soviet Union could hardly fail to profit; and it would probably have meant for the incumbent administration in Washington a far larger loss of support on election day than could be gained by condoning the attack. Moreover, even if successful in toppling Nasser and re-establishing Western control of the Canal, the attacking powers could hardly expect anything but an intensification of the nationalist hostility which had led them to the use of force in the first place. For the United States to be associated with such a victory at such a cost would have been short-sighted in the extreme.

President Eisenhower's forthright stand on principle came as a shock and a disappointment to the governments of Britain, France, and Israel; but to the Arabs it was a gratifying surprise. For a brief period, indeed, it seemed as if the clock might be turned back, that the United States might recover much of the respect and influence it once enjoyed in the Arab world. But United States opposition to aggression, even by friends and allies, did not mean any change of view about Nasser; and Arab hopes for a new American beginning in Middle Eastern policy were soon seen to be illusory. The moment of opportunity was lost. Instead of now conceding that neutralism was not, after all, immoral as Secretary Dulles had asserted, that the dream of Arab independence and unity was not necessarily a threat to the West, that Arabs were entitled to choose their own leadership, and that they could with some justice regard the Israelis and the Western imperialists as more immediate threats than the Soviet Union, the United States continued as before. Nasser, as an obstacle to United States policy objectives, was to be opposed, isolated, and discredited in all feasible ways. Even in petty ways. In contrast to its humanitarian airlifts and relief supplies for the Hungarian refugees, the United States not only declined urgently needed medicines for the bombed-out victims of Port Said but even refused to release frozen Egyptian dollars so they might be purchased. The CARE program, providing free lunches for three million Egyptian school children, was stopped. The United States refused to sell oil or surplus wheat despite the urgency of Egyptian need. Instead, responding at once, the Soviet Union provided the medicines, oil, and wheat. During the Western economic boycott of Egypt that followed the Suez episode, Iron Curtain markets for cotton provided Egypt with a life-saving alternative to the West. By actions such as these, the United States soon erased the good effect of its stand in November and made clear its continuing hostility to Nasser.

Opposition to Nasser, however, did little to encourage Arab cooperation in Western defense arrangements—which now seemed more urgent than ever. The Soviet Union, on the other hand, basking in the after-glow of its stand, rocket threats and all, against the tripartite aggression, was proceeding to reap the political harvest the United States had failed to secure. To the advantages of weapons supply and the lion's share of Egypt's trade were now to be added cultural exchanges, Iron Curtain scholarships, economic and technical assistance, and, in symbolic climax, an agreement to help build the celebrated High Dam. By the end of 1958 the United Arab Republic (Egypt and Syria) had accepted from the U.S.S.R. in addition to military equipment, some $600 million in long term low interest credits "without political strings," dwarfing Point IV aid since the beginning to all the Arab Countries combined.

As Soviet influence grew, the post-Suez phase in the persistent United States effort to win Arab support began. This sixth phase, coupled with hostility to Nasser, involved efforts to win the support of other states whose leaders distrusted the Egyptian Saladin, his propaganda against monarchs and feudal oligarchies, and his huge popularity among their own populations. These other states—Saudi Arabia, Jordan, Lebanon, and possibly even Syria—together with Iraq might with skill be made to constitute a zone of Western strength in the Arab world; and even the Egyptian leader, his obduracy softened by isolation, might in time, it was hoped, be induced to join.

The vehicle of the new approach was the so-called Eisenhower Doctrine. Proposed by President Eisenhower early in January, 1957, and approved by Congress two months later, the Doctrine authorized the President to extend economic and military assistance, including troops if necessary, to any Middle Eastern nation desiring protection against "overt armed aggression from any nation controlled by International Communism." A fund of $200 million was provided, and the Richards Mission was sent to the Middle East in the spring of 1957 to line up adherents.

Meanwhile, however, King Saud had become, in a sense, the first focus of contention in the post-Suez Eisenhower Doctrine competition between Nasser and the United States. In January 1957, en route to the United States, King Saud paused in Cairo, and under Nasser's urging signed with King Hussein and Shukry Kuwatly, president of Syria, the Arab-Solidarity Agreement. The four leaders agreed to replace the British subsidy to Jordan with an Arab one in return for Hussein's promise to end his treaty with Britain and never to join the Baghdad Pact. Also, and most important from the viewpoint of President Nasser who was already convinced of United States hostility, they affirmed a common opposition to the Eisenhower Doctrine. Although spurned in New York, King Saud was warmly received and feted in Washington as the royal statesman whose years and rank and oil income entitled him to a far more prominent (and pro-Western) role in Middle Eastern affairs than heretofore. Within three weeks after the Cairo Solidarity Agreement the pliable monarch had agreed to renew the American air base lease for a further five years in return for $50 million in economic and military aid, had praised the Eisenhower Doctrine in public, and had undertaken to impress the other Arab leaders with its possibilities. Back in Cairo again, however, he was rebuffed by Nasser; and the four Arab Solidarity leaders separated without having been able to agree.

To an extent, the United States was thus successful in this first round with Nasser in keeping Saudi Arabia on friendly terms with the United States and in preventing whole-hearted implementation of Arab Solidarity opposition to the Doctrine. King Saud himself, however, was to fare less well. In the spring, an assassination plot was discovered, presumably Egyptian-sponsored, and in March of the following year, Saud was accused of paying $5 million as an initial installment toward having Nasser killed in an "air accident." As a result of nationalist anger in the towns of Saudi Arabia against this "traitorous" act, along with dissaffection among the tribes, pinched in their subsidies by the royal squanderlust, Saud was forced to put control of the government into the hands of his less extravagant, less anti-Nasser brother, Feisal.

Meanwhile, in the spring of 1957, the Richards Mission had begun its travels. Except for those non-Arab nations already committed to the West, however, for whom the Doctrine was a welcome windfall, the mission was seemingly a failure. No Arab country, excluding Libya and the small Western-oriented half-Christian state of Lebanon, not even Nuri al-Said's Iraq, dared risk the popular outrage certain to greet any endorsement of the Doctrine. Ostensibly a result of the Suez crisis, the new instrument seemed instead to be a total *non sequitur* and could hardly fail to rouse the deepest suspicion among the Arabs. It offered protection against Communist aggression which Arabs did not fear, and said nothing about an enemy, still occupying part of Egypt, they had good reason to fear: Israel. In attempting to isolate Egypt and Syria it violated the popular ideal of Arab unity. In seeking to enlist the Arab states as partisans in the Cold War—and in the view of many Arabs on the wrong side at that—it violated the principle of neutralism or non-alignment. In addition to the failures of formulation, the Doctrine was presented in such a way as to be insulting to populations still highly sensitive about recent colonial domination (in effect: "Either you're with us or against us; we'll make it worth your while to be with us.") And finally, during the weeks of gestation in Washington, adverse Soviet and Egyptian propaganda had portrayed the Doctrine night and day as a nefarious new imperialism with all the old tactics—gunboats, bribes, and puppet regimes—and the same old aim: "divide and rule."

Unfortunately, this hostile view seemed to be confirmed by the first overt American action under the Doctrine in April 1957, while the Richards Mission was still in the Middle East. King Hussein at the end of April suddenly overruled his freely elected but pro-Nasser government and imposed martial law, alleging a "communist" plot supported by Egypt and designed to take over the country. The United States response was electric. Units of the Sixth Fleet were rushed to the Eastern Mediterranean with warnings that United States paratroops were ready to protect "the integrity and independence" of Jordan and its young king. King Hussein was awarded an unconditional $10 million, weapons were promised, and by the end of April it was all over. Jordan had been detached, at some cost to the principles of democracy in that country, from the January Arab Solidarity Agreement and had been established instead as an American client state under the authoritarian rule of King Hussein. To an Arab eye, the Eisenhower Doctrine in action seemed to fit the Soviet-Egyptian prescription: gunboats, bribes, puppet regime.

King Hussein had not endorsed the Doctrine publicly, but the speed with which the United States responded to his need suggests there was nevertheless an understanding. Indeed, at least one Western authority (and many Arabs) believe the alleged plot was a fiction and the April crisis was an American contrivance from start to finish.

Whether this is true or not, the events of April erased any lingering doubts in Arab minds that the new American approach to the Arab World was anti-Nasser, anti-nationalist, and that it had clandestine dimensions. It was clear too that Nasser would not sulk in his tent but would oppose American efforts at every level.

The first and second rounds in the competition for Arab favor had gone, from one point of view, to the United States. The third round went decisively and popularly to Nasser—and to the Soviet Union. When accusations about an American-sponsored plot to unseat the pro-Nasser, pro-Soviet regime in Syria began to circulate following a major Syrian-Soviet arms and aid agreement during the summer of 1957, Arabs were ready to believe the worst; and again, as the Syrian crisis grew, American actions seemed to confirm the charge: the State Department emissary's hasty visit to Istanbul and Beirut, avoiding Damascus and Cairo; his reputation among the Arabs as the *coup*-maker who had supported General Zahedi's overthrow of Mosaddeq in Iran in 1953; the shipment of arms to Middle Eastern allies bordering on Syria including an airlift of weapons to Jordan; an American task force off the Syrian coast; mobilization of Turkish forces on the Syrian frontier with American officers present—all this seemed to fit. When Secretary Dulles at the United

Nations in September spoke of the danger to Turkey (23 million people and the strongest field force in NATO—half a million men battle-tested in Korea) from Syria (4 million people and a small untried army only beginning to receive modern equipment from the U.S.S.R.) the evidence seemed complete. Meanwhile, the Soviet Union continued to champion Syrian independence and integrity against "American aggression," threatening use of nuclear force if necessary. When no *coup* materialized, the popular conclusion was not that no *coup* had been planned but that the United States had been forced to back down. The prestige of the Soviet Union rose to new heights, and so too that of Nasser, who had sent a token force to Syria as a gesture of support during the crisis and whose government had agreed in September to conclude an economic union with Syria and in November to begin negotiations toward implementing that abiding Arab dream, a federal union itself.

A few weeks later (February 1958), the United Arab Republic suddenly came into being. Syrian leaders, fearing the worst from a combination of the pro-Soviet Syrian Chief of Staff, local Communists, and Soviet prestige, had gone in something like panic to Nasser, urging full and immediate union. In such a union, Nasser's domestic rigor against communist activity would be extended to Syria, and the present Syrian leadership could preserve something of its existing role. With some reluctance Nasser agreed, and formation of the U.A.R. was announced to enormous popular acclaim. The Soviet Union accorded immediate recognition. In the "competition" over Syria, it was clear enough who had won. The American reaction to the new union was less than enthusiastic, and for most Arabs the real American response seemed to be in the creation two weeks later of the ill-fated rival federation of Jordan and Iraq.

The fourth Arab state to be involved in an Eisenhower Doctrine crisis was Lebanon. A small nation approximately half Muslim and half Christian, the basis of its political stability lay in the "National Pact of 1943" when the Muslims agreed not to press for union with Muslim Syria and the Christians agreed to sever their political ties with the West, France in particular. Under this arrangement, the country prospered. But in 1957, after the Egyptian defeat in Sinai when Lebanese enthusiasm for Nasser had cooled and the growth of Soviet influence in Syria was cause for apprehension, the government of President Chamoun decided to endorse the Eisenhower Doctrine. There was also a financial inducement—$10 million as an initial installment. But all this was viewed in Lebanon as a departure from the National Pact, particularly by certain political leaders excluded from Parliament as a result of the 1957 elections, who made it an issue in street demonstrations. In May 1958, after President Chamoun had indicated his intention of altering the constitution so as to remain in office, the assassination of a Christian pro-Nasser newspaper editor brought matters to a head. Confronted with public disorder and actual fighting but no longer enjoying majority support in Lebanon and unable even to count on the Muslim-Christian army in view of its divided loyalties, the Chamoun government began to draw on United States assistance in the name of the Doctrine. Opposition groups similarly found the U.A.R. a source of funds, weapons, volunteers, and propaganda support. The internal dispute thus acquired an international dimension, thereby being made more dangerous; and the United States found itself pitted once again against President Nasser. Following the Lebanese government's appeal to the United Nations against "massive intervention" by the U.A.R., Mr. Hammarskjold and the United Nations Observer Corps, finding little evidence of intervention, seemed to have turned the tide toward solution. But at this moment, in July 1958, the Revolution in Iraq occurred.

Convinced that the Iraqi revolution was all part of a Nasserite-Soviet plot which might set loose forces that would engulf Lebanon, President Chamoun urgently reiterated his earlier request for American troops, and King Hussein similarly demanded British support. This posed for the United States a painful dilemma; honor the moral commitment to an ally, thus going to the brink, risking the nuclear war that Middle East policy was supposed to prevent and incurring at the very least a new increment of opprobrium among the anti-imperialist peoples of the world? Or back down, with a chilling effect of all United States allies?

The United States chose to land troops, and the result was another international crisis, fully exploited as usual by the Soviet Union and from which the United States was eventually rescued in the United Nations by an Egyptian Resolution to which all the Arab states adhered: expressing their confidence in each other, they desired the Secretary-General to "facilitate the early withdrawal of the foreign troops from the two countries." American forces were withdrawn as smoothly and efficiently as they had arrived.

What did the troops accomplish? The only visible result was the demise of the Chamoun government in favor of a neutralist government led by one of the opposition leaders in the fighting, and a Lebanese repudiation of the Eisenhower Doctrine. But in retrospect, it is evident that there have been other consequences, less visible perhaps, but far-reaching. For the world in general, it was a demonstration that in support of its commitments in the Middle East the

United States was ready to confront the Soviet Union, with force if need be, whereas the U.S.S.R. itself was seen to be less ready. To Nasser and Arab nationalists, it showed that the promise of Soviet backing could be relied on only up to a point—the point at which Soviet interests ceased to coincide with Arab interests. It showed also that United States imperialism did not, after all, run true to form: there had been no violence, no tampering with the Lebanese political process, no mounting of a counterrevolutionary invasion of Iraq; and there had been a speedy unconditional withdrawal. For Arabs in general it was a demonstration of the danger of trying to utilize great power support to fight local issues; but also in a subtle way, it was a kind of reassurance in the new era of independence that the West, even after having been thrown out, was still nearby in case of need.

For the United States it was a clear illustration of the perils of lending American power for local purposes in blank checks such as the agreement with Lebanon under the Eisenhower Doctrine. But in a larger sense, the Lebanese episode came as a liberating shock, making it possible finally to put an end to what one writer has called the "inexorable blindness" of American-Arab policy during the eight years preceding.

Phase VII: The Fruits of Disengagement 1958-62—By the end of the summer of 1958, United States Arab policy was unmistakably in ruins. Egypt, by long odds the strongest Arab country with the only outstanding and outstandingly popular Arab leader, far from being won to an association with the United States, had been made actively and effectively hostile. Syria, hostile to begin with, had only been made more so, and was now united with Egypt under Nasser. Iraq, the linchpin of Baghdad Pact defense against the U.S.S.R. under Nuri al-Said, had now under revolutionary leadership become openly hostile too. Lebanon, from being warmly pro-Western, had been converted to a cool neutrality. Only Jordan, and to an extent Saudi Arabia, remained. Jordan, utterly dependent on outside subsidy, and pro-Western solely in virtue of the military control of the King over a mainly hostile population; and Saudi Arabia, also with its pro-Western monarchy but little in the way of modern military strength or facilities—these were weak pillars at best. The elimination of Nuri al-Said and the monarchy in Iraq were a reminder of how tenuous an advantage they could be.

Moreover, if American policy was designed to keep Soviet influence out of the Arab world or at least keep it unimportant, it seemed in practice to have had opposite results. Having achieved the status of a great world power, the Soviet Union would surely have made its presence felt in the Arab Middle East sooner or later in any case. But up until 1954, there was little evidence of the U.S.S.R. in the Arab world—mainly propaganda against the imperialist West and local ruling classes, and a few communists and front groups. By 1958 however, having used to great advantage every unpopular new turn in Western policy, the Soviet Union had made itself welcome. Russian power and prestige were everywhere evident—arms, trade, aid and technical assistance, cultural missions and all the rest—and the U.S.S.R. had acquired a commanding voice in Middle Eastern affairs. American mistakes had helped to make the Soviet path an easy one.

All this seemed to justify, in the summer and fall of 1958, the most gloomy forecast for the future of American influence in the Arab Middle East. But since then it is clear that matters have changed, dramatically, for the better. Now it is the United States that is everywhere desired as the major great power friend. President Nasser and his nationalist supporters throughout the area are now on something approaching good terms with the United States, despite Israel, and without benefit of military pacts or treaties, even without the Saudi air base agreement which lapsed in 1962. It has at times become necessary to deny that Nasser is now the American "chosen instrument" in the Arab world. The Arab monarchs continue to be as friendly as before. A pro-Western government in Iraq has replaced the hostile Kassim regime of 1958, and even Syrian intransigence has softened to the point of allowing American loan and economic assistance agreements. The tidal shift eastward in Arab public opinion between 1955 and 1958 has been reversed—to the point one can now propose that the Cold War has been won in the Middle East, for the present at least, and even entertain assertions that a not unwelcome *pax Americana* has come into being.

To an extent, to be sure, this has been a consequence of the very success of the Soviet Union between 1955 and 1958. In those years, having suddenly become a dominant, perhaps *the* dominant, power in the Arab Middle East, with vital interests of its own, a major economic and political stake in the area, with commitments to honor and investments and prestige to protect, the U.S.S.R. began in its turn to run into policy conflicts with the Arabs, to make unpopular decisions, to generate disillusionment. Whereas Soviet absorption of Egyptian cotton, for example, during the Western boycott after the Suez crisis had been a welcome alternative, discounted Russian sales of this same cotton in other hard currency markets, displacing direct sales by Egypt, was an unpleasant discovery. Or again, whereas, during the formation of the U.A.R., the

Russians had tolerated the loss of their left hand in Syria (the local communists) for the sake of making headway with Nasser, a year later in Iraq during the abortive pro-Nasser Shawaf uprising, they elected to back the Iraqi communists instead. Discomfited in Iraq, Nasser cracked down on local communists in the U.A.R. who had enjoyed a certain toleration since the big Russian aid agreements. When Premier Khrushchev protested, Nasser lashed out at "interference in internal affairs" and noted publicly it was no longer possible to make a distinction between local communists and their foreign sponsor. Communism was just as much a threat as Zionism. Khrushchev's threatening rejoinder that Nasser was a "rather hotheaded young man" who might "strain himself" was gratifyingly reminiscent of earlier Western comment.

This flurry was soon composed, but the *Life* magazine essay (of 1956) on the Hungarian uprising appeared for the first time in the Arab world in 1959, in Arabic, as part of an effective undercover campaign against the U.S.S.R.; and Nasser began to show a renewed interest in the Western alternative, as indicated, for example, in new surplus wheat, loan, and technical aid agreements with the United States.

In general, the massive influx of the Soviet Union at all levels and in a multiplicity of ways allowed the Arabs for the first time to make direct comparisons between Soviet promise and fulfillment. Given the unreality of Arab expectations, the fulfillment was inevitably found to fall short. The Arabs were also able to make comparisons between Soviet fulfillment and that of the West, especially the United States. By the end of 1962, on almost every level of performance, in machinery and equipment, trade policy, interpersonal relations, economic and technical assistance, in dealings with other nations allied and neutral, and in economic and military power, the United States on balance was seen to be superior. The confrontation over Cuba in October 1962, seemed to be a crystallization and epitomization of this new state of affairs.

But if the American rise in Arab estimation is partly to be explained by the Soviet fall, both developments are even more the result of the sea change in United States policy following the shambles of 1958.

The new approach might be characterized as one of disengagement, or non-alignment. This has meant in practice a standing aloof from quarrels within and among the Arab states. It has meant non-intervention, and a relaxation of the unsuccessful effort to line up the Arabs with military pacts and assistance agreements. It has meant a turning away from the attempt to preserve or re-establish empty "vital interests." Having lost so much, it has no longer seemed necessary so rigidly to support the status quo and a new flexibility has been possible in contemplating inescapable change. It has meant an end to the sterile and unsuccessful opposition to the Soviet Union which had formed the basis of United States actions—as if the Russians (along with the Israelis) were the only people who really mattered in the Middle East—and a recognition that the Arabs could no longer be approached solely as a means, or obstacle, to Cold War ends. At the same time it has meant an impartial responsiveness to Arab initiative in extending economic and technical assistance, without "political strings."

In essence, the new policy approach meant a recognition by the United States that the Arabs had achieved independence and would henceforth have to be approached on a basis of equal respect; that if "vacuum" there was, the Arabs were the ones who should fill it; that the Arabs themselves were the proper and most important ends of policy in the Arab world; and that such policy, to be successful, would have to be based on the common ground of mutual advantage. This in turn involved a recognition that the overriding objectives of the Arabs, summed up in the nationalist drive for political independence and unity, economic growth, and social reform, were not incompatible with United States objectives but were, on the contrary, directed toward achieving precisely that free, strong, stable, peaceable society the United States was seeking everywhere to foster. This had been President Nasser's contention from the beginning, and there is some irony that he was forced at such cost to demonstrate the point over the determined opposition of the United States. But his victory and the victory of the decisive new force of Arab nationalism of which he remains the towering leader and symbol, has turned out in the sequel to be a United States victory too. Endorsing Nasser and Arab nationalism, the Soviet Union had helped Nasser and the Arabs achieve independence from the West. But real independence, unless their purposes have radically changed, is not what the Soviets have in mind for the Arab world; and who can doubt, as this becomes clear and if United States support of independence continues to be genuine, where the Cold War sympathies of the Arabs will remain?

Since 1958, as a result of the policy of disengagement, of stepping back from immediate involvement, the United States has been able to view events in the Arab Middle East with relative equanimity. Developments that in the earlier period would have produced shocks of alarm and international crises have since then hardly claimed American attention. The breakup of the U.A.R. in 1961, for example, and the continuing factional struggles and military *coups* in Syria; Premier Kassim's abortive attempt to annex Kuwait to Iraq in 1961 and his overthrow in the spring of 1963; the renewed attempt to form a greater Arab union, including this time Iraq as well as Egypt and Syria; even the revolt in Yemen and the subsequent Egyptian and Saudi intervention and fighting—despite a few excited American headlines and editorials all this has hardly disturbed American calm. In the Arab world itself, events and conflicts of recent years have occasioned relatively little disturbance too. Partly no doubt this is a result of growing Arab maturity, but mainly it is because the local issues have not been magnified and made more lethal by Cold War intervention. In terms of this relaxation as well as the favorable westward shift in Arab opinion, the fruits of disengagement have been substantial.

Toward a Successful Policy

Can it now be said that the United States has succeeded in filling Professor Speiser's 1946 prescription for a successful Middle Eastern policy? The answer seems to be a qualified yes. The American approach, to take up Professor Speiser's first requirement, is independent of British and other domination—the United States stand in the 1956 Suez crisis was a decisive demonstration of this. The interests of foreign countries, particularly those of Israel in view of the active support of Zionists and other sympathizers in the United States, continue to be taken into account, but not unduly so. American policy approaches the ideal set by George Washington in his Farewell Address:

> . . . nothing is more essential than that permanent, inveterate antipathies against particular nations and passionate attachments for others should be excluded; and that in place of them just and amicable feelings toward all should be cultivated. The Nation, which indulges toward another an habitual hatred or an habitual fondness, is in some degree a slave. It is a slave to its animosity or to its affection, either of which is sufficient to lead it astray from its duty and its interest. . . .

Moreover, having disassociated itself from "European imperialism," the United States has also mostly put aside the self-defeating legacy of imperialistic tactics and attitudes taken over from Europe with all the demeaning implication that local populations are inferior: the conception of "vital interests" (meaning military bases, pacts and treaties, ownership or control of canal and oil companies); the exercise of gunboat diplomacy; the support of puppet individuals, parties, and regimes; the interventions in local affairs.

Again, Professor Speiser's second requirement seems to have been met. American policy may be said to rest on a clear conception of the long-term American interest in the area: fulfillment of the best aspirations of the Middle Eastern peoples themselves—to remain free, to better themselves economically and in other ways, to achieve social justice, and the rest. It is recognized that they would thus constitute the best possible barrier to communism and the growth of Soviet power and control. This conception is not new. What is new is the recognition that attainment of these objectives by Middle Eastern society, even with United States support, does not necessarily entail alliance with or even friendship for the United States, and that it need not do so. Far from being "immoral," nonalignment, neutralism, even "positive neutralism," reflect the normal desire of newly independent peoples to preserve independence, to "avoid foreign entanglements." It has become apparent that respect for such desires not only does not imply defeat for American policy, but can be a factor of success instead.

Thirdly, in the Speiser prescription, American policy would have to be consistent within the area. The policy of disengagement in the Arab world has made it possible to eliminate destructive inconsistencies of the kind evident during the period before 1958, the simultaneous involvement with the mortal rivals Nasser and Nuri al-Said between 1954-56, for example, or the professed American allegiance to the principles of democracy versus support or (if not connivance in) the suppression of democracy in Jordan in 1957.

In the Middle East as a whole, ambivalances with policy consequences remain in abundance—necessary reform versus constituted governments slow to reform; Arab unity versus separate independence; civil liberties and democratic sovereignty versus stability and order; the security of Israel versus the security of its Arab neighbors. But in all of these, the principle of disengagement and withdrawal, of nonintervention and the impartiality ("nonalignment") thus made possible and plausible has helped to bring such inconsistencies within the limits of toleration for all parties concerned.

It might be argued that the resumption of nonintervention or "friendly noninvolvement" in the Arab world is inconsistent with the very real involvement represented by the military arrangements with Turkey. But this is an inconsistency more apparent than real. In Turkey, the multifold association with and the protective backing of the United States has reflected popular desire as well as government policy, and is consonant with Turkish aspirations no less than nonintervention is in the Arab world. In Turkey, it is not construed as United States intervention but rather an association on an equal basis for a common purpose.

The same may be said, with reservations, about Iran. United States intervention, real or imagined, in unseating the enormously popular nationalist hero Premier Mosaddeq in 1953 has not been forgotten and United States backing for the Shah, reform-minded as he seems to be, is resented by many sections of Iranian society, not least the students who approve of reform but not authoritarian rule. Even in the event of violence and revolution, however, it seems likely that the long Persian memory of Russian pressure and war would make a continuance of United States support attractive to successor regimes.

If American policy, by and large, now approaches Professor Speiser's principle of intra-area consistency, it is no less consistent with United States foreign policy in general: military preparedness at home; let live toleration and respect for peaceminded peoples abroad, with aid and protection in judicious response to need. This is not to say that there are no departures from the ideal with respect to other areas of the world—as if the lessons painfully learned in one area or by one section of government are transferable only with difficulty to other areas. But as far as the Middle East is concerned there are grounds for reasonable satisfaction.

The fifth principle was that a successful policy would have to be based on a clear and up-to-date understanding of the changing social and political realities and trends in the area. Perhaps, after the painful lessons of 1950-58 and the belated recognition that the new—but not unfamiliar—and decisive social force at work in the Middle East is nationalism, one may say that an understanding now exists. A danger is that formulations which apply today are certain, in an era of rapid and fundamental change, to change themselves. The problem will be to keep accurately aware of the changing reality. Fortunately, successful implementation of the final Speiser principle should make this task manageable. The development of a corps of able, conscientious, and experienced personnel through which to formulate and carry out policy has progressed to the point that satisfaction is more than justified. There are exceptions, to be sure. The effectiveness of able men may be diluted by the Parkinsonian inflation of numbers and complicated by the operations of other United States agencies in the Middle East. But United States State Department and Foreign Service personnel concerned with the area from the meager beginnings before World War II, have come to constitute a corps of a quality second to none.

Thus, despite the distracting push and clamor of domestic partisans or foes of one or another cause or interest or country in the Middle East, despite the endless conflicts of views in Washington and all the difficulties of establishing and pursuing a coherent and consistent policy, and despite the frequently divergent and sometimes violent opinions and demands of the United States allies elsewhere, the United States has been able, by and large, to implement the principles of Professor Speiser's farsighted prescription for policy success in the Middle East; and the empirical evidence, generally speaking, suggests his principles are correct.

Current Policy Problems

Even if the Cold War has seemingly been won in the Middle East, however, or to put it in minimum terms, a *modus vivendi* with the Soviet Union or a great-power standoff arrived at; and even if the threat of a nuclear holocaust has accordingly receded; and even if optimism about the future of United States policy in the area is justified, problems and dangers remain. A hard core of dilemmas continues to confront United States policy makers, and others will surely arise, to which a general allegiance to the principle of nonintervention and impartial support toward creating free, strong, stable, and peaceable societies does not supply specific and ready answers. This policy in practice, for example, may in some situations be construed by interested parties to represent exactly the opposite of impartiality and nonintervention. Or again, "hands off" may on occasion seem likely to lead to even greater evils than intervention.

The definition of evil in this connection rests on a conception of what concerns of the United States in the Middle East may be of such importance as to require intervention, and perhaps in the last resort the use of force, to protect.

A reasonable definition of these major concerns might be: prevention or suppression of overt aggression by or against *any* state or states within the area; continuation of the flow of Middle Eastern oil to Western markets; limitation of Soviet influence; and continuation of United States access to and passage through the area. It seems clear that in the long run, these things are best achieved by a continuing United States identification with and support for the constructive aspirations of the peoples concerned. But, in the shorter run, dilemmas remain.

One set of these surrounds United States economic support for Egypt. More than half a billion dollars, mainly in the form of foodstuffs, has been supplied to Egypt since 1958. Under Public Law 480, the United States is currently providing a third of the wheat and about 20 per cent of all the food grains consumed. This aid has been extended on very favorable terms, and without political strings in response to Egyptian requests and is quite properly intended to support Nasser's promising internal program of social and economic betterment. At the same time, however, it undeniably releases Egyptian resources for use in other ways. For most Arabs, United States economic aid to Egypt thus carries an implied United States approval of or acquiescence in Egyptian foreign policies—propaganda, incitements and threats, subversion, military intervention and all. Nasser has become identified as the American "chosen instrument" in the Arab world. Nonintervention and impartial support thus turns out to be intervention after all.

Most politically conscious Arabs approve of Nasser's policies and the implied United States endorsement. But Egyptian bombing of Saudi villages from bases in Yemen—aggressions no less real than the Israeli military raids in Jordan, Syria and Egypt between 1953 and 1956 which brought Security Council censure of Israel in every case—and the vehemently resented Nasserite threat to the Saudi regime and its oil industry raises the baffling problem of what (if anything) the United States should do about it. If minor actions—such as calls at Saudi Red Sea ports by United States destroyers, paratroop exercises and jet fighter training visits at Saudi bases, and the attempt to secure Egyptian withdrawal from Yemen in return for United States recognition of the new Yemeni republican regime—are unsuccessful, the temptation (and the pressure from Congress) would be strong to threaten cancellation of the aid program, or a refusal to extend it, as political leverage against Egypt. This would be construed in Egypt as overt intervention by the United States, and viewed with great hostility. The existence of a Soviet alternative for Nasser, and the whole experience of the past decade suggest the dangers involved in such a course. The nub of the dilemma is to decide what United States actions would be effective in persuading Nasser to abandon his aggressive policies vis-à-vis his neighbors while avoiding a rupture with him—the man still acclaimed as leader and hero, the symbol of reform and modernization everywhere in the Arab world.

United States concern about the Egyptian-Saudi confrontation arises in part from the potential threat to the flow of Middle Eastern oil to free world markets, principally in Western Europe. The

Saudi Monarchy is vulnerable to Egyptian pressures. Saudi armed forces cannot wholly be relied on, as witness the defections of Saudi pilots to Cairo during the fighting in Yemen. Some, even, of the royal family have preferred Nasser and the nationalist cause. But from a Western point of view there is no visible alternative in Saudi Arabia to the present regime. Its demise would in all probability usher in a period of chaos and strife, with interruption of oil production and transport a clear possibility. Hence the temptation to intervene, on the one hand to dissuade Nasser, and on the other to persuade Prince Feisal as the present head of government to win a wider domestic support by implementing nationalist objectives in Saudi Arabia—economic development, mass education, emancipation of women, freedom of press, radio and TV, and elimination of corruption and royal profligacy.

Such policies may not be enough however, in a republican age, to preserve the monarchy; and the dilemma of whether further intervention with all its adverse effects would be necessary to prevent (assuming it could prevent) an overthrow would then confront United States policy makers. A decision would rest in part on the degree of importance attached to maintaining the old flow, which in turn is the product of a great many variables, political, economic, social, and psychological, in the United States and the world at large as well as in the Middle East itself. (It is clear, as a consequence, that the importance of oil as of all other particular United States concerns in the Middle East must constantly be redefined.) In a period of general oil shortage in the world and severe Cold War tension (as was the case in the mid-1950's) the flow from the Middle East would probably be construed as vital, and more than a temporary interruption intolerable. At the time of the Suez crisis, Western Europe depended on the Middle East for 80 per cent of its oil needs, and even the partial and temporary interruption of supply imposed by blockage of the Suez Canal and the Mediterranean pipeline from Iraq imposed severe hardship.

At the present time, in contrast, there is a world glut of oil and tankers, with new supplies available in Libya and North Africa as well as in the Middle East itself. Even the Soviet Union is emerging as a provider of oil to Europe. Interruption of the Middle Eastern flow might be withstood for a time, perhaps as long as a year, even though the higher grade crudes of Libya and North Africa could not go far toward replacing the industrial grades of the Persian Gulf region. But it is apparent that in the longer term the Middle Eastern supply will continue to be of first importance. At the rate of six million barrels a day, the Middle Eastern production now supplies Western Europe with half its needs, Japan with approximately eighty per cent. West European consumption is growing fifteen per cent per year, that of Japan twenty per cent. It seems altogether likely as time goes on that the Middle East, with two-thirds of the world's oil reserves and two-thirds of its exportable surplus, will provide the bulk of the West European and Japanese increment. In such circumstances, should more than a temporary or partial stoppage of the Middle Eastern flow be threatened, the risks of intervention to preserve it might seem justified.

However, until markets alternative to those of the West should emerge (China perhaps?), the likelihood of a general stoppage of the oil flow seems remote. For the foreseeable future, the oil producing countries of the Middle East will continue to be more vitally dependent on their earnings from oil, and on free world markets, than the free world is on the oil exports of particular producing countries. It is a buyer's market. Even the anti-Western regime of Premier Kassim in Iraq, having learned the lessons of Mosaddeq's Iran, was careful not to jeopardize its oil sales to the West. In Saudi Arabia, should the monarchy be overthrown, it seems likely the successor regime or regimes would be similarly anxious to maintain (or re-establish) the income from oil.

Singly, or in combinations such as the Organization of Petroleum Exporting Countries (OPEC), which is intended to increase bargaining power of its members vis-à-vis the Western oil companies and their customers, the interest of the producing states is not to hinder the flow of oil, but rather to maximize their own income and control. Their pressure to do so will continue to raise difficult problems for the Western oil companies, who quite naturally seek the support of their own governments. But the vital interests of the companies are not always and not necessarily the vital concern of the United States; and the experience of Iran in 1951-53 suggests that governmental backing of oil company interests may actually endanger what is really more important: the continuing flow of oil. To decide if, how, and to what extent United States intervention in support of oil company interests is necessary is part of the policy maker's dilemma.

A third set of dilemmas, perhaps the most touchy of all, surrounds the problem of Jordan, Israel, and the U.A.R. The United States has continued its economic, military and diplomatic support of King Hussein (who remains utterly dependent on that support) and of Jordanian "independence" against the hostile majority of the population and against all the forces of Arab nationalism, as wielded by President Nasser, to which this majority responds. This is intervention in the oil imperialist tradition with all its negative implications; but withdrawal of United States support would almost certainly mean, with or without the fall of Hussein, a closer association in the name of Arab unity of Jordan with Egypt. To minimize the threat they assume such a development would pose, the Israelis have promised in the event of a Jordanian disruption to occupy the Jordanian West Bank, former Palestinian territory that compresses central Israel to a vulnerable sea coast corridor only a few miles wide. Few doubt Israel's determination or ability to carry out this threat, which would in all likelihood be accompanied by a direct attack on Egypt. War with Egypt would in any case be a probable result, possibly with rockets and nuclear weapons, although both states have signed the test ban agreement, and with great power conflict a possible, if not likely, consequence. In such circumstances, should the United States continue to guarantee Jordan? Or, for the sake of nonintervention, Jordanian self-determination, and Arab approval, should it withdraw support? Could Israeli aggression in Jordan then be tolerated? To prevent it should the United States reassure Israel with a specific military guarantee against Egypt and the other Arab states, with all the unhappy consequences for United States policy in the Arab world? Or should the United States make clear its determination to prevent or reverse, by force if necessary, any Israeli move into Jordan? Should it do both? Should the United States intervene with respect to the U.A.R., pointing out the possible consequences of its propagandistic and subversive attempts to induce regicide in Jordan, and the possible results of a closer union with that country? Should it insist on Egyptian disengagement? No doubt the United States has acted in some or all of these directions in its effort to preserve the status quo in Jordan, artificial as it may be. No doubt it has endeavored at the same time to help the young King to become less unpalatable at home by diverting him from unpopular causes, such as supporting the dispossessed Imam of Yemen, in favor of attention to economic and social progress in Jordan instead. Perhaps an agreement by all parties to keep the West Bank free of heavy weapons—tanks, rockets, artillery—under United Nations supervision might provide a *modus vivendi* compatible both with Israeli security and Jordanian self-determination, and might allow a gradual United States disengagement. Meanwhile, however, the multifold dilemma with the attendant dangers remains, and United States involvement seems likely to continue.

Whatever the original motivations, it is clear that the present basis of the United States position in Jordan is to prevent events in that country from becoming the occasion of renewed fighting between the Arab States, Egypt in particular, and Israel. There is no lack of causation external to Jordan however; and given the arms race between Egypt (drawing mainly on the U.S.S.R.) and Israel (drawing mainly on France) in jet aircraft and tanks, rockets, and perhaps even weapons of mass destruction, the consequences of war, should it occur, grow steadily more lethal. Even if the threat of Soviet involvement seems for the moment to have receded and with it the likelihood of great power conflict, it is surely a major interest of the United States to prevent a new outbreak of fighting. The American purpose in this situation is impartial as far as the Arab-Israel issue is concerned—opposition to aggression or attack from whatever quarter—and might well be carried out through the United Nations. But perhaps United States determination should be made unmistakably clear.

* * * *

Problems and dangers thus remain, which may on occasion require a degree of United States intervention, or even at a remote extreme, the use of force. Lord Morley's description, on a muted scale, may still apply. But thanks to the comparative success of United States Middle Eastern policy in recent years, together with the Cold War success of Western policy in general, such problems seem to have been reduced to a manageable minimum. For the future of United States relationships in this area, a reasonable optimism seems justified.

The American Assembly

Since its establishment by Dwight D. Eisenhower at Columbia University in 1950, The American Assembly has held Assemblies of national leaders and has published books to illuminate issues of United States policy.

The Assembly is a national, nonpartisan educational institution, incorporated under the State of New York. It was the official administrator of the President's Commission on National Goals, which reported to President Eisenhower late in 1960.

The Trustees of the Assembly approve a topic for presentation in a background book, authoritatively designed and written to aid deliberations at national Assembly sessions at Arden House, the Harriman Campus of Columbia University. These books are also used to support discussion at regional Assembly sessions and to evoke consideration by the general public.

All sessions of the Assembly, whether international, national, or local, issue and publicize independent reports of conclusions and recommendations on the topic at hand. Participants in these sessions constitute a wide range of experience and competence. Over sixty institutions of higher education have cosponsored one or more regional Assemblies.

American Assembly books are purchased and put to use by individuals, libraries, businesses, public agencies, nongovernmental organizations, educational institutions, discussion meetings, and service groups. Current American Assembly books:

1958——United States Monetary Policy
1959——Wages, Prices, Profits and Productivity
1960——The Secretary of State
——Goals for Americans
1961——Arms Control: Issues for the Public
——Outer Space
1962——Automation and Technological Change
——Cultural Affairs and Foreign Relations
1963——The Population Dilemma
——The United States and the Middle East
1964——The United States and Canada
——An Effective Congress

Early Editions Revised:

1962——The United States and the Far East
1963——The United States and Latin America
——The United States and Africa
1964——The Federal Government Service
——United States Monetary Policy
——The Representation of the United States Abroad